An American quarter century

US politics from Vietnam to Clinton

edited by
Philip John Davies

Manchester University Press
Manchester and New York
distributed exclusively in the USA and Canada by St Martin's Press

Copyright © Manchester University Press 1995

While copyright in the volume as a whole is vested in Manchester University Press, copyright in individual chapters belongs to their respective authors, and no chapter may be reproduced wholly or in part without the express permission in writing of both author and publisher.

Published by Manchester University Press
Oxford Road, Manchester M13 9NR, UK
and Room 400, 175 Fifth Avenue,
New York, NY 10010, USA

Distributed exclusively in the USA and Canada
by St Martin's Press, Inc.,
175 Fifth Avenue, New York, NY 10010, USA

British Library Cataloguing-in-Publication Data
A catalogue record for this book is available from the British Library.

Library of Congress Cataloging-in-Publication Data
An American quarter century : US politics from Vietnam to Clinton /
    edited by Philip John Davies.
        p.   cm.
    ISBN 0-7190-4514-2 (hbk). — ISBN 0-7190-4515-0 (pbk.)
    1. Political planning—United States. 2. United States—Politics
and government—1974–1977. 3. United States—Politics and
government—1977–1981. 4. United States—Politics and
government—1981–1989. 5. United States—Politics and
government—1989–   J. Davies, Philip, 1948–
JK468.P64A54   1995
973.92—dc20   95-3503
                                                                 CIP

ISBN 0 7190 4514 2 hardback
ISBN 0 7190 4515 0 paperback

First published in 1995

99 98 97 96 95   10 9 8 7 6 5 4 3 2 1

Typeset in Great Britain
by Northern Phototypesetting Co Ltd, Bolton

Printed in Great Britain
by Bell & Bain Ltd, Glasgow

Contents

Figures and tables

Contributors

Michael E. Bradley is Professor of Economics and Director of International Programs at the University of Maryland Baltimore County, and adjunct Professorial Lecturer in Economics at the Johns Hopkins University School of Advanced International Studies. He has published articles in the areas of comparative economic systems and history of economic theory. He has published two basic texts, *Macroeconomics* and *Microeconomics*, and is completing an intermediate microeconomic text.

Philip John Davies is Reader in American Studies, and head of the American Studies program at De Montfort University, Leicester. His books include *Elections USA*, *Science Fiction*, *Social Conflict and War*, and recent articles have appeared in *Electoral Studies*, *Politics Review*, *Talking Politics*, and *History Today*. He is currently working with Fredric A. Waldstein on 'Political Issues in America: The 1990s Revisited'.

Richard Davis is Associate Professor of Political Science at Brigham Young University. He is author of *The Press and American Politics*, *Decisions and Images: the Supreme Court and the Press*, and *Politics and the Media*. He specializes in the role of the mass media in American politics.

Georgia Duerst-Lahti is Associate Dean of the College and Associate Professor of Political Science at Beloit College. She has published on gender politics in journals including *Political Science Quarterly*, *Women and Politics*, and *Administration and Society*. She is currently working on a collection entitled 'Gender Power, Leadership, and Governance'.

John A. Kromkowski is Associate Professor and Associate Dean at the Catholic University of America. Author of an award-winning study, *Juvenile Crime and Neighborhood Deterioration*, and President of the National Center for Urban Ethnic Affairs, he is also editor of the multi-volume series, *Annual Editions: Race and Ethnic Relations and Cultural Heritage and Contemporary Change*.

Thomas C. Mans is Associate Professor of Politics and Department Chair at Creighton University, Omaha, Nebraska. His doctorate is from the University of Iowa and he specializes in American political institutions.

F. Dale Parent is Associate Professor of Sociology at Southeastern Louisiana University. Although his research concerns encompass a variety of social problems in the United States, the current focus of his published work is on the politics of health care.

Wayne Parent is Associate Professor and Acting Chair of the Department of Political Science at Louisiana State University. He is coeditor of *Blacks and the American Political System*.

G. Wyn Rees is Lecturer in International Relations at the University of Leicester. He has published on European security issues, and, with David Sadler, has recently been awarded a NATO Research Fellowship.

David Ryan is Lecturer in History and International Studies at De Montfort University, Leicester. He is the author of *US–Sandinista Diplomacy, 1979–1990*. He is currently working on two further books on the history of US foreign relations.

David Sadler is Head of Politics and Senior Lecturer in Politics at De Montfort University, Leicester. He has published in the field of European security, and, with G. Wyn Rees, holds a joint NATO Research Fellowship.

John E. Schwarz is Professor of Political Science at the University of Arizona. He is the author of *America's Hidden Success*, *The Forgotten Americans*, and numerous articles in political science journals.

Fredric A. Waldstein holds the Irving R. Burling Chair in Leadership at Wartburg College where, among his other responsibilities, he serves as coordinator of the Environmental Studies minor and teaches public policy. He is currently coediting with Philip John Davies 'Political Issues in America: The 1990s Revisited'.

John Kenneth White is Professor of Political Science at the Catholic University of America. He is author of *The New Politics of Old Values*, and *The Fractured Electorate*, and coeditor of *Challenges to Party Government*. He has published widely in national and international journals.

Abbreviations

AAUW	American Association of University Women
ABM	Anti-Ballistic Missile
AFDC	Aid to Families with Dependent Children
CAWP	Centre for the American Woman in Politics
CCC	Civilian Conservation Corps
CEQ	Council of Environmental Quality
CFE	Conventional Forces in Europe
CIA	Central Intelligence Agency
CJTFs	Combined Joint Task Forces
CPI	Consumer Price Index
CPSC	Consumer Product Safety Commission
CSCE	Conference on Security and Cooperation in Europe
CWA	Concerned Women for America
DENR	Department of Environmental and Natural Resources
DOD	Department of Defense
EA	Environmental Assessment
EEOC	Equal Employment Opportunity Commission
EIS	Environmental Impact Statements
EITC	Earned Income Tax Credit
EMILY	Early Money Is Like Yeast
EPA	Environmental Protection Agency
ERA	Equal Rights Amendment
ESDI	European Security and Defence Identity
FBI	Federal Bureau of Investigation
FDA	Food and Drug Administration
FEC	Federal Elections Commission
FECA	Federal Election Campaign Act

FMLN	Frente Farabundo Marti para la Liberacion Nacional
FOFA	Follow On Forces Attack
GATT	General Agreement on Tariffs and Trade
GDP	gross domestic product
GFD	gross federal debt
HEW	Health, Education and Welfare (Department of)
IMF	International Monetary Fund
INF	Intermediate Nuclear Forces
IRLG	Interagency Regulatory Liaison Group
MACT	Maximum Achievable Control Technology
NAAQS	National Ambient Air Quality Standards
NACC	North Atlantic Cooperation Council
NARAL	National Abortion Rights Action League
NARRAL	National Abortion and Reproductive Rights Action League
NATO	North Atlantic Treaty Organization
NDP	net domestic product
NEPA	National Environmental Policy Act
NFBPW	National Federation of Business and Professional Women
NI	net investment
NIH	National Institutes of Health
NIPA	National Income and Product Accounts
NNP	net national product
NNS	net national saving
NOW	National Organization for Women
NWPC	National Women's Political Caucus
OMB	Office of Management and Budget
OPEC	Organization of Petroleum Exporting Countries
OSHA	Occupational Safety and Health Administration
PAC	Political Action Committee
PDD	Presidential Decision Directive
PfP	Partnership for Peace
RACT	Reasonably Available Control Technology
RARG	Regulatory Analysis Review Group
RCRA	Resource Conservation and Recovery Act
SALT	Strategic Arms Limitation Treaty
SARA	Superfunds Amendment and Reauthorization Act
SDI	Strategic Defense Initiative

START   Strategic Arms Reduction Treaty
UNCED   United Nations Conference on the Environment and
                    Development
UNPROFOR   United Nations Protection Force
WEU   Western European Union
WIC   Women, Infants and Children (Nutrition)
WPA   Works Progress Administration

1 *Philip John Davies*

The end of the American century: the shape of the closing quarter

The calendar provides a convenient tool to bracket the examination of societal events, but historic developments rarely remain conveniently bound by arbitrary time scales. Time can be defined by the clock or the calendar, but political, social, and economic processes are driven not by clockwork, but by complex dynamics and stimuli. Within "the American Century," several individual decades attract regular attention, but even while these are legitimately important, they are not discrete. For example, while mention of "the Thirties" brings to mind a particular combination of privations and crises, that decade cannot be understood without reference to the policy failures of preceding years, and the unexpected economic stimulation provided in the 1940s by World War II.

Once one moves beyond the strict definitions provided by calendar time, the beginning and ends even of apparently well-defined periods become loosened, and defined increasingly by the perception of the observer. It has always seemed to me, for example, that the 1960s began with the death of Buddy Holly in 1959, but did not end until the resignation of President Richard Nixon in 1974. That, though, was a decade in which popular culture and politics melded with unusual force.

While the borderlines offered by dates alone are fragile and frayed, the last quarter of the twentieth century offers a period defined reasonably well by political and social events. The activism and problem-solving approach of the 1960s which somehow united as natural outgrowths of American politics the targeted and social policies of the War on Poverty, the first manned flight to the moon, and intervention in South-East Asia appeared ready to stumble to a close at the beginning of the 1970s. A new conservatism was developing as the reshaping of the Republican Party by zealous supporters of Barry Goldwater's failed 1964 presidential campaign, was consolidated by Richard Nixon's victories, and taken further by Ronald Reagan's supporters.

But the 1960s' challenge to entrenched interests continued to have effect. The roots of the congressional reforms of the early 1970s were set in the previous two decades during which unrepresentative congressional committee chairs were able to frustrate progressive policy making. When Nixon's conduct of the presidency and his subsequent resignation created the opportunity, Congress was in the mood to assert authority through legislation on budget impoundment, international military involvement, and campaign finance restrictions. Even as the voters were beginning to move to more conservative leaders, the environment was being restructured by prior initiatives. The interplay of these forces has molded the character of the past twenty-five years.

The USA entering the 1970s seemed a nation in turmoil and shock. The Vietnam War was an economic drain, and divided the country internally. The difficult course of the 1968 presidential campaign, and the vicissitudes of the 1968 Democratic Convention were testament to this, as were events such as the trial of celebrity child care expert Dr Benjamin Spock for aiding those avoiding the military draft (1968), the conviction of US soldiers for atrocities against the Vietnamese villagers of My Lai (1969), the tightening of military conscription with the draft lottery (1969), the conviction on conspiracy charges of the Chicago Seven, organizers of political street protests (1970), the "secret" bombing of Cambodia, a noncombatant nation, on the sole authority of President Nixon (1970), the shooting dead of protesting students at Kent State University and Jackson State University (1970), and the publication of the Pentagon Papers exposing the cynicism in American conduct of the Vietnam War (1971). Political leadership was decimated by failure, death, and resignation, as President Lyndon Johnson withdrew his bid for reelection, Senator Robert Kennedy and Rev. Dr Martin Luther King were assassinated, Vice President Spiro Agnew and President Richard Nixon left executive office in disgrace, Attorneys General Richard Kleindeinst and John Mitchell were convicted of offenses related to the Watergate scandal and the conduct of the 1972 Nixon election campaign. The troop commitment in Vietnam fell from its peak of half a million in 1968 to total land force removal in 1972, followed by total victory for North Vietnam in 1975, made more bitter for America because of the loss of over 50,000 dead in this ultimately futile venture.

Not all was problematic and divisive. The 1969 moon landing by Neil Armstrong and Buzz Aldrin was a cause for great celebration. The Supreme Court, newly led by Chief Justice Burger, finally decided that states and localities had deliberated long enough about school desegregation, and indicated that speed was now the watchword. While the public reaction in some areas took the form of white communities rioting against integration by school bussing, the shift toward a calmer approach to the problems of racial discrimination was helped by the firmness of this decision. The voting age was reduced to eighteen by Constitutional Amendment in 1970. The Nixon administration initiated new approaches to China and the USSR that lay the foundations for substantial later developments. Domestically, Nixon's proposals on family assistance, and the price freeze of 1971, can be seen as examples of consensual politics, being policies that could have come from either party. Earth Day (1972) may well have been intended to divert movement politics away from anti-war agitation, but also helped give the environmental movement momentum. Pressure for the Equal Rights Amendment was strong, and while ultimately the states did not rally in the required numbers, the 84 to 8 vote of support during 1972 in the US Senate was just one sign of the shift in the political clout exercised by women.

Reapportionment had reformed state and local government, and even some congressional constituencies, to the advantage not merely of overlooked population groups, such as African-Americans, but also of cities – the needs of which were themselves often overlooked by the rurally dominated gerrymandered state legislatures. A new politics was taking root, especially in the South, but it was a new politics that nurtured not only the Democrats' two successful presidential candidates of this era, Jimmy Carter and Bill Clinton, but also the rising stars of the Republican right who opposed them most vigorously, exemplified by Representative Newt Gingrich, who became Speaker of the House of Representatives in 1995.

Urban areas, and their communities, had only a brief time to benefit from fair representation at state level. While central cities, suburbs, and non-metropolitan areas each held about one-third of the total population in 1970, by the mid-1990s over half of the

nation's people live in suburban areas. Central cities have historically nurtured many of the great developments of the American
nation, but they have also attracted a great proportion of its problems. These cities, which often failed to gain support in an earlier age
because the political structure was stacked against them, now gain
less support than they would like because urban flight has eroded the
state and national power of this group of communities.

The population of cities has declined, but the problems have not
disappeared at the same rate. Urban migration has been racially and
economically selective. In 1990 the population of the nation was
around 12 percent African-American, but the average African-
American proportion of the population in cities over 100,000 was
almost 19 percent, and in the nation's 20 largest cities the proportion
increased to almost 30 percent. In the 1970s cities were losing
individuals and families with an aggregate income approaching
$7,000 million annually, and in spite of some "gentrification" it is
still clear that most cities are losing household income as a result of
migration, with consequent dramatic influence on the purchasing
power of the cities' neighborhoods.

Urban migration was not the only significant movement of the last
quarter century. The US Bureau of the Census has calculated the
geographical position of the "center of population" for each census
since the first was taken in 1790. This notional "center" moved
steadily west through the nineteenth and the first half of the
twentieth centuries. Movement of the "center of population" slowed
as the political boundaries became fixed, and the nation became
more populated, but it continued to edge west. In the second half of
the twentieth century the "center of population" developed a distinct
swing toward the South. At the end of World War II the "center"
lay on the Indiana/Illinois border, in between, and somewhat south
of, a line drawn between the two state capitals. By 1970 the "center"
approached the Illinois/Missouri border, a little south of St Louis. A
quarter century later the "center" lies about 100 miles south-west of
St Louis, apparently heading towards Arkansas. This single,
cumulative indicator traces the growing significance of the West and
the South in attracting settlement, and with it, gaining fresh political
clout.

The total population in 1970 was 203 million persons, a figure
that increased by more than 25 percent over the next quarter
century. Through this period employment growth in the South and

West has significantly outpaced the rest of the nation. Periods of growth have helped the South and West most, while periods of recession have bitten deepest in the Northeast and Midwest. For example, in the 1980s the healthier regions expanded at double the pace of the Northeast and Midwest, while in the early 1990s percentage job losses in the Northeast were four times higher than in the rest of the nation. In the early 1970s over 52 percent of the the nation's jobs were in the Northeast and Midwest, but by the early 1990s over 55 percent of the jobs were in the South and West.

Figures on regional change do hide local differentials. The relatively poor states of the Deep South have had low growth rates, as have the more northerly Mountain states of the West. The states sharing the South Atlantic coastline have done well, as have the Pacific coast states, but the massive growth of Florida, Texas, and California have been the touchstones of this expansion.

Regional political power has been given a fresh look by this population movement. At the end of the 1960s the Northeast and Midwest states held 233 of the 435 House seats, and 275 votes in the Presidential Electoral College. By the mid-1990s this share fell to 193 House seats, and 235 Electoral College votes. Since the South and West contain the majority of states (29), these expanding regions now hold regional majorities in all the branches of federal government. Over the same period Texas has increased its number of Electoral College votes from 25 to 32, Florida from 14 to 25, California from 40 to 54. With growth continuing in these states, it is possible that early in the next century these three states alone could hold half the votes needed for a presidential victory. The accumulation of such influence ensures that these states will never be far from the minds of national politicians (see Table 1.1).

Regions rarely act as wholly reliable voting blocs, but to a degree they do tend to share social, historic, economic, and therefore political characteristics which help define the political agenda. It has been widely predicted that this shift of influence toward areas that have voted conservatively in the presidential elections of the last quarter century would benefit Republican candidates. The combination of recession in the early 1990s, and the intervention in the 1992 presidential election of popular independent candidate Ross Perot, allowed Democrats Bill Clinton and Albert Gore to win the election with only 43 percent of the vote, the second-lowest victory percentage in over a century.

Table 1.1a Distribution of House seats 1968 and 1994

	1968	1994
Northeast	108	88
Midwest	125	105
South	133	149
West	69	93
Totals	435	435

Table 1.1b Electoral College votes 1968 and 1994

	1968	1994
Northeast	126	106
Midwest	149	129
South	168	184
West	95	119
Totals	538	538

Note: Number of votes needed for presidential election =270.

President Clinton, at 46 the third-youngest president, is the first person in the White House to come from America's "baby boom" generation. For the generally more liberal Democratic Party to win the presidency with an all-Southern ticket is itself a remarkable comment on the changes in the nation in recent years. In 1957 Little Rock, Arkansas was the location of riots stimulated by the local community's defense of racially segregated schools. By the 1980s progressive Democrat Clinton had been elected governor of Arkansas, and in 1992 the headquarters of the Clinton presidential campaign were located in Little Rock.

The problems of racial friction have not disappeared nationally, and migration patterns have further concentrated racial isolation, inter-group tension, social deprivation, and democratic decline in the nation's cities. Presidents Ronald Reagan and George Bush gained prestige in foreign affairs, but seemed less interested in domestic policy, and were accused of being neglectful of urban matters. In 1993 the White House was occupied by an incumbent with a confirmed interest in domestic, regional, and urban affairs. However Clinton's room for maneuver is limited by long-term shifts in the political landscape, by changes in the role of presidential leadership that had originated in earlier decades, as well as by the economic situation he inherited, and the need to build enough public support to be reelected. The new South that has brought Clinton and Gore to the executive, has also made Newt Gingrich the first southerner ever to become Republican Speaker of the House of Representatives. Republican leadership has moved to the South, as the South has increased its political clout, and the new Southern Republicanism is significantly more conservative than traditional Republicanism of the Northeast and Midwest.

A quarter century after the crises of Vietnam and Watergate the United States appears more calm. The reunification of Germany, the fall of Communist governments, a break out of democracy, or at least apparent moves to democracy, in Latin America and South Africa, feed the claim that America has led the West to a Cold War "victory." However, it may be that a world order less clearly defined has an even greater need for visionary foreign policy leadership. President Clinton won in 1992 with a campaign that adopted the mantra "It's the Economy, Stupid!," but the failure to meet challenges of Bosnia, Rwanda, Somalia, and Haiti with the uncompromising actions typical of his predecessors have met with skeptical reactions at home and abroad.

Domestically, issues such as those encompassed by the environmental agenda are now impossible to ignore. Social policy has shifted, but the foundations are strong. Politicians and electorate alike perceive a need to act within constraints. The greater opportunities available for participation by women and formerly disregarded racial and ethnic groups have added a new vitality to politics. None of these developments has prevented a massive decline of individual confidence in government. Surveys of public opinion find that general trust in government has fallen dramatically, as has belief in the selflessness of senators and representatives, and regard for the leadership provided by the executive. Beliefs that government is wasteful, run to benefit a few big interests, and uncaring of ordinary people have increased as rapidly as trust has fallen. Some candidates for office have found it expedient to adopt an "antipolitics" stance, simultaneously exemplifying the failure of leadership, and stoking the fires of an increasingly cynical and detached electorate.

The scene is set for a dramatic battle for power at presidential, senatorial, and House level, between political groups, and on a transformed political landscape. The essays that follow analyze the route that has been taken over the closing quarter of the American century, and the base from which the nation will enter the new millennium.

Part I
Policy agendas reconstructed

America's silent revolution: social policy in the United States

During the past three decades a revolutionary change has occurred in American social policy. This revolution has gone largely unnoticed, but it is a revolution nonetheless. Three decades ago social policy in the United States was founded upon the presumption that individuals, if they were motivated, decently educated, and treated fairly, could provide for themselves through employment in the private economy. That historic tenet, which reflects the American ethos of self-reliance, no longer remains the premise of social policy. Social policy now both acknowledges and accepts the reality that the economy is unable to absorb all willing and able workers at minimally acceptable levels of living. The story behind this crucial, long overdue transformation of American social policy and an examination of the shortcomings of policy that still remain are the subjects of this essay.

In the process of transformation, American social policy over the past three decades earned a number of successes. For example, the community action program begun by the War on Poverty coupled with the Voting Rights Act and its various renewals provided the impetus for more than a quadrupling of the number of elected black officials in the United States, from about 1,000 such officials in 1965 to 4,700 in 1990. In addition, amendments to the Social Security program in 1972 (which raised benefits and then tied those benefits to inflation) and the enactment of Supplemental Security Income were crucial to halving the rate of poverty among the elderly during the twelve year period from 1972 to 1984. A substantial expansion of the food stamps, school meals, and Women, Infants and Children Nutrition (WIC) programs virtually eliminated flagrant malnutrition among children. Medicaid gave the poor greater access to health care as Head Start did to better education. From the very young to the very old and from political needs to income and other crucial needs, social policy made a positive difference during the past three decades.

Nonetheless, the dominant opinion today is *not* that social policy succeeded, but instead that it failed both the nation and the poor. By the end of the 1980s, the overall rate of poverty was barely lower than it had been two decades earlier. More rather than fewer families were on the welfare rolls. The eradication of flagrant malnutrition notwithstanding, a higher proportion of children, not a lower proportion, lived in poverty. Conditions in the inner cities had grown worse, not better. Not surprisingly, liberals and conservatives began to find common ground in the view that social policy, and particularly welfare policy, had malfunctioned. Why the failure? Liberals believed that the social programs had done too little to prepare welfare recipients for work or, once on the job, to help them meet child care, health insurance, transportation, and other costs important to keeping them employed. Conservatives countered that social policy created dependency by being too generous in permitting recipients to stay on welfare indefinitely. As for the recipients themselves, they said that assistance was too miserly and administered too often in a degrading and humiliating manner. By the close of the 1980s social policy satisfied literally no one.

Social policy's transformation

Save for the period of the Great Depression, social policy in the United States historically has been grounded in the view that the vehicle of upward economic mobility for able-bodied individuals of working age is employment within the private economy.[1] According to this perspective, the proper role of social policy is to provide income assistance to people deemed legitimately outside the private economy, such as the elderly or the disabled, and to provide a "ladder" to all other people that will enable them to climb out of poverty, and into self-sufficiency, through private employment.

Social policy during the Kennedy and Johnson administrations was based on an expansive view of this philosophy, particularly in regard to the role of government in providing the able-bodied with a ladder enabling them to climb into self-sufficiency through the private economy. Both the New Frontier and the Great Society attacked barriers to successful entry into the private economy. They did so on numerous fronts. The minimum wage was raised; a multitude of job training programs to prepare workers for the private market were enacted; civil rights legislation to combat job discrimination got through Congress as did federal aid to improve education in poorer communities and a separate Head Start program for very young children; medical and various nutritional programs, intended to keep the poor healthy, and expansion of public housing, providing them with more adequate shelter, were enacted or greatly expanded. The philosophy behind all of these programs was that enough economic opportunity existed in the private economy (which was growing, seemingly exponentially, under Keynesian economic policies) to provide for everyone who had adequate health, education, and training and who was not artificially barred from decent employment by discrimination. If the government prepared the disadvantaged effectively and protected them from discrimination, the private economy could do the rest.

At first glance, statistics seemed to confirm this conclusion. During the years from 1960 to 1973, poverty declined precipitously, from 18.1 to 8.8 percent of the American population (these figures include income from in-kind programs). Such stunning results, however, momentarily hid from view the growth taking place from 1967 onwards in the proportion of Americans who would be poor except for assistance they received from the government.[2] The philosophy behind social policy that the private economy would do most of the job conflicted with the reality that government transfer payments in one form or another – not well-paying jobs in the private economy – were primarily responsible for the drop in poverty.

A group that by the end of the 1960s comprised about one-third of the poor – recipients of welfare – brought this contradiction between the philosophy and results of social policy home both to policy makers and the public. Welfare recipients were an anomalous group because their condition once was perceived as closer to that of the elderly and the disabled than to able-bodied workers. At one time, widowed and divorced mothers who were raising children were not expected to be able to compete successfully in the labor market. This perception changed especially during the 1960s, when it grew far more common for married women with children to enter the labor market and become employed, indeed to become employed full time. In addition, the characteristics of adults on welfare began to change in ways considered objectionable. Increasingly single mothers became eligible for welfare not because of widowhood or even divorce but because they had given birth outside of marriage. Tripling in the decade from 1960 to 1970, from 800,000 to 2.6 million, the growth in the number of households on Aid to Families with Dependent Children (AFDC) alarmed the public. The largest increase, proportionately, occurred among families headed by never-married mothers.

By the early 1970s, therefore, the world of social policy with respect to the able-bodied was in disarray. Nonworking poverty among able-bodied adults appeared to be growing, not declining.[3] In turn, the philosophy behind social policy underwent a subtle and largely unnoticed change. It is generally believed that the amount of funding devoted to social policy has been on the decline for a number of years. To the contrary, social policy was not so much scaled back as redirected. Less emphasis was devoted to overcoming the barriers to successful employment in the private economy – to education, training, and protection against discrimination – which had been the foundation of the New Frontier and the Great Society; instead, social policy began to use more of its resources toward providing assistance that would supplement the earnings of low-wage employed workers and, for a brief time (from 1972 to 1980), toward programs that would provide employment itself (750,000 public service jobs were created in the 1970s).[4] Instead of attempting to enable individual workers to succeed in the private market through education, training, decent health, and protection against discrimination, the ladder provided by social policy after 1970 increasingly was in the form of social assistance intended to bolster the extent and quality of the job opportunities themselves. At the same time, income assistance granted to able-bodied nonworkers, such as welfare recipients, was reduced in real terms and increasingly made contingent upon the recipients preparing for and seeking employment.[5]

This redirection of policy continues today. The role of the federal government now is only minimally one of preparing individuals to get work and to be successful in the private market. Funds for job training have become an ever lower proportion of total social assistance, as has federal aid-to-education (there are a few exceptions here in the area of education, such as Head Start). Direct assistance provided through AFDC has been cut significantly in real terms, as well. The focus of attention for the past two decades has been directed to reforming the rules of welfare so as to require work (a law specifying that certain AFDC recipients look for work was enacted in 1967, and experiments with workfare began in earnest in 1982) and to providing supplements to private sector earnings in order to raise the attractiveness of work. In 1965, very little social assistance was available to employed workers. Since the late 1960s, food stamps, for which all low-wage workers are eligible, have been accorded substantial real increases in funding. The biggest increase in assistance, however, came in the form of the Earned Income Tax Credit (EITC), for which *only* employed workers are eligible. First enacted in 1975, the EITC is essentially a supplement to the wages of workers with low household incomes. It is administered through the tax system. Amounting in total assistance to only $2 billion in 1980, the program grew to more than $7 billion in 1990 and $13 billion in 1993, rivaling federal expenditures devoted to AFDC. The program will outgrow AFDC in 1995; its expenditures are expected to reach more than $20 billion by 1998.[6]

The redirection that took place in social policy had a good measure of rationale. A problem American families encountered, throughout the period, was the scarcity of economic opportunity available to them in the private market. Wages had declined for a host of reasons, including the development of a surplus of labor following the mid-1960s due to the entry of an avalanche of baby boomers and women into the job market.[7] By 1990, the average hourly wage was 14 percent beneath what it had been in 1973 (declining from $11.38 an hour in 1973 to $10.02 in 1990, using 1990 dollars). Social policy began to concentrate first on creating more public service jobs to reduce the labor surplus and thereafter on enhancing pay levels through programs that operated, essentially, as supplements to wages. On the other hand, as we will see below, the redirection of policy in this area did not go nearly far enough, and this accounts for a good part of the dissatisfaction with social policy that mounted and continues to exist today. In addition, much more needed to be done to help prepare individuals to be successful in the private market – especially those individuals who did not go on to college after high school (comprising half of all workers entering the labor force). Preparation for success in the private market once had been a focus of social policy, during the days of the New Frontier and Great Society, yet despite the growing disadvantage (and rates of poverty) Americans experienced if they had not gone beyond high school, social policy actually retreated in this area following 1980.

Defining and measuring poverty

The redirection of social policy, designed to bolster the quality of economic opportunities available to low-wage individuals, had the key end objective, implicitly, that few individuals who worked year-round full-time should remain in poverty. This laudable goal tied in with the historic American ethos that people willing to work hard and persevere ought to be able to make their way. Obviously, however, a good part of the decision as to how much is needed by way of supplements, as well as a good part of the assessment as to success or failure in meeting the new policy's objective, would depend upon how one defines and measures poverty.

A measure of poverty had become available to the federal government in the early 1960s.[8] The measure was based on the lowest realistic cost necessary to feed a family of given size meals that would meet minimum nutritional requirements, set by the federal government, for maintaining adequate health. To determine the poverty line, this food budget was multiplied by three. This multiple of three came from the budget of the average American family since, for the last year for which data were available at the time, in 1955, the average American household spent one-third of its income on food. In essence, then, there were two components to the poverty index. The food component was based on the idea of the cost necessary to attain minimally adequate health while the multiplier, derived from the budget of the average family, built on the idea that poverty is related to the average or prevailing standard of living. Putting these ideas together, the original poverty index could be described as attempting to measure the cost to reach "the lowest level of the prevailing standard of living." This is a common meaning of the term among Americans, according to the *Merriam Webster's Collegiate Dictionary*, which defines poverty as "the state of one who lacks a usual or socially acceptable amount of money or material possessions."

The government has continued to use this poverty index over the years, with one crucial alteration.[9] Rather than refiguring the formula to reflect changes in the proportion that food comprised of the average family budget (necessary to keep the index linked to the prevailing standard of living), the government simply tied the index to the rate of inflation, adjusting it each year to take the rise in consumer prices into account. In effect, then, the federal poverty line today measures the same income in purchasing power as it did at the start. The consequence is that the government transformed a measure of income intended to be relative to the prevailing standard of living into a constant that does not change over time. The income figure for 1990 thus is based on the living standard of 1955 updated only for inflation; it is not based on the living standard of 1990. In 1990, the poverty index as the federal government measured it came to $13,300 in annual income for a family of four. Yet, food in 1990 no longer comprised one-third of the budget of the average family as it did in 1955; it had fallen to below to one-fifth. If the index with which the federal government began were updated to account for the living standard in 1990, the poverty line for a family of four would have been more than $22,000.

The implications of the poverty measure for working poverty

This change in the way the federal government measures poverty has important implications for workers. Most workers who are employed year-round full-time expect and want their employment to earn them a level of living that is minimally appropriate to the standards of today, not minimally appropriate according to some bygone era in the past. Examining a budget explains why it took an income of $22,000 in 1990, not $13,300, for a family of four to be able to attain the lowest level of the prevailing standard of living. More than $22,000 in income in 1990 was necessary just to cover the poverty line food budget for a family of four ($3,970 per annum, or about $80 per week); the cost for a two-bedroom apartment defined by the government as low-cost housing ($6,190 per annum, which comes to $385 per month rent plus all utilities); transportation ($3,250 per annum, which averages the yearly costs, including insurance and financing, for *one* intermediate size car traveling 100,000 miles over 10 years); medical expenses ($1,570 per annum, the average for a four-person family in 1990); clothes ($1,000 per annum divided between the four family members); incidental personal items ($1,700 per annum, which includes personal hygiene and household cleaning products, all household repairs and replacements, school supplies, and other such items); entertainment ($250 per annum); summer activities or child care for the children while the adults are at work during the non-school months ($600 per annum); a small amount ($500 per annum) for emergencies; and taxes ($3,450 for federal income, social security, and state income taxes).

This is a bare-bones budget, difficult to reduce by much and yet continue to live within the minimum prevailing standard. This point is reinforced by Gallup opinion polls, which found throughout the 1980s that precisely the same income level (about 165 percent of the federal poverty line) is what scientifically selected samples of Americans considered to be the minimum amount of income a family of four needs to be able to live in their communities.[10] I call it the "realistic poverty line." It is the income families needed to attain the lowest level of the prevailing standard of living. Falling beneath it is, according to *Webster's*, what people often mean when they use the words "poor" and "poverty." There are some complications with the measure, to be sure. Families residing in a central city may have access to good mass transportation and so might not need a car, but those same families then likely will face higher prices for rent which, in combination with the cost of mass transportation, approximately balance out the cost of a car. The reverse takes place outside central cities. Roper surveys find that at the basic level of living to which we are referring here, total costs normally do not differ significantly between central city, suburban, and rural areas. There are some exceptions, of course, but the total income of the budget outlined above, or a reasonable approximation of it, is applicable to a large majority of locales in the country.

In a family of four that contains two adults, two potential workers exist. Say that one of the adults works year-round full-time while the other, to save after-school child care costs, works two-thirds time. If so, for the family income to reach the realistic poverty line, the prime (full-time) earning adult would need to occupy a job that at minimum paid $6.60 an hour year-round (for 2,000 hours of work over the year). The difficulty of finding these jobs is indicated by the fact that nearly 20 percent of all year-round full-time jobs in 1990 paid less than this (including about 13 percent of all such jobs occupied by male workers). With respect to male workers, another 5 percent were employed part-time because they were unable to get adequate full-time work, and still another 5.6 percent were unemployed. In total, then, nearly 25 percent of the male workforce was unable to locate employment able to bring families of four up to a realistic poverty line, even if a second adult in the family were employed two-thirds time. It was all the more difficult still, of course, for a single parent to support a family with two children at a minimally acceptable level.

This is why supplementation of private market earnings was so crucial and why social policy needed to incorporate this approach. On its own, the private market itself failed to deliver the economic opportunities necessary to lift all (or, even, nearly all) steady year-round full-time workers to a minimally acceptable standard of living.

The implications for social policy

At the same time, some crucial flaws remain in the present policy of wage supplements. The supplements themselves have weaknesses. Food stamps, for example, are stigmatizing in character, or are perceived so by many low-wage workers, with the result that often low-wage workers opt against using them. For its part, the EITC is available to most workers only once a year, which makes the subsidy difficult to use to maintain one's standard of living on a weekly or monthly basis as the usual bills become due.

In addition, the government calculates the subsidies based on the outmoded federal poverty line rather than a realistic poverty line. Recall the point that workers expect their earnings will support a level of living somewhere within minimal standards prevailing today, not within minimal standards of some forty years ago. In 1992, the maximum EITC credit coupled with food stamp assistance for a family of four with both adults working at a combined income of, say, $14,000 was approximately $3,000, resulting in a total income for the family of about $17,000. Yet, the realistic poverty line for a family of four in 1992 was just beneath $24,100, or $7,000 higher. Thus, the wage supplements may have brought the family beyond the official poverty line of $14,300; but, by common usage of the term, the family still was left clearly poor.

The situation is no less dire for single heads of families with children, who comprise the vast majority on welfare. Consider a single parent working year-round full-time who earns $9,000 per annum. The EITC and food stamps, taken together, would add more than $3,000, enabling the family's effective income to surpass $12,000, which is above the official poverty line of $11,300 for a

family of three in 1992. However, the realistic poverty line in 1992
for such a family was $18,500, and this does not consider the costs of
after-school child care the family may have to bear when a sole
parent is working full-time the whole year.

The example helps to make clear the situation many welfare
parents face. They cannot live minimally acceptably on a federal
poverty line income, which is approximately the amount year-round
full-time employment coupled with the EITC and food stamps will
yield them. So, a large number of them stay on welfare (where, in
addition, they retain access to Medicaid and thus to health care) and
work under the table part-time or even full-time so as to raise their
incomes to something approaching what is actually needed to make
ends meet.[11] As it now stands, neither welfare alone, nor steady
work combined with wage supplements, is a realistic alternative for
single parents, unless the fathers also are employed in well-paying
jobs. Otherwise, the only realistic choice is to take full welfare
benefits and to add income from hidden part-time work (or from
illicit activities and other sources) to them.

Such a calculus lies at the heart of the welfare problem. With the
creation of an extraordinary 40 million new jobs in the United States
during the past three decades, it is plausible, during periods of
normal recovery, that nearly enough jobs exist for the overall
number of workers seeking them. It may be that there is a need for a
modest public service jobs program. However, with respect to
remedying welfare, far more critical is that employment must be
made to pay not simply more than does welfare, but enough so that a
family can live minimally acceptably. The growing emphasis on
wage supplements has taken American social policy in the correct
direction, but has not yet gone nearly far enough.

Because the wage supplements and thus the returns from employment remain unsatisfactory, none of the scores of workfare experiments implemented during the past decade has succeeded by much in
diminishing the number of recipients on welfare.[12] True, some of the
experiments have reduced unemployment very moderately and
increased the level of work among the recipients somewhat (and
thereby have reduced, once more by extremely modest amounts, the
public expenditures that are paid to families on welfare). On the
other hand, few experiments have led to more than marginal
increases in the total income actually available to welfare recipients
(after including the income from employment), so that very few

families have been lifted out of poverty due to the experiments (even measured by the official poverty line). Most importantly, no experimental treatment has enabled a significantly greater number of welfare recipients to leave the rolls as compared to natural reductions, most often occurring through marriage, that otherwise would take place. These natural reductions are measurable through the experience of control groups. It is a disheartening set of results, but fully predictable given the calculus described above. That calculus must be changed, and changed decisively, in order for welfare reform to be placed on a road to success. To change the calculus, supplements for low-wage employment must be set at higher levels.

All the same, we should pause to consider the transformation that did occur in social policy in America during the past twenty-five years, almost all of it silently, absent of fanfare, indeed without much by way even of notice. During those twenty-five years, a revolutionary philosophical change undercut the historic assumptions behind social policy. By acknowledging that a ladder to the private economy is not enough, social policy came to reflect a recognition that inadequate opportunity exists in the private market, no matter how hard and diligently a person tries, including able-bodied persons, and that therefore the government's assistance is needed to augment those opportunities which the private market does make available. Thus, today, assistance by government on an ever larger scale is offered to able-bodied persons even when employed, and also is available to individuals on a permanent rather than time-limited or transitional basis, and during normal economic circumstances rather than simply in times of economic depression or severe recession. In so doing, the past twenty-five years reversed the direction of two centuries of American social policy. During the first two centuries, the American world view held that in a land of boundless opportunity, able-bodied people may need preparatory and other transitional assistance but otherwise can and should be able to take care of themselves. As a foundation for public action, this longstanding philosophical tenet was eroded away by a silent revolution in social policy lasting the past twenty-five years, presided over, ironically, mostly by conservative presidents.

Education and economic opportunity

When contemplating the level of available economic opportunities, people sometimes need reminding that not everyone in America has a college degree. It is true that virtually all federal policy makers – whether elective, appointive, or civil service – do have college degrees, many of them advanced degrees. Living in a world where everyone has gone to a university may tempt policy makers to the conclusion that failing to go beyond high school is atypical, something peculiar having to do with the individual person. The reality, of course, is otherwise. Throughout the 1980s, barely one-quarter of all workers entering the labor force had earned a college degree; about half (among workers aged 20 to 30 included) had no education at all beyond high school. In America, a high school degree, and no more, was typical, not atypical.

Despite its typicality, however, workers with no education beyond high school experienced severe disadvantage in the economy, which can be seen by comparing their fortunes with those of workers who had earned college degrees. The earnings situation for workers with college degrees has been a reasonably good one. Consider male workers who are married with two children and who work year-round full-time. In 1989, only 6.1 percent of these workers earned beneath the minimally acceptable wage necessary to bring their families at least to the lowest level of the prevailing standard of living ($6.60 an hour working year-round full-time). It was quite a different situation for workers with only a high school degree. Despite working year-round full-time, 21.4 percent of these male workers who were married with two children earned beneath the minimally acceptable wage. If one adds the workers who were employed part-time because they could not find adequate full-time jobs along with those who were unemployed, approximately one-third of male workers with a high school degree and two children were unable to attain the earnings necessary – even if their spouses were working two-thirds time at $6.60 an hour – to pull their households up to the lowest level of the prevailing standard of living.[13]

Considering that about half of the workforce has no education beyond a high school degree, the reality does not portend well that fully one-third of these workers earn too little adequately to support a family. It is not a healthy situation. Should this reality persist, sooner or later it will become destabilizing. There is, as a result, a special need for education and training alternatives for the large number of workers in the United States for whom education now ends with high school.

Such an alternative needs to transition teenage students from school to employment, providing them with advanced skills in the process. The United States not only provides no substantial program of this kind, but as we have seen the federal government's participation in aid-to-education actually declined considerably over the past decade.

Here American social policy may be able to learn from its German counterpart, and particularly from the German apprenticeship program. A program along similar lines in the United States for students not intending to enter college would last three years and would perhaps commence following the first semester of the eleventh grade. Thereafter, enrolled students would continue to take language, math, science, and history or social science courses that would be integrated with classes leading to credentials in any one of dozens of applied fields. Simultaneously, students would receive appropriate training in on-the-job internships in local industries and businesses. The approach, then, is to couple continuous in-class education with continuous on-the-job learning in the student's chosen field. Certification of specialized training in the student's chosen field would occur after the program's sixth semester. Such a program would provide a strong link between school and employment that does not exist today for about half of the young adult population. Because they will be trained with job skills at a level of competency and experience significantly beyond high school, many students likely would end up with employment within the firms in which they held internships.

Following President Clinton's election to office, the federal government has begun to articulate the need for alternative education and training programs such as the kind just described. The administration proposed and Congress enacted a start-up program that, years from now, might come to be seen as the first steps toward a major reorganization of the later years of education for students who presently finish with no education beyond high school. Another revolution of policy may be in the offing.

Conclusion

Few Americans have regarded federal social policy over the past three decades with anything other than disdain. Most observers believe that social policy not only has been unsuccessful, but that it has been stagnant and, indeed, perhaps incapable of fundamental change given the intense existing division of opinion about policy coupled with the exceptionally diffuse nature of political power in the United States. Such a perspective fails to penetrate beneath the surface. The past thirty years have proven to be a historic turning point for social policy in the United States. A revolution has occurred concerning the social role of government. Thirty years ago virtually no assistance existed for workers who were able-bodied and employed; today the levels of assistance available to such persons have begun to rival the amount devoted by the federal government to its most famous welfare program. In addition, although it is still too soon to tell, we may be witnessing the start of a second revolution in social policy as well, which if successful ultimately would replace many of the federal government's present job training activities. This is the provision of a comprehensive program of education and training available to all high school students who do not go on to college. Should these twin policy innovations to assist low-wage employed workers and to provide advanced skills training continue to grow, we will come to look back upon these years, perhaps three decades from now, as ones of an exceptional redirection of thinking that created the superstructure for an enduring social policy founded upon the actual economic realities facing the disadvantaged rather than upon myths about self-sufficiency in a land of opportunity.

Notes

1   A history of social assistance in the United States during the twentieth century is found in James T. Patterson, *America's Struggle Against Poverty, 1900–1985* (Cambridge, MA: Harvard University Press, 1986).

2   Charles Murray, *Losing Ground: American Social Policy, 1950–1980* (New York: Basic Books, 1984), p. 65, Figure 4.5.

3   The change in public perception that occurred after the mid-1960s is described in Lawrence M. Mead, *The New Politics of Poverty* (New York: Basic Books, 1992).

4   Judith M. Gueron, "The Route to Welfare Reform," *The Brookings Review*, vol. 12, no. 3 (summer 1994), pp. 15–16.

5   The decline in welfare payments in real dollars after 1970, and its contrast with social security, is documented in Christopher Jencks, *Rethinking Social Policy: Race, Poverty, and the Underclass* (Cambridge, MA: Harvard University Press, 1992), p. 77, Table 2-2. See also Hilary

Hoynes and Thomas MaCurdy, "Has the Decline in Benefits Shortened Welfare Spells?," *The American Economic Review* 84 (May 1994), p. 44, Figure 1.

6 For figures on the growth of the Earned Income Tax Credit and how the program works, see Christopher Howard, "Happy Returns: How the Working Poor Got Tax Relief," *The American Prospect* 17 (spring 1994), pp. 46–54.

7 John E. Schwarz, *America's Hidden Success: A Reassessment of Twenty Years of Public Policy* (New York: W. W. Norton, 1983), pp. 115–144.

8 On the origins of the federal poverty line, see Mollie Orshansky, "Counting the Poor: Another Look at the Poverty Profile," *Social Security Bulletin* 28 (January 1965), pp. 3–29 and Mollie Orshansky, "How Poverty is Measured," *Monthly Labor Review* (February 1969), pp. 37–41.

9 For an examination of the limitations of the federal poverty line, see John E. Schwarz and Thomas J. Volgy, *The Forgotten Americans: 30 Million Working Poor in the Land of Opportunity* (New York: W. W. Norton, 1992), pp. 32–52 and Patricia Ruggles, *Drawing the Line: Alternative Poverty Measures and Their Implications for Public Policy* (Washington, DC: Urban Institute Press, 1990).

10 The results of the polls are reported in Schwarz and Volgy, *The Forgotten Americans*, p. 41, Table 3.

11 See Kathryn Edin and Christopher Jencks, "Reforming Welfare," in Christopher Jencks, *Rethinking Social Policy: Race, Poverty and the Underclass* (Cambridge, MA: Harvard University Press, 1992), pp. 205–208.

12 For the results of some of the better programs, see Schwarz and Volgy, *The Forgotten Americans*, pp. 102–106.

13 The figures in this paragraph are calculated from the tapes of the Panel Study of Income Dynamics.

3 Fredric A. Waldstein

The environmental agenda and the Environmental Protection Agency

The Environmental Protection Agency protects and enhances our environment today and for future generations to the fullest extent possible under the laws enacted by Congress. The Agency's mission is to control and abate pollution in the areas of air, water, solid waste, pesticides, radiation, and toxic substances. Its mandate is to mount an integrated, coordinated attack on environmental pollution in cooperation with state and local governments.[1]

The simple fact is that the Environmental Protection Agency cannot possibly do all the things its various mandates tell it to do.[2]

The account of the Environmental Protection Agency (EPA) offers a microcosm of the relationship between the environmental movement and environmental policy in the United States during the past twenty-five years. Created in 1970 by President Richard Nixon with an executive order (Reorganization Plan No. 3), the EPA was and remains a product of political as much as environmental interest. The purpose of this chapter is to examine the evolving relationship between politics and the environment over time using the EPA as the touchstone for discussion. It is, of course, impossible to cover such a broad topic comprehensively given the space constraints imposed by a single book chapter. Rather, the goal here is to provide the reader with enough context to begin to appreciate the complexity of the environmental policy making process with the many competing actors and agendas at work throughout that process.

The modern environmental movement

Historically, the utilization of natural resources fell within the domain of state and local governments. County park commissions, city planning and zoning boards, and municipal waste collection and disposal systems reflect this traditional orientation. The federal government took responsibility for managing the natural resources it owned, but, with few exceptions such as the creation of the national parks system, these resources were mostly managed to maximize human economic gain. Consequently, the management of natural resources fell under the authority of entities such as the departments of Agriculture and Interior and the Army Corps of Engineers, each of which had policy agendas that generally did not give high priority to environmental preservation and conservation.

The modern environmental movement is commonly traced to the 1962 publication by Rachel Carson of *Silent Spring*, a book which captured and focused the public's attention on the potential negative impact that human activity can have on the natural environment.[3] Subsequent calamities given prominent attention by the media such as the discovery of toxic waste at the Love Canal housing development, the Three Mile Island nuclear accident, oil washing on the beaches of California, and the "burning" of Cleveland's Cuyahoga River by a cigarette tossed from a boat into its polluted waters served to keep the public focused on the environment. Such incidents were ideally suited to the mass marketing of television news much the same as were the civil rights marches in the South. Helpless birds floundering and dying on beaches as the result of being victimized by oil spills offered the elements needed of a news segment to hold a large audience: stark visual images and a clear story line with which viewers could readily identify.[4]

It did not take long for existing environmental interest groups such as the Sierra Club, the Audubon Society, the Izaak Walton League, the Wilderness Society, and the National Wildlife Federation to capitalize on this unprecedented public attention. And several new groups were founded as well including the Environmental Defense Fund, Friends of the Earth, and the Natural Resources Defense Council.

The combination of media attention, public concern, and interest group expansion moved the "natural environment" as an issue across the political threshold onto the public policy agenda. Elected officials and their potential successors recognized this reality and reacted from one of two perspectives: (1) grudging recognition that the environment demanded attention by the public and had to be addressed among other policy issues; or (2) the environment offered an opportunity to gain visibility and legitimacy that may not have been as readily available through other issues. In short, the political climate dictated that public decisions would be made which impacted the environment for better or worse. Such political "heavyweights" as Richard Nixon and Henry Jackson were among those who early on utilized the environment as a policy issue to their political advantage.

Few politicians capitalized on the environmental issue more effectively than Edmund Muskie, senator from Maine.[5] His appointment to the Public Works Committee was intended as punishment by then-Senate Majority Leader Lyndon Johnson. But the very undesirability of the committee allowed Muskie to rise rapidly within its ranks as more senior senators left for more desirable committee assignments. In 1963 he became chair of a new subcommittee on the environment, and recruited a talented staff which shared his interest in promoting an active environmental agenda. No member of the House pursued at this early stage an environmental agenda as ambitious as Muskie's. Consequently, he had no peer during the early years in the environmental policy field, and no one had greater influence on the Clean Air Act of 1963 and its 1965, 1967, and 1970 amendments; the Water Quality Act of 1965; and the Clean Water Restoration Act of 1966. These pieces of legislation, in addition to others, reflected Muskie's philosophical proclivities about both environmental policy and relations between the federal and state governments. Muskie viewed the federal government's role primarily as one of engaging in scientific research, setting pollution control standards based upon that research, and engaging in oversight to ensure compliance with the standards set. The individual states were the agents given primary responsibility for formulation and implementation of pollution control policy within the established federal standards.

The judicial branch of the federal government was another early participant in the establishment of environmental policy. The initial rationale for court intervention regarding the environment was the Rivers and Harbors Appropriations Act passed by Congress in 1899 which, among other matters, limited refuse that could be discharged into certain navigable waters.[6] Although not primarily an environmental statute, the Supreme Court, in a series of decisions in the 1960s and 1970s beginning with *United States* v. *Republic Steel Corporation* 362 US 482 (1960), interpreted the Rivers and Harbors Act to make it unlawful to discharge material into a navigable stream without a federal permit. Other courts followed suit. Given the willingness of the courts to rule on issues pertaining to the environment it is not surprising that litigation has played a prominent role in the evolution of environmental policy. The federal and state governments as well as private individuals and organizations have not been reluctant to utilize the courts in pursuit of their respective environmental policy agendas. The propensity to use litigation as a strategy of first resort has led policy makers to anticipate litigation and incorporate it into the rules and regulations they craft. This has had a tendency to reenforce the use of litigious strategies over time.

Judicial strategies employed by governments, interest groups, and individual citizens include utilization of both public and private law remedies.[7] One distinction between the two is that private law generally involves compensation after injury while public law seeks to prevent injury before the fact. The boundaries between public and private law can become somewhat nebulous, however. What happens, for example, when a private party brings suit against another private party, but on behalf of the public? Such *qui tam* actions have been discouraged by the courts in the environmental as well as in other policy arenas in the absence of a clear legislative mandate permitting such action.[8] Part of the court rationale is that *qui tam* actions may limit state discretion to pursue criminal and civil remedies. For example,

> the private enforcer may be incompetent or in collusion with the defendant, in which case a judgement may be rendered that fails to protect the public interest and subsequent prosecution by public officials . . . Another risk is the potentially adverse effect of the availability of private enforcement on official efforts at negotiated settlement.[9]

Congress has written provisions into much environmental legislation (e.g. the Clean Air Act of 1970) at the behest of environmental lobbying organizations which permit private citizens and others to sue alleged polluters or force the EPA to sue for compliance with extant regulations.

The National Environmental Policy Act

The National Environmental Policy Act (NEPA), sponsored by Senator Henry "Scoop" Jackson of Washington, was passed by Congress and signed into law by President Richard Nixon in 1969. It declared that the federal government had responsibility for the protection of the environment. NEPA created the Council of Environmental Quality (CEQ) as a body within the executive branch to advise the president about matters pertaining to the environment. But the real significance of the CEQ evolved with its role in developing regulations governing Environmental Impact Statements (EIS), a role which has been sanctioned by the Supreme Court. Perhaps the most important feature of NEPA is the requirement that all "major federal actions significantly affecting the human environment" must include an EIS.[10]

Three major issues pertaining to the EIS provisions of NEPA have been litigated in the courts. These are: (1) the determination of whether an EIS is necessary; (2) a time frame within which it should be executed; and (3) an understanding of what it should include. There are two considerations that have been raised with respect to the first issue. One has to do with determining what constitutes "major federal action." The other is the determination of what constitutes "significant environmental impact." The courts have provided guidelines which suggest that a substantial commitment of federal government resources to a project constitutes "major action." More problematic has been the determination of what constitutes "significant environmental impact." Here the courts have interpreted "environment" in a broad sense and developed a two-stage standard (qualitative change in land/water use and the quantity of the land/water impacted by the proposed change) to determine whether or not impact is significant. The Supreme Court has ruled that the EIS process should begin at the time of a proposal for federal action.[11] The third issue, what the EIS process should include, has also resulted in a two-stage process. The first stage is the preparation of an Environmental Assessment (EA) to determine the impact. If impact is found then the second stage must be completed, a full EIS. Again, the courts have insisted that the EIS process be taken seriously by all parties involved to make a determination of the overall impact of the complete project.[12]

NEPA represents the culmination of the pre-EPA era and was a harbinger of what was to come with respect to the environmental policy process. Congress passed laws designed to impact environmental quality, which as often as not, lacked specificity and precision, executive branch officials struggled internally and externally attempting to implement these laws, and lobbying groups sought judicial remedies in pursuit of their own interpretation of environmental law. In short, the milieu into which the EPA was born was not atypical in a rapidly evolving policy arena.

The genesis of the Environmental Protection Agency

The creation of the EPA cannot be wholly understood independent of the political climate of the early 1970s. Richard Nixon, serving his first term as president of the United States, looking ahead to the 1972 campaign, saw a field of Democratic presidential hopefuls led by the 1968 Democratic vice presidential candidate, Senator Edmund Muskie from Maine. Both men sought to enhance their environmental credentials in the public mind, with consequences for environmental policy in the US that, if not unintended, at least were not motivated entirely by their commitment to protecting the natural environment.

Senator Muskie, an early proponent of environmental protection, was being criticized in 1970 by environmental interest groups and in the press for the apparent ineffectiveness of the 1967 amendments to the Clean Air Act. Muskie, a former governor, had supported the position that the states should be the parties primarily responsible for implementing environmental policy. But by 1970 the federal government had not approved even one state implementation plan. Some ascribed Muskie's action as a "sell out" to industrial and labor interests for the political support they could generate on his behalf in a presidential campaign. Muskie, in response, sought to shore up his environmental credentials by taking a strong environmental position on the 1970 reauthorization of the 1967 Clean Air Act.

> Muskie proposed a revised bill that contained the most stringent federal pollution control program that had ever been attempted . . . States retained primary responsibility for devising plans for implementing these requirements, but these plans had to be approved by the federal government.
> The enormous weight of Muskie's leadership was put behind four

ideas that were to prove central to later debates over environmental policy: (1) nationally uniform ambient standards, (2) no balancing between health risks and economic costs, (3) rigid deadlines to be adhered to regardless of economic and technological obstacles, and (4) uniform emission limits for new sources, even in areas without pollution problems.[13]

In addition, Muskie abandoned his traditional position of ensuring executive continuity and accountability by drafting legislation in a manner which would make implementation of environmental policy more independent of the presidency than had been his previous position.

President Nixon and his aides developed a political strategy that allowed him to defuse environmental protection as a campaign issue with minimal concessions to the environmental movement. He signed into law such visible legislation as NEPA and the Clean Air Amendments of 1970. But one may argue that his *pièce de résistance* in this game of environmental one-upmanship was the creation of the EPA. The initial plan proposed by the Nixon White House called for the creation of a new Department of Environmental and Natural Resources (DENR) which would have replaced the Department of the Interior and assumed responsibilities then housed in the Department of Health, Education and Welfare (HEW), the Department of Agriculture, and the Army Corps of Engineers. Nixon was initially receptive to this plan, but ultimately abandoned it in light of the following factors: (1) opposition from existing departments which would lose jurisdiction over responsibilities they held; (2) the possibility of congressional opposition to any reorganization plan that might make obsolete existing congressional committee oversight responsibilities; and (3) the political advantage to the president of creating independently an agency with which he was identified.

> From the president's point of view, a separate agency had two very attractive features. First, it was a highly visible and innovative action. Second, it represented a compromise between those who totally wanted to redesign the executive branch and those who wanted to change nothing. Ironically, then, the creation of a powerful environmental advocacy agency was a compromise devised for parties virtually none of whom was an environmental advocate.[14]

The new EPA came into existence on September 9, 1970 by

presidential order, sixty days after the proposed reorganization plan was submitted to Congress. It had responsibilities for conducting and sponsoring environmental research, establishing standards, and monitoring and supporting state and local environmental activity. Initially the EPA was little more than a collection of existing bureaus and offices from other agencies and departments with their concomitant personnel which both helped define and reinforce its future orientation. From the Department of Agriculture came the Pesticides Regulation Division. From the HEW came the Bureau of Radiological Health, the Bureau of Solid Waste Management, the Bureau of Water Hygiene, the National Air Pollution Control Administration, and the Office of Pesticides Research. From the Department of the Interior came the Federal Water Quality Administration and the Office of Research on the Effects of Pesticides on Wildlife and Fish. From the Atomic Energy Commission came the Division of Radiation Standards. The Interagency Federal Radiation Council was also integrated into the EPA.

Major environmental laws and initiatives

Since the creation of the EPA a number of major legislative initiatives have become law. These have been spawned by a number of committees and subcommittees in both chambers which jealously guard jurisdiction over their respective progeny. Table 3.1 suggests how the committee structure and jurisdictional boundaries impact on environmental policy. The committee system was never designed for the convenience of the executive bodies which are subject to congressional oversight. Consequently, agencies such as the EPA are placed in the position of serving many masters simultaneously, and they too often have conflicting agendas. This system complicates significantly the development and implementation of environmental rules and regulations, and helps explain the sometimes tortured path that environmental policy takes.

The most significant laws that involve the EPA with their major provisions are identified in Table 3.2. In addition, other examples of significant environmental legislation (and the entity responsible for its implementation) include: the Coastal Zone Management Act of 1972 (Commerce Department) which authorized federal grants to states for purposes of developing coastal zone management plans in compliance with federal guidelines; the Endangered Species Act of

Table 3.1
*Congressional standing committees with
environment-related responsibilities*

Senate	
Agriculture, Nutrition and Forestry	Agriculture in general, soil conservation, forestry, pesticide policy
Appropriations	Appropriations for all programs
Commerce, Science, and Transportation	Coastal zone management; marine fisheries; oceans, weather, and atmospheric activities; technology research and development
Energy and Natural Resources	Energy policy in general; nuclear waste policy; mining; national parks and recreation areas; wilderness; wild and scenic rivers
Environment and Public Works	Air, water, and noise pollution; toxic and hazardous materials; Superfund; nuclear waste policy; fisheries and wildlife; ocean dumping; solid-waste disposal; environmental policy and research in general
House	
Agriculture	Agriculture in general; soil conservation; forestry; pesticide policy
Appropriations	Appropriations for all programs
Energy and Commerce	Clean Air Act, nuclear waste policy; safe drinking water; Superfund; hazardous waste and toxic substances
Interior and Insular Affairs	Public lands; wilderness; surface mining; nuclear waste policy
Merchant Marines and Fisheries	National Environmental Policy Act; oceanography and marine affairs; coastal zone management; fisheries and wildlife
Public Works and Transportation	Water pollution; rivers and harbors; oil pollution; water power
Science, Space, and Technology	Nuclear waste policy; environmental research and development; energy research

Source: Norman J. Vig and Michael E. Kraft. 1991. *Environmental Policy in the 1990s.* Washington, DC: Congressional Quarterly Press. p. 6.

Table 3.2

Major environmental laws passed since the creation of the Environmental Protection Agency for which it has had principal jurisdiction

Law	Major provisions
Nixon administration	
Resource Recovery Act of 1970 (transferred from Dept of Health, Education and Welfare at creation of EPA)	Created grants for solid waste management systems; provided technical and financial assistance to state and local agencies to develop waste disposal systems
Clean Air Act Amendments of 1970	Required EPA administrator to set air quality standards and emissions limits; required states to develop air quality implementation plans; required reduction in auto emissions
Federal Water Pollution Control Act (Clean Water Act) Amendments of 1972	Set water quality goals; established pollutant discharge permit system; increased grants to states to construct waste treatment plants
Federal Environmental Presticides Control Act of 1972	Required registration of all pesticides in US commerce; allowed administrator to cancel or suspend registration
Marine Protection Act of 1972	Regulated dumping of waste materials into the oceans' coastal waters
Ford administration	
Safe Drinking Water Act of 1974	Authorized government to set standards to safeguard the quality of public drinking water supplies and to regulate state programs for protection of groundwater sources
Toxic Substances Control Act of 1976	Allowed EPA to ban or regulate the manufacture, sale, or use of any chemical presenting an "unreasonable risk of injury to health or environment"; prohibited most uses of PCBs

| Resource Conservation and Recovery Act of 1976 | Required EPA to set regulations for hazardous waste, treatment, storage, transportation, and disposal; provided assistance to states for hazardous waste programs under federal guidelines |

Carter administration

| Clean Air Act Amendments of 1977 | Amended and extended Clean Air Act; postponed deadlines for air quality standards and auto emission compliance; set standards for "prevention of significant deterioration" in clean air areas |

| Clean Water Act Amendments of 1977 | Extended deadlines for industry and cities to meet treatment standards; set national standards for industrial pretreatment of wastes; increased funding for sewage treatment construction grants and gave states flexibility in determining priorities |

| Comprehensive Environmental Response, Compensation, and Liability Act of 1980 (Superfund) | Authorized federal government to respond to hazardous waste emergencies and to clean up chemical dump sites; created $1.6 billion "Superfund"; established liability for cleanup costs |

Reagan administration

| Resource Conservation and Recovery Act Amendments of 1984 | Strengthened EPA procedures for regulating hazardous waste facilities; authorized grants to states for management of solid and hazardous waste; prohibited land disposal of certain hazardous liquid waste; and required states to consider recycling |

| Safe Drinking Water Act of 1986 | Reauthorized Safe Drinking Water Act of 1974 and revised EPA safe drinking water programs; accelerated schedule for setting standards for maximum contaminant levels of 83 toxic pollutants. |

Superfund Amendments and Reauthorization Act of 1986	Provided $8.5 billion through 1991 to clean up abandoned chemical dumps; set standards and timetables for cleaning up such sites; required that industry provide local communities with information on hazardous chemicals used or emitted
Clean Water Act Amendments of 1987	Amended Federal Water Pollution Control Act of 1972; revised EPA water pollution control programs, including implementation of nonpoint-source pollution management plans; expanded EPA enforcement authority; established national estuary program
Ocean Dumping Act of 1988	Amended Marine Protection Act of 1972 to end all ocean disposal of sewage sludge and industrial waste by 1992; revised EPA regulation of ocean dumping fees, permit requirements, and civil penalties for violations

Bush administration

Clean Air Act Amendments of 1990	Established controls for acid rain; established new air quality attainment standards; introduced Maximum Achievable Control Technology (MACT) as standard to evaluate potentially toxic air pollutants

Clinton administration

None to date

Source: Norman J. Vig and Michael E. Kraft. 1991. *Environmental Policy in the 1990s.* Washington, DC: Congressional Quarterly Press. pp. 393–397.

1973 (Interior Department) which authorized the federal government to protect all threatened and endangered species; the Federal Land Policy and Management Act of 1976 (Interior Department) which ended longstanding policy of conveying public lands into private ownership, and generally to manage public lands for long-term public benefits; the National Forest Management Act of 1976 (Agriculture Department) limited clearcutting and otherwise changed forest management practices to a greater conservation orientation; the Surface Mining Control and Reclamation Act of 1977 (Interior Department) established environmental controls over strip mining; the Public Utilities Regulatory Policies Act of 1978 (Energy Department) intended to promote energy conservation and efficiency; the Nuclear Waste Policy Act of 1982 (Energy Department) established plans and guidelines for construction and operation of nuclear power plants including disposal of spent fuel; the Food Security Act of 1985 (Agriculture Department) promoted conservation of farm land; and the Global Climate Protection Act of 1987 (State Department) which authorized the development of a strategy to address global climate change. These examples demonstrate that environmental concerns now permeate the federal government even though the focus for this chapter is limited principally to those measures which fall within the jurisdiction of the EPA. Table 3.3 offers an overview of executive branch departments with environmental responsibilities.

The full regulatory consequences of most environmental laws do not immediately manifest themselves and not infrequently implementation is left to future administrations. An important example is the Resource Conservation and Recovery Act (RCRA) of 1976 which was passed literally just days before the presidential election. Such actions are especially problematic for the EPA and place pressure on it because laws like RCRA tend to be highly prescriptive and incorporate mandates using formulae and targets based in part on faith and untested assumptions, and not only on scientific merit.[15]

Three significant environmental laws were passed during the Carter administration for which the EPA had jurisdiction, amendments to both the Clean Water and Clean Air Acts and Superfund. The amendments to the Clean Air and Clean Water Acts suggest two different orientations by Congress with respect to regulatory policy. The 1977 amendments to the Clean Water Act set national standards for industrial pretreatment of waste which suggests a tightening of control by the federal government. At the same time, it extended deadlines for industries and cities to meet water treatment standards and it gave the states greater flexibility to establish water treatment priorities. The amendments to the Clean Air Act extended deadlines for meeting air quality standards. They were also more prescriptive and reduced the discretion states had prior to the 1977 amendments. In addition, the EPA was mandated to use a new Reasonably Available Control Technology (RACT) to evaluate state compliance of

Table 3.3
*Executive branch departments and agencies with
major environmental responsibilities*

Executive branch authority	Environmental responsibility
White House Office	Overall policy; agency coordination
Council on Environmental Quality	Environmental policy coordination; oversight of National Environmental Policy Act; environmental quality reporting
Office of Management and Budget	Budget; agency coordination and management
Environmental Protection Agency	Air and water pollution; pesticides; radiation; solid waste; Superfund; toxic substances.
Dept of the Interior	Public lands; energy; minerals; national parks
Dept of Agriculture	Forestry; soil conservation
Dept of Commerce	Oceanic and atmospheric monitoring and research
Dept of State	International environment
Dept of Justice	Environmental litigation
Dept of Defense	Civil works construction; dredge and fill permits; pollution control from defense facilities
Dept of Energy	Energy policy coordination; petroleum allocation; research and development
Dept of Transportation	Mass transit; roads; airplane noise; oil pollution
Dept of Housing and Urban Development	Housing; urban parks; urban planning
Dept of Health and Human Services	Health
Dept of Labor	Occupational health
Nuclear Regulatory Commission	Licensing and regulating nuclear power
Tennessee Valley Authority	Electric power generation

Source: Council on Environmental Quality. 1987. *Environmental Quality, Sixteenth Annual Report to the Council of Environmental Quality.* Washington, DC: US Government Printing Office.

clean air standards. But how RACT was to be utilized was not clearly defined by Congress and it was left to the EPA to struggle with formulating a working definition which turned into a source of friction between the states and the EPA.

The Comprehensive Environmental Response, Compensation and Liability Act (Superfund) was passed in 1980 to provide the means necessary to clean up abandoned hazardous waste sites. In 1986 the Superfund Amendments and Reauthorization Act (SARA) broadened the base of corporate taxes to support Superfund. The initial budget was set at $1.6 billion to be funded by a special tax on chemicals and petroleum. It became apparent rather quickly that this amount would be inadequate to clean up the Superfund priority sites identified by the EPA (approximately 2,000) and the authorization was increased to an additional $8.5 billion over five years.[16] In passing Superfund Congress once again adopted an approach whereby the EPA was given the responsibility to identify toxic sites and clean them up with little guidance regarding the establishment of priorities for program design such as site selection methodology and how resources should be allocated.

The eight years of the Reagan presidency witnessed the passage of several major environmental laws in spite of the administration's open hostility to the environmental movement. All, however, came in the wake of the political mismanagement of the EPA that culminated in the subsequent criminal conviction and imprisonment of the assistant administrator for solid waste, Rita Lavelle, and the resignation of the administrator, Ann Gorsuch. Public furor and the loss of credibility left the administration politically impotent to mount sufficient opposition to congressional initiatives to prevent them from becoming law. Congressional distrust of the administration to execute faithfully environmental laws resulted in legislation that was highly prescriptive in detailing what the EPA could and could not do with respect to substantive policy issues. One might characterize this strategy as preemptive micro-management. Congress also increased its public profile with respect to its oversight responsibilities safe in the knowledge that public opinion remained opposed throughout Reagan's tenure to his perceived virulent anti-environmental perspective.

The legislative landscape had changed significantly by the time George Bush became president in a way that favored a renewed surge in environmental activity. Senator Robert Byrd of West Virginia, an unwavering supporter of the sulfurous coal industry, stepped down as Senate Majority Leader and was replaced by George Mitchell of Maine, a leading environmental advocate. Henry Waxman, a representative from the Los Angeles area and staunch proponent of raising clean air standards, became chairman of the House Commerce Committee's subcommittee on the environment. In addition, reapportionment and redistricting increased representation of suburban and exurban constituencies which gave environmental protection high priority as a policy issue.

Nonetheless, the pace of environmental legislation slowed substantially during the Bush administration. The single major substantive environmental protection initiative to become law was the collection of amendments to the Clean Air Act. But it was substantive legislation indeed. The 1990 amendments represented the first effort to address seriously the issue of acid rain in addition to the establishment of new air quality attainment standards and standards to evaluate potentially toxic pollutants. But once again Congress, suspicious of the former Reagan vice president, used the amendments to impose upon the EPA very prescriptive regulatory formulae.

No major environmental legislation was passed by Congress during the first two years of the Clinton administration which is not surprising given the president's priorities of health care and welfare reform. A proposal by the administration to elevate the EPA to a cabinet-level department was stalled in congressional committees.

Environmental Protection Agency administration and organization

The EPA is headed by an administrator, the first of whom was William Ruckelshaus. He established the first organizational structure of the EPA by dividing it into five divisions, each headed by an assistant administrator. They were the divisions for: Categorical Programs (Office of Pesticides Programs, Office of Radiation Programs, and the Office of Solid Waste Management Programs); Media Programs (the Office of Air Program and the Office of Water Program); Enforcement and General Counsel; Planning and Management; and Research and Monitoring.[17] This organizational structure was somewhat awkward in the sense that the first two divisions were identified by substantive policy issues while the later three were identified by generic functions. In addition, the distinctions between media programs and categorical programs were hardly mutually exclusive. This resulted in jurisdictions that over-lapped among divisions which had different professional and organizational orientations. There were also ten regional offices throughout the country, each headed by a regional administrator who reported to the administrator.

The broad organizational structure initiated by Ruckelshaus has remained largely intact, although a number of programs are now headed by assistant administrators which is indicative of their elevated status within the Agency. Also, some additions have been made to reflect the increased responsibilities with which the EPA has been charged over time. Currently there are assistant administrators for: Administration and Resource Management; Enforcement; Policy, Planning and Evaluation; International Activities; Research and Development; Air and Radiation; Pesticides and Toxic Sub-stances; Water; and Solid Waste and Emergency Response.

The EPA has grown since its inception from an organization with approximately 5,000 employees and a budget of $900 million to an organization with approximately 17,000 employees and a budget of

Table 3.4

Approximate Environmental Protection Agency budget and personnel figures (selected years)

	Government outlays $ million	% of total Government outlays	Number of full-time employees
1970	384	0.2	3,702
1971	701	0.3	5,959
1972	763	0.3	7,835
1973	1,114	0.5	8,270
1977	4,365	1.1	9,159
1981	5,242	0.8	9,872
1985	4,490	0.5	10,307
1989	4,906	0.4	11,094
1993	5,930	0.4	13,443
1994	6,539 (estimate)	0.4 (estimate)	13,566 (estimate)

Sources: US Government. 1994. *Budget of the United States Government Historical Tables: Fiscal Year 1995.* Washington, DC: US Government Printing Office. US Government. selected years. *Appendix to the Budget of the United States Government.* Washington, DC: US Government Printing Office.

more than $6 billion. Table 3.4 offers a perspective on the growth of the EPA over time. In spite of the growth in the number of laws and rules for which the EPA has administrative responsibilities, its Fiscal Year 1993 operating budget, in constant dollars, was roughly the same as it was in Fiscal Year 1979.[18]

The Environmental Protection Agency under the Nixon and Ford administrations

There is general agreement among students of environmental policy that Richard Nixon and his political advisers approached the environmental issue as one that had to be addressed but not embraced. They appear to have approached their role as one of balancing the political need to avoid alienating the various constituencies of what they perceived as comprising an environmental juggernaut, on the one hand, against their general ideological proclivity to minimize government regulation of and restrictions on the private economy on the other. From a purely political perspective they were generally successful. In spite of complaints by the pro-environmental lobbyists and their congressional allies that the Nixon administration was "soft" on environmental issues, it never evolved as a campaign issue as it would in later presidential elections, especially in 1988 and 1992.

The first administrator of the EPA, William Ruckelshaus, was an assistant attorney general who had the support of Nixon confidant, Attorney General John Mitchell. Among his credentials, Ruckelshaus had successfully prosecuted water pollution violators when he had served as an Indiana assistant attorney general. Ruckelshaus chose to give agency priority to enforcement. This is in keeping with his professional background as a prosecutor. In addition, he believed that the EPA had to establish its credibility quickly, and he judged that high visibility legal action against large corporations charged with polluting the environment would serve such a purpose. Also, there already existed a team of lawyers on staff that could begin litigation with little delay.[19] The Ruckelshaus strategy worked in establishing quickly the legitimacy of the EPA as an agency that was serious about its mandate to protect the natural environment.

But this strategy brought with it potential political and organizational costs. Politically, this strategy was not the preference of the Nixon White House which sought a more accommodating relationship with the business community. It also reinforced suspicions in the business community that the EPA agenda was primarily as an advocate for environmental interests, an image which it has maintained throughout its existence with the exception of a few years during the Reagan administration. From an organizational perspective, devoting substantial agency resources to the enforcement strategy meant long-terms needs such as developing a coherent, integrated organizational structure were sacrificed for short-term image building that litigation generated. Yet, one of the justifications for creating the EPA was precisely the need to bring a comprehensive perspective to environmental policy. In addition, the simple lack of scientific knowledge about the causes, effects and treatment of pollution cried for attention through research and development. However, these were long-term strategies by the very nature of the issues they sought to address and inconsistent with the priority of demonstrating the impact of the Agency immediately.

Nixon won reelection and Ruckelshaus was reappointed as EPA administrator which seems to confirm the political wisdom of the strategy he adopted. But there remained tension between the EPA and the Executive Office of the president. This is illustrated by the relationship between the Office of Management and Budget (OMB) under the direction of George Shultz and the EPA. The Clean Air Act of 1970 required the EPA administrator to establish National Ambient Air Quality Standards (NAAQS) as a means to promote the improvement of air quality. George Shultz, in an effort to ensure that economic interests were being given adequate consideration by various government agencies, established the "Quality of Life Review" process which required all agencies to submit proposed regulations to OMB prior to implementation. Ruckelshaus's claims to the contrary notwithstanding, representatives of the environmental community argued that this procedure stripped the EPA administrator of his statutory duty to establish clean air standards. This kind of initiative to keep the EPA "on the reservation" with respect to administration priorities has been characteristic of its relationship with various elements in the Executive Office of the President ever since, especially with members of the White House staff.

Ruckelshaus departed the EPA in the spring of 1973 to become director of the FBI. His replacement was Russell Train, a career public servant who had served in a variety of capacities in all three branches of the federal government. He was well known and well respected in Washington circles. Train survived the presidential transition following Nixon's resignation, and, not unlike Gerald Ford, served primarily in a caretaking capacity. He kept the organizational structure developed by Ruckelshaus, and he continued to pursue Ruckelshaus's policies.

The Environmental Protection Agency under the Carter administration

Douglas Costle served as the EPA administrator throughout the presidency of Jimmy Carter. Much of his career up to the time of his appointment had been spent as a public servant in federal and state Republican administrations. He had been a member of the team that originally designed the EPA under the Nixon administration. The selection of someone outside the traditional Washington Democratic hierarchy was characteristic in an administration which had won election running against the Washington establishment and which appeared suspicious of those who were part of it. Consequently, Costle and the EPA under his tenure enjoyed substantial independence in setting an environmental agenda. But that independence also meant the EPA had few people in the administration outside the agency who had a vested interest in helping to promote its agenda. Indeed, Carter established in the White House the Regulatory Analysis Review Group (RARG) to ensure that the potential economic benefits and costs of proposed environmental policies were given careful consideration.[20]

Costle was intent on changing the image of the EPA from that of protector of the natural environment to protector of public health. This in fact accurately reflected the overall mission of the agency, but it would demand significant resources in time and energy to project this new image and supplant the traditional environmental image of the EPA which had a strong ecological orientation. Costle spent his entire tenure trying to achieve this end. To concentrate on this change in image he left the organizational structure much as he had found it and he retained the advocacy orientation of the agency. In this respect he resembled Ruckelshaus. Both administrators were willing to invest substantial resources to influence public perception of the EPA and its mandate at the expense of long-term strategic planning about the primary function of the Agency and how it should organize itself to achieve those objectives.

In 1977 the Carter administration formed the Interagency Regulatory Liaison Group (IRLG) comprised of representatives from the Consumer Product Safety Commission (CPSC), the Food and Drug Administration (FDA), the Occupational Safety and Health Administration (OSHA), and the EPA to coordinate their respective agendas. Was the IRLG useful? One can hardly argue against the potential utility of representatives from different agencies coordinating their efforts. But the ultimate effectiveness of the final report of the IRLG on carcinogenic risk, for example, is highly questionable. The political compromises necessary to get the various participants in the IRLG to sign on to the final document left it largely irrelevant.[21]

The EPA agenda during the Carter administration may be best characterized as ambitious. It struggled to implement several major pieces of legislation that became law at the end of the Nixon/Ford administrations, worked with Congress to forge new legislation, and sought to change the Agency's orientation from one of ecology to one of health. The record suggests that in trying to accomplish so much in the short term the Agency lost an opportunity to set for itself a long-term agenda that would transcend the four years of the Carter presidency.

The Environmental Protection Agency under the Reagan administration

The Reagan administration was openly hostile to the environmental movement. Reagan's position reflected the traditional Western conservative belief that natural resources were meant to be exploited for the economic benefit of humankind. Three strategies were pursued to change the EPA from its perceived image as an advocate for the interests of the environmental movement: (1) personnel changes; (2) the imposition of a broad administrative structure intended to check the development of policy initiatives within the federal bureaucracy generally; and (3) budgetary initiatives. Ann Gorsuch was appointed administrator of the EPA. Closely associated with Reagan Republicanism, she had made her reputation as a member of the Colorado legislature where she was known for her opposition to the environmental movement. But she was not well known within Reagan's inner circle and Gorsuch was given little discretion with respect to EPA appointments. Most of the top positions were filled by the White House. This ensured the administration that the EPA would be staffed by personnel it perceived would be loyal to the White House and to its agenda. In addition, the administration simply opted to move very slowly filling a number of positions which impeded the ability of the EPA to fulfill its legislative mandates.

The determination of the Reagan administration to bring the bureaucracy of the federal government (including the EPA) in line with its ideological orientation resulted in the creation of an administrative structure whereby domestic policy initiatives were screened by cabinet councils comprised of cabinet officers or their designees and White House personnel.[22] The Cabinet Council for Natural Resources and the Environment was chaired by Secretary of the Interior James Watt, a strident opponent of the environmental movement. Neither Gorsuch nor any other representative from the EPA served on this council which is indicative of the low priority the EPA and its agenda had in the Reagan administration. The EPA also fell victim to the general policy of cutting the domestic budget. Measured in constant dollars, the EPA budget was cut just over 19 percent from Fiscal Year 1980 to Fiscal Year 1990, the last Reagan budget.[23]

Ultimately, the strident anti-environmental policy posture of the Reagan administration led to a backlash in the wake of congressional investigations for misfeasance and nonfeasance by EPA officials which culminated in the resignation of administrator Gorsuch in the fall of 1983 and the subsequent imprisonment for criminal conduct of Superfund administrator, Rita Lavelle. The administration recruited William Ruckelshaus from the private sector to once again take the helm of the EPA to restore its credibility as an environmental agency. Perhaps the greatest contribution Ruckelshaus made by his return was to buoy the sagging morale of agency employees. He assembled a senior staff with substantial government and environmental experience that was widely acknowledged as of superior quality. However, his substantive accomplishments were relatively minor. He attempted to develop a policy to address acid rain but that proposal was not favorably received by the Cabinet Council for Natural Resources and the Environment.

Ruckelshaus left government to return to the private sector after Reagan's reelection. He was succeeded by Lee Thomas, a career public servant, who had succeeded Rita Lavelle as the head of Superfund. Thomas made changes in the senior staff and brought with him to the position as administrator a reorientation to an ecological focus on the environment and a more global perspective than was characteristic of his predecessors. He took special interest in the depletion of ozone in the upper atmosphere attributed in part to chlorofluorocarbons (CFCs) used as refrigerants and cleansers. The interest and leadership of Thomas in this issue helped to bring about an international agreement on CFCs known as the Montreal Protocol which has been presented as a model for multinational environmental agreements. A second area of international concern on which Thomas focused was global warming. Again, under his leadership the US maintained a high profile at international conferences on this issue and helped move the global environmental dialogue that shaped the United Nations Conference on the Environment and Development which took place in Rio De Janeiro, Brazil in 1992. Encouraging a stronger international orientation was perhaps the most lasting legacy that Thomas left with the EPA.

The Environmental Protection Agency under the Bush administration

George Bush came from a very different Republican Party tradition than did Ronald Reagan. This was perhaps no more evident than in their respective relationships with the environmental movement. Reagan sought to challenge the environmental movement outright as a matter of ideological principle. George Bush sought to defuse the environment as a policy issue that would clearly distinguish him from his opponent. The campaign of 1988 once again witnessed both principal presidential candidates, Bush and Massachusetts governor Michael Dukakis, trying to claim rightful ownership of the environmental mantle. George Bush said he wanted to be known as the "Environmental President."

Upon his election Bush appointed William Reilly to head the EPA. Educated in the Ivy League followed by a service career planted squarely in Washington environmental policy circles (Reilly's positions before becoming administrator included a tour of duty with the Council on Environmental Quality, and president of both the Conservation Fund and the US World Wildlife Fund), he was the archetypal Bush appointee. His environmental credentials were substantial and the president promised him he could appoint his own staff. The staff Reilly put together to run EPA was experienced in Washington politics and environmental protection, not unlike himself. Perhaps not surprisingly, no new organizational initiatives or designs for EPA came out of this rather conventional group of Washington insiders. Working against Reilly were: (1) the staggering budget deficit which would limit his budget and (2) individuals in key White House positions and elsewhere in the executive branch who were philosophically more compatible with the Reagan administration.

George Bush had campaigned to address the problems of acid rain, global warming, and the disappearance of wetlands. But the two issues which defined the Bush administration's environmental policy were the revision of the Clean Air Act and the United Nations Conference on the Environment and Development (UNCED), perhaps better known as the "Earth Summit," held in Rio De Janeiro, Brazil. Pressure had built in Congress to revise the Clean Air Act throughout the 1980s, but it was not until Ronald Reagan left office that revisions had any chance politically of becoming law.[24] In many respects, the position of the Bush administration on the Clean Air Act resembled the Nixon administration's position on environmental issues generally: that is, protect the interests of the business community and their view of the economy without alienating the environmental movement and losing credibility with it and with Congress.

The team assembled to develop the appropriate policy from the perspective of the administration included Roger Porter, assistant to the president for Economic and Domestic Policy; C. Boyden Gray, White House counsel; Robert Grady, associate director of OMB; and William Rosenberg, assistant administrator for Air and Radiation. Once again an administration did not trust the EPA to be sensitive enough to a range of policy concerns broader than environmental interests and chose to deny the EPA exclusive jurisdiction of a major environmental policy initiative. Whatever the rationale, the strategy worked. The proposed Clean Air Act amendments sent to Congress were presented by an administration unified in its support, and they were very similar to those which eventually became law. The most significant changes from an administrative perspective were the mandates and statutory deadlines Congress imposed on the EPA for fear that without them a future administration might try to scuttle the intent of the law. This, however, ignored the lack of success historically that such mandates on the EPA have had for a variety of reasons, including mistaken technical assumptions written into the law. Politically, the Bush administration and Reilly's EPA came through the process with their environmental credibility unimpaired.

Quite the opposite resulted from the administration's encounter with the UNCED held in June 1992. The purpose of UNCED was to bring together the developed and developing countries of the world to produce a set of agreements reached through consensus about how to promote economic development through sustainable environmental policies. Reilly had played a leadership role in establishing the agenda of the Rio Summit which was to culminate in the signing of a set of five accords by the political leaders of virtually every country in the world. Most of the debate in preparation for the conference had been between the developed countries who urged preservation of natural resources and slow growth by the developing world, and the developing countries who countered that they were unfairly being asked to bear most of the sacrifices. The heart of the accords were the "Biodiversity Convention" and the "Global Warming Convention." The Biodiversity Convention was intended as a legally binding treaty that required, among other things, countries to share in the research, profits and technology that resulted from harvesting genetic resources. This measure was opposed by the US biotechnology industry in particular. The Global Warming Convention, a legally binding treaty, originally set targets for reducing "greenhouse" gasses into the atmosphere. The other three accords were non-binding principles and blueprints.

While the summit was in progress a political battle raged at home between the conservatives led by Vice President Dan Quayle who argued that the biodiversity treaty was directed expressly at American industry, and that the emissions targets posed a threat to existing jobs with insufficient scientific evidence to support the utility of the targets. All of the G-7 countries agreed to sign the accords with the exception of the United States. At the last minute a compromise was reached which allowed Bush to attend the summit. In return the targets were eliminated from the Global Warming Convention, and the US simply declined to sign the Biodiversity Convention. But the political fallout in the US was severe. The organized environmental movement would use the Rio summit as evidence that George Bush was different more in style than in substance from his predecessor, a charge he was unable to escape in the 1992 election.

The Environmental Protection Agency under the Clinton administration

Presidential candidate Bill Clinton shored up his questionable environmental credentials substantially when he chose as his vice presidential running mate Senator Al Gore from Tennessee. Gore's environmental credentials were acceptable by any mainstream political standard, but they looked absolutely impeccable to the environmental community compared to those of his Republican counterpart, Vice President Dan Quayle. To date Gore's interests as vice president have been focused on the theme of "reinventing government" rather than the environment. It remains to be seen whether or not he will become more visible in the environmental policy arena. He did play a role in the selection of personnel to environmental positions, including former governor of Arizona and president of the League of Conservation Voters, Bruce Babbitt (Secretary of the Interior) and former senator from Colorado, Timothy Wirth (counselor for the State Department).

Clinton's choice to head the EPA was Carol Browner, former secretary of the Florida Department of Natural Resources. Prior to that she had served as a staff member to both Senators Gore and Lawton Chiles (currently governor of Florida). In an interview she commented, "We can't just continue to put out the same old environmental regulations and expect to get solutions . . . We need to change the process."[25] Changing the process, according to Browner, means working more closely with business and industry to develop voluntary pollution control standards. This "go slow," accommodating approach has drawn criticism from some environmentalists. It remains to be determined whether or not this represents substantive change in the philosophical orientation of the Agency designed to enhance the mission of the EPA or simply an excuse to justify minimal action in meeting the Agency's mandate. The Clinton administration's substantive policy initiatives have been few, and its proposed elevation of the EPA to a cabinet-level department has not enjoyed the advocacy by the White House of such issues as health care and welfare reform.

An assessment of the Environmental Protection Agency and environmental policy

Since its creation in 1970 the EPA has served six presidents and had eight administrators (counting Ruckelshaus twice). Each administrator, acting in consort with the White House or not, has attempted to put his or her own *imprimatur* on the EPA and the policies for which it is responsible. Simultaneously, the EPA has not traditionally had close relations with the Executive Office of the President. Attempts by the EPA to initiate closer contacts have normally been met with indifference at best. A more familiar scenario has been the initiation of closer contacts with the EPA by one or more of the EOP constituencies to ensure, either overtly or covertly, that the EPA's environmental agenda remained subordinate to other domestic policy agendas. This has created strong centrifugal forces which encourage discontinuity over time. These forces are aggravated by the creation of laws which mandate broad but vague targets and standards that have little grounding in scientific research. Consequently, the idiosyncratic environmental proclivities of members of Congress and ranking officials in the EPA drive the Agency careening along a path with few parameters to help it retain a long-term orientation. The centrifugal consequences of this are exacerbated by the Congress's recent proclivity to pass laws which mandate EPA action on an ever increasing environmental policy agenda without concomitant increases in the Agency's resources, a dilemma articulated by the quotes which preface this chapter.

Counterbalancing these centrifugal forces are specific recurring themes that seem to act as centripetal forces helping to maintain a sense of continuity within the EPA and the evolution of environmental policy. Among the more important substantive issues is the determination of the appropriate balance between the command and control orientation of direct regulation with the market incentives and quasi-market incentives such as "bubbles" and "offsets" with which the EPA has experimented since the early days of the agency.[26] Among the more important recurring process issues is the utilization of risk assessment and risk management to make policy decisions. Critical to this debate is the understanding that environmental policy decisions necessarily involve appreciation that setting standards and targets are political decisions as well as scientific decisions, and that the public as well as policy makers must accept the ambiguity that issues as complex as the environment necessarily entail.[27]

Finally, perhaps the single most important consequence of the EPA is its very existence. It serves both as the principal forum for the environmental policy debate, and as a focal point for a broad range of participants including the Congress, the environmental lobby, the

judiciary, other executive branch entities, state and local governments, and individual citizens. That in itself is no small contribution
to the dialogue of democracy.

Notes

1   Office of the Federal Register. 1993. *The United States Government
Manual*. Washington, DC: Government Printing Office. p. 564.

2   Executive Office of the President, Council on Environmental Quality.
1985. *Environmental Quality*. Washington, DC: Government Printing
Office. p. 14.

3   Rachel Carson. 1962. *Silent Spring*. Greenwich, CT: Fawcett Publications.

4   Edwin Diamond. 1975. *The Tin Kazoo: Television, Politics, and the
News*. Cambridge, MA: MIT Press.

5   Muskie's role in particular and the early stages of environmental
policy in general are developed thoroughly in Marc Landy, Marc J. Roberts,
and Stephen R. Thomas. 1994. *The Environmental Protection Agency:
Asking the Wrong Questions from Nixon to Clinton* (expanded edition).
New York and Oxford: Oxford University Press, chapter 2.

6   For a more comprehensive treatment of the relationship between
rivers and harbors legislation and environmental policy see Jerry L. Mashaw
and Richard A. Merrill. 1975. *An Introduction to the American Public Law
System*. St Paul, MN: West Publishing, chapter 1.

7   Broadly speaking, public law pertains to the operation of government
or the relationship between the government and other parties including
private individuals. Private law, by comparison, pertains to the relationship
between private individuals.

8   E.g., *Connecticut Action Now, Inc.* v. *Roberts Plating* Co., US Court
of Appeals, Second Circuit, 457 F.2d 81 (1972).

9   Mashaw and Merrill, *An Introduction to the American Public Law
System*, p. 82.

10   A concise and insightful discussion of the EIS and NEPA in general
may be found in: Zachary A. Smith. *The Environmental Policy Paradox*.
Englewood Cliffs, NJ: Prentice Hall. pp. 52–54.

11   *Aberdeen and Rockfish Railroad Company* v. *Students Challenging
Regulatory Agency Procedures*, 422 US 289 (1975).

12   E.g., *Calvert Cliffs' Coordinating Committee, Inc.* v. *United States
Atomic Energy Commission*, US Court of Appeals, District of Columbia
Circuit, 449 F.2d 1109 (1971).

13 Landy et al., *The Environmental Protection Agency*, p. 30.

14 Landy et al., *The Environmental Protection Agency*, p. 32.

15 See: Charles O. Jones. May, 1974. "Speculative Augmentation in Federal Air Pollution Policy-Making." *Journal of Politics*. vol. 36, pp. 438–464.

16 *Congress and the Nation: 1985–1988*. 1989. Washington, DC: Congressional Quarterly, p. 421.

17 Office of the Federal Register. 1972. *United States Government Organization Manual: 1971–72*. Washington, DC: US Government Printing Office. pp. 405–409.

18 *Congressional Digest*. February, 1994. Washington, DC: CQ Press. p. 37.

19 Alfred A. Marcus. 1980. *Promise and Performance: Choosing and Implementing Environmental Policy*. Westport, CT: Greenwood Press. pp. 85–99.

20 Susan J. Tolchin. July/August 1979. "Presidential Power and the Politics of RARG." *Regulation*. pp. 44–49.

21 See Landy et al., *The Environmental Protection Agency*, chapter 6.

22 See Nolan J. Argyle and Ryan J. Barilleaux. 1986. "Past Failures and Future Prescriptions for Presidential Management Reform." *Presidential Studies Quarterly*. vol. 16, no. 4. pp. 716–733. See also Fredric Waldstein. 1990. "Cabinet Government: The Reagan Management Model," in *The Reagan Years: The Record in Presidential Leadership*. Joseph Hogan (ed.) Manchester and NY: Manchester University Press, chapter 3.

23 Norman J. Vig and Michael E. Kraft (eds.) 1990. *Environmental Policy in the 1990s*. Washington, DC: CQ Press, p. 400.

24 For a full account of the Clean Air Act as amended in 1990 see Gary C. Bryner. 1993. *Blue Skies, Green Politics*. Washington, DC: CQ Press.

25 Margaret Kriz. June 18, 1979. "The Greening of Environmental Regulation." *National Journal*. p. 1467.

26 For a useful introduction to these and other economic concepts see: Myrick Freeman III. 1990. "Economics, Incentives, and Environmental Regulation," in Norman J. Vig and Michael E. Kraft (eds.) *Environmental Policy in the 1990s*. Washington, DC: CQ Press, pp. 145–166.

27 See, for example, Richard N. L. Andrews. 1990. "Risk Assessment: Regulation and Beyond," in Norman J. Vig and Michael E. Kraft (eds.) *Environmental Policy in the 1990s*. Washington, DC: CQ Press, pp. 167–186.

The inexorable rise of the national debt

The American public places the federal debt near the top of economic policy issues because it is so large, and because it has grown so rapidly over the past 15 years. While there are some potentially serious consequences of a large and growing debt, it is not the most important economic problem in contemporary America. Urban decay, poverty, inequality, the quality of education, equal opportunity, creating jobs that pay decent wages, integration into the world economy, sluggish economic growth, and the inability to sustain low unemployment rates without generating inflation are all more serious problems than the debt. Draconian measures to reduce the debt may well make the other problems worse. On the other hand, doing nothing about the debt could have its own set of negative consequences.

The numbers

The federal budget and the national debt are numbingly large numbers. As the late Republican Senator Everett Dirksen of Illinois often remarked, "a billion here, a billion there, and pretty soon you're talking about real money."

The national debt and the federal budget deficit are not the same thing, but they are closely related. The budget surplus (+) or deficit (−) is the difference between the federal government's receipts and outlays in a given Fiscal Year. The federal debt is the accumulated debt of the federal government, or the accumulated budget deficits from the past. A budget deficit requires the government to borrow, and this increases the federal debt. A balanced federal budget would stabilize the debt. Should one ever occur, a federal budget surplus would reduce the debt.

Between Fiscal Years 1970 and 1993, the gross federal debt of the US government (GFD) grew from $380.9 billion (38.7 percent of gross domestic product, GDP) to $4.35 trillion (69.1 percent of GDP). To put this into historical perspective, Figure 4.1 shows the GFD since the end of World War II.

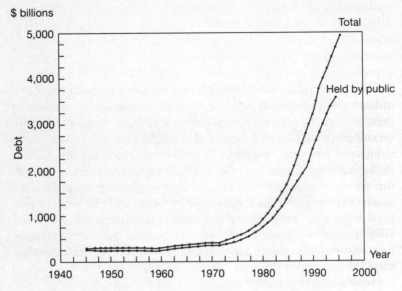

Figure 4.1   Gross federal debt, Fiscal Years 1945–1995 ($ billions)
Source: Economic Report of the President, 1972–1975, 1979, 1981, 1989, and 1994. Washington, DC: US Government Printing Office.

From 1945 through the 1960s, the debt grew at a modest pace despite changes in the political climate and administrations, the economic impact of the Korean War (1950–1953) and policy changes in the Truman (1945–1953), Eisenhower (1953–1961), Kennedy (1961–1963) and Johnson (1963–1969) administrations. Even the effects of the Vietnam War on the debt seem modest in hindsight.

Beginning in 1970, the debt began to grow at an accelerating pace. The growing expenditures to finance the Vietnam War and expand social programs, oil shocks in 1973 and 1979, a recession in 1973, inflation and high nominal interest rates all contributed to greater federal budget deficits and growth of the federal debt in the 1970s.

Ironically, it is during the Reagan (1981–1989) and Bush (1989–1993) administrations – the two most conservative administrations since Herbert Hoover (1929–1933) – that the federal debt really exploded, more than quadrupling between Fiscal Years 1982 and 1993. Although they continued to advocate a balanced budget amendment to the US Constitution, conservative Republicans, who traditionally decry "fiscal irresponsibility" and the massive national debt, expressed minimal concern over the debt in the 1980s. Democrats, accustomed to defending programs and fiscal policies that contributed budget deficits and growing federal debt, began to express great alarm over deficits and growth of debt in the 1980s.

The absolute size of the debt, impressive as it is, is not a very useful indicator of its significance. Most economists consider the size of the debt relative to Gross Domestic Product (debt/GDP) as a more meaningful indicator of the economic significance.

Figure 4.2 shows the debt/GDP ratio since the end of World War II. With a few bumps along the way, the debt/GDP ratio fell during the entire period 1945–1974. Although the growth of the debt accelerated in the 1970s, compared with the years 1945–1969, GDP grew faster than the debt and the ratio of debt/GDP fell. The debt/GDP ratio rose slightly between 1974 and 1976 following a recession in 1973 and oil price shocks, leveled off and rose through the 1980s and early 1990s.

Historically, a sharply rising debt/GDP ratio is associated with wars or such economic disasters as the Great Depression of the 1930s. In 1939, after a decade of high unemployment, economic stagnation and moderately expansionary fiscal policy during the Great Depression, the federal debt was 55 percent of GDP. Military spending to prosecute World War II raised the debt/GDP ratio to its all-time high of 122.7 percent in 1945.

In every Fiscal Year since 1981, the debt/GDP ratio has risen, reaching 69.1 percent of GDP at the end of Fiscal Year 1993, the highest since 1955. The Treasury Department and the Office of Management and Budget estimate that it will rise to 70.6 percent of GDP by the end of Fiscal Year 1995. Such a sharp rise in the debt/GDP ratio in a period which saw no major wars, the end of the Cold War, reduced international military tensions among the major military powers, and no economic catastrophe comparable to the Great Depression is unique in American history.

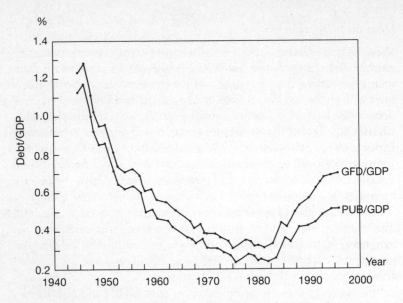

Figure 4.2   Gross federal debt/gross domestic product, Fiscal Years
1945–1995
Key:
GDP   gross domestic product
GFD   gross federal debt
PUB   government debt held by the public
Source: Economic Report of the President, 1972–1975, 1979, 1981, 1989,
and 1994. Washington, DC: US Government Printing Office.

Virtually nobody really expects the federal government to run
budget surpluses that would reduce the debt, or realistically to run
balanced budgets that would stabilize it. The most realistic expecta-
tion is for budget deficits to continue and for the debt to continue to
rise. A smaller federal deficit merely reduces the *growth* of the debt.
Reducing the federal debt would require federal budget surpluses,
which would in turn require some combination of higher taxes and
reduced spending – hardly a strong plank in any political platform.
The question is whether the debt will rise more rapidly than aggregate output and gross domestic produce (in which case, the debt/
GDP ratio will rise), at the same rate as GDP (in which case, the
debt/GDP ratio will be stable) or more slowly than GDP (in which
case, the debt/GDP ratio will fall).

Does the debt matter?

Views of the economic significance of federal deficits and the national debt range from panic to complacency. Traditionally, arguments on deficits and the debt ran fairly clearly along ideological lines with conservatives tending to be alarmist and liberals seeing the debt as no cause for concern and even beneficial economically. Charles Schultze of the Brookings Institution, formerly Professor of Economics at University of Maryland and Chair of Lyndon Johnson's Council of Economic Advisers, has identified three broad classifications of views of the significance of the debt – "wolves," "termites", and "pussycats." [1]

Schultze's "wolves" see the seeds of economic disaster in the debt. The "wolves" include many of the traditional opponents of an extensive economic role for government – the political and ideological right, financial interests, and modern "classical" economists.

"Pussycats" are a surprisingly diverse group. They include liberals (most notably, Professor Robert Eisner of Northwestern University), as well as such conservative economists as Professor Robert Barro of Harvard and (in recent years) Milton Friedman.

Eisner argues that the official measures of the budget deficit and federal debt are misleading and distort the their size and significance. Taking a strongly Keynesian approach, he asserts that in a period of relatively high unemployment and crumbling infrastructure, the budget deficit (and therefore the debt) are probably too small. [2]

Friedman, a Nobel laureate and arguably the best known spokesman for a minimal economic role for government, has taken a rather benign view of the debt in recent years because he sees the large federal debt as a constraint on further expansion of the size of government. [3] Barro argues from a proposition known as the Ricardian Equivalence Theorem that the economic significance of financing government expenditures through debt instead of through higher taxes – thus increasing the size of the debt – is not particularly important because individuals will simply save now to pay the higher taxes that will be required to service or retire the debt in the future. [4]

Schultze compares the debt with a termite infestation. "Termites" see potential problems with a large public debt if it is ignored. Their main concern is that large deficits and a rapidly growing public debt will reduce national saving, investment, and economic growth – all of which will contribute to lower future living standards. However, toxic "cures" for the rising debt could cause more serious problems than the debt itself.[5]

"The debt will bankrupt the country"

This is an intuitively appealing argument against a growing national debt, but it doesn't hold up very well under closer examination. Even with the rise in the debt/GDP ratio in the 1980s, there is little concern over national bankruptcy (whatever that means). Creditors will not be descending on Washington to attach the assets of the government. The federal government could (if it wished and cared nothing about inflation) simply print up enough money to pay off the debt.

There *are* absolute limits on the debt. The interest on the debt, for example, cannot exceed the net domestic product. Short of this absolute limit, if fiscal policies and the debt were generally viewed as so completely out of control that the owners of financial wealth would not purchase government bonds and currency would not be accepted in exchange, one could say that the country is bankrupt. In this event, the debt would be a much less serious problem than social and economic disintegration and chaos.[6]

"The debt is a burden on current and future generations"

Alarmists often point out that every person in the United States is in debt from the time he or she is born. If we divide the 1993 national debt of \$4.676 trillion by the US population of 258.233 million, this "debt burden" amounts to \$18,108 for every man, woman, and child in the United States.

Since it is highly unlikely that the national debt will be paid off or reduced significantly, future generations will bear the obligation of making interest, and conceivably principal payments on the debt. But is this a *net* burden on the current generation and generations to come? The answer is the economist's favorite: "It depends."

The real burden of the debt on any generation is the "other things" it must give up to pay the interest and principal. The government, like other borrowers, borrows and repays in current dollars. Inflation lowers the real value of the debt to the lender and the real burden of the debt on the borrower. For example, if prices rose by 4 percent between 1993 and 1994, the real value of the \$4.35 trillion debt outstanding at the end of fiscal year 1993 would fall by \$1.74 billion. Inflation thus imposes a tax on the holders of the debt by reducing the real value of the debt.[7] In the extreme, a government can virtually completely repudiate its real debt with hyper-inflationary monetary policies.

The net burden of the debt, if any, depends on to whom it is owed. As shown in Figure 4.1, not all of the federal debt is held by the public. About $1.35 trillion, or about 30 percent of the outstanding debt was held by the government in 1992 – i.e. the government owes this portion of the federal debt to itself. Of this amount, about $1.048 trillion was held by the Treasury and in trust funds (such as the Social Security trust fund) and about $302.5 billion was held by the Federal Reserve banks.

The Federal Reserve ("the Fed") is the monetary policy authority in the United States. Its holdings of government securities largely reflect the Fed's open-market operations (purchases and sales of government securities), the main tool for controlling the money supply. The burden of the federal debt held by the Fed is insignificant because the Fed's interest earnings on the debt are income to the federal government.

However, at least some of the debt held in trust funds may impose a distributional burden on future generations. For example, some of the interest paid on the debt held by the Social Security trust fund finances pensions, virtually all of which are spent on current consumption. This part of the government-held debt will generate an inter-generational transfer between the working and wage-earning population and the pensioners.

The publicly-held debt that is held internally by US households, firms, and financial institutions imposes a distributional burden on those who hold none of the debt, but not a net burden on society. Society as a whole is responsible for principal and interest payments on the debt, but these payments are also income to domestic holders of the debt.

The debt that is owed to foreign creditors may be a net burden to society. To meet its debt obligations, the US government may have to either raise taxes, cut other government programs or increase borrowing. To the extent that the interest and principal payments by the US government to foreign creditors do not generate income to Americans, the externally held debt is a net burden on the United States.

The burden of a public debt on current and future generations also depends on the types of expenditures it finances. Critics of government spending tend to assume that it is inherently "wasteful," or at least that it is current consumption spending that neither raises productivity nor generates any future benefits.

Indeed, a substantial portion of total government outlays are for current consumption. Many "entitlement programs" – such as Social Security pensions and some federally funded public assistance benefits that support consumption expenditure by their recipients, as well as most military spending – fall into this category. Some public spending on "pork barrel" projects that are locally popular with members of Congress and their constituents are either wasteful or add little to productivity, but the significance of this type of spending is overstated by critics.

If the government borrows to finance current consumption, only the debt remains in the next period. As Adam Smith put it over 200 years ago, the person who borrows to finance current consumption can "neither restore the capital nor pay the interest without either alienating or encroaching upon some other source of revenue"[8] Smith's argument applies equally to government borrowing.

If consumption spending is financed by an internally held debt, there is no net burden on the generation that does the consuming. However, future generations have a debt and receive no benefits from the consumption by the current generation.[9] Future benefits from other government programs may have to be cut to meet the debt obligation. Maintaining other programs will require higher taxes in the future, lowering disposable income. Future living standards may fall because paying the interest and principal on the debt lowers national saving and investment.

This is not to suggest that entitlement programs and public assistance expenditures should be eliminated or savaged to reduce the growth of the debt. Many of the beneficiaries of entitlement programs are among the economically most vulnerable groups in society (children, the elderly, widows, widowers, and the disabled). However, financing them by borrowing is in essence borrowing to finance consumption, and this imposes a net burden on society, at least on future generations. The burden on future growth and living standards is particularly heavy if the government borrows from foreign creditors to finance current consumption, as was the case with much of the Latin American public debt incurred in the 1970s and 1980s.[10]

Some government spending is investment that increases the country's capital stock, raises productivity, and promotes the growth of capacity and potential GDP (the highest level of aggregate output that can be sustained without accelerating inflation). Expanding and maintaining social overhead and infrastructure (roads, ports, railways, sanitation facilities, etc.); spending on education and public health (human capital investment); and expenditures on research and development of new technologies and products are examples of this type of spending.

Government borrowing to finance expenditures that raise productivity and output (presumably by a value at least equal to the amount borrowed) does not impose a net burden on society because society gains assets and the benefits from the additional output generated by economic growth.[11] If capacity and output grow at least as rapidly as the debt, there is no need to reduce future private consumption and investment, raise taxes or reduce the benefits from government programs to finance the debt.

Some government expenditures do not have a measurable direct effect on productivity and output, but provide benefits over a long period of time. We in the United States are still enjoying the benefits of public works, parks, and reforestation projects undertaken by the Works Progress Administration (WPA) and the Civilian Conservation Corps (CCC) in the 1930s. Public hospitals, schools and universities are other examples of public spending projects that provide benefits over more than a single generation. Future generations will inherit the benefits of the assets created by these projects as well as the debt that financed them – i.e. they do not impose a net burden on future generations. If the social rate of return on these types of projects is greater than the private rate of return that would attract sufficient private capital to finance them, there is a net benefit to society from the government debt incurred to provide them through the public sector.

"The debt has made the US the world's greatest debtor"
This argument sounds dramatic in the thirty-second sound bites that pass for real political discourse in the United States. There are some reasons for concern about the rapid shift from international creditor to international debtor in the 1980s, but it is not necessarily the portent of economic and political doom that it is often portrayed to be.

The terms "creditor" and "debtor" nation refer to the net international investment position of the US – the difference between the

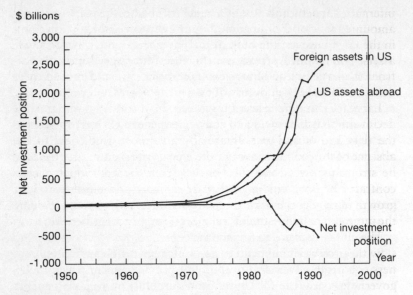

Figure 4.3   Net investment position of the US 1945–1992 ($ billions)
Source: Economic Report of the President, 1972–1975, 1979, 1981, 1989, and 1994. Washington, DC: US Government Printing Office.

value of US assets abroad and the value of foreign assets in the US. Figure 4.3 shows the US net international investment position (in billions of dollars) from 1972 through 1992. The net investment position had been falling consistently since 1950, but the decline after 1980 was precipitous. The US was a creditor nation (US claims on foreigners exceeded foreign claims on the US) until 1987. By 1992, foreign claims on the US exceeded US claims on foreigners by $521.3 billion.

One of the reasons that the US has become a net debtor is because it is an attractive haven for foreign assets.[12] There is no risk of losing assets in the US due to social or political upheaval or revolution. The US faces no threat of military hostilities with its neighbors. There is virtually no risk that the US government will repudiate its bonds. In short, US interest rates and the minimal risks of loss account for a large part of the increase in the value of foreign assets held in the US from $220.5 billion in 1975 to $2,524.7 billion in 1992.

The growing US federal debt accounts for part of the increase in foreign assets in the US and the shift from international creditor to international debtor. In 1992, foreign owned US Treasury securities amounted to $560.7 billion, or about 22 percent of the foreign assets in the US. However, the bulk of foreign assets in the US are private assets. Foreign-held private debt in the US increased in large part from the large inflow of foreign capital that financed record trade deficits in the 1980s and early 1990s.

Large foreign purchases of US government securities mitigate the decline in US bond prices and consequent rise in US interest rates as the debt grows and the Treasury issues more securities. In the absence of foreign purchases of US Treasury securities, there would be stronger upward pressure on US interest rates (which would contract economic activity and probably increase the deficit and the growth of the debt) and/or on the Federal Reserve to accommodate the increased debt by purchasing more Treasury securities.

The ability of the US to sustain even reduced budget deficits and slow the growth of public debt depends increasingly on the willingness of foreign governments and owners of wealth to purchase US government securities.[13] This reduces the ability of the Fed to pursue monetary policies that lower interest rates because it may precipitate an exodus of foreign capital.

Some critics argue that the US international debtor status reduces its international political and economic influence.[14] A large creditor, the argument goes, can use its clout to influence domestic and international policies of debtors. As the only real remaining superpower in the post Cold War world, the US international political position does not seem to have deteriorated. Moreover, a large debtor has considerable influence over its creditors who want to protect their assets.

"Government deficits and the federal debt reduce saving, investment, and economic growth"

The effect of deficits and a growing national debt on national saving, investment, and economic growth is the real economic reason to be concerned about the debt. Growth of the economy's productive capacity and aggregate output of goods and services (GDP) requires investment, and investment requires saving. There are many things that Americans do well as a society, but saving is not one of them.

The following national income accounting identity shows the links between the budget deficits (the growth of the national debt), the trade deficit, national saving, and investment. In the US National

Income and Product Accounts (NIPA), national saving is

$$NS \equiv PS + GS \equiv NI + NX$$

where NS is national saving, PS is private saving, GS is government saving – the combined budget surplus (+) or deficit (−) of all levels of government, NI is net investment (investment, less depreciation) and NX is net exports or the balance of trade.

Net investment is the change in the capital stock, which is critical for sustained economic growth. This brings us to a valid concern over the high deficits that have caused the national debt to grow.

Although state and local governments typically run budget surpluses, their combined surplus has been falling since 1980. Adding the small combined saving by state and local governments to the large dissaving embodied in the federal budget deficits, public saving in the US (GS) is negative. In some countries – Italy, for example – high government budget deficits and public dissaving are offset by a high rate of private saving (PS). This is not the case in the US, which has a very low rate of private saving. In 1992, net private saving amounted to $329 billion, only about 11 percent of the net domestic product (NDP = GDP less depreciation).

Public and private borrowing is all financed from the same flow of saving. The traditional "neoclassical" macroeconomic concern over public dissaving and a rising public debt is that it depresses private investment and thus hinders economic growth. The combination of a low private saving rate and growing public dissaving reduces the domestic sources of funds for private investment. This would predict that growth of the national debt relative to gross domestic product would depress private investment, and the evidence since the 1960s seems to support this prediction.

Figure 4.4 shows the ratios of gross federal debt to gross domestic product (GFD/GDP), net national saving to net domestic product (NNS/NDP) and net investment to net domestic product (NI/NDP) for the US between 1960 and 1992. While GFD/GDP was falling, the ratios of net national saving and net investment to NNP (NNS/GDP and NI/GDP) fluctuated slightly around 15 percent. In the period of a sharply rising debt/GDP ratio since the early 1980s both NNS/NDP and NI/NDP fell. In 1981, both ratios were about 12 percent. By 1992 NNS/NDP had fallen to about 2.1 percent and NI/NDP had fallen to 4.5 percent. The NI/NDP ratio would have fallen even further had there not been a large flow of foreign assets into the US.

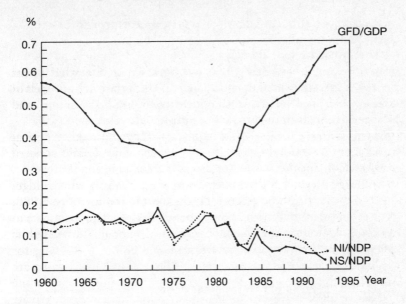

Figure 4.4 Gross federal debt, net investment, and net saving 1960–1992
Key:
GDP   gross domestic product
GFD   gross federal debt
NDP   net domestic product
NI   net investment
NS   net saving
Source: Economic Report of the President, 1972–1975, 1979, 1981, 1989,
and 1994. Washington, DC: US Government Printing Office.

This contradicts the "pussycats'" generally benign view of the debt,
but does it indicate the doomsday scenario promoted by the "wolf at
the door" view of the debt?

If the current generation reduces national investment and saving in
favor of greater consumption, we leave the next generation with a
larger debt and a smaller capacity to produce. In short, we pass the
debt on to our children. We have known, since at least the days of
Adam Smith, that capital is required to employ labor. In an economy
with high unemployment and unused capacity, expansionary fiscal
and monetary policies can increase output and employment, as John
Maynard Keynes explained in the 1930s. However, eventually, low
rates of saving and net investment slow the growth of the capital

stock and capacity sufficiently to constrain the growth of employment, output, and income.

The effect of low domestic ‚saving on investment and capital
formation since the early 1980s has been eased somewhat by the
inflow of foreign capital that has balanced the large trade and current
account deficits (NX in the NIPA identity above).

If the profits from foreign-owned capital are reinvested in the US,
this will at least partially offset the effects of low national saving and
investment rates. However, to the extent that foreign owners
repatriate the profits earned on assets employed in the US they will
not contribute to US investment, output, and employment. If the
foreign owners of these assets get favorable tax treatment compared
with domestic owners, the government's tax revenue from foreign
assets is less than if they were domestically owned, and will reduce
the tax base for all levels of government.

Economic policy implications of the debt

Being "against" deficits and a rising national debt – like being "for"
motherhood, baseball, apple pie and "family values" – in the
abstract is much easier than supporting specific policies that would
reduce the growth of the debt. Running on a platform of reducing
benefits from popular public programs and even suggesting tax
increases is the political equivalent of self-immolation in America.

Fiscal policy

Fiscal policies have the most obvious impact on the federal budget
deficit and the growth of the federal debt. At first glance, the fiscal
strategy seems simple. To reduce the deficit and growth of the debt,
simply enact some combination of higher taxes and lower government spending. Unfortunately, too many voters and the candidates
they elect to federal office labor under the delusion that cutting only
"wasteful" government spending will do the job without raising
taxes or reducing real benefits from government programs. Many
even think that cutting government waste alone will get the deficit
and the debt under control and allow for tax cuts.

Nobody likes to pay taxes, but Americans have a particularly
strong aversion to higher taxes. It has been argued that the American
Revolutionary slogan "No taxation without representation!" was
only half accurate.

In the 1984 presidential campaign debates, Walter Mondale made the ill-fated statement that he might have to raise taxes. His opponent, Ronald Reagan, promised lower taxes with no cuts in spending and no increase in the deficit or the debt. The economic growth unleashed by lower tax rates would, according to Reagan, raise total tax revenue enough to finance existing levels of federal expenditure, including a substantial increase in military spending. The Reagan landslide in the 1984 election illustrates the pitfalls of economic realism and fiscal bluntness.

Reducing the budget deficit and slowing the growth of the debt isn't even as simple as cutting spending and raising taxes. Federal fiscal policies affect aggregate output and income, and hence government receipts and outlays. Raising taxes and cutting spending reduce aggregate demand, which reduces GDP (at least in the short run). Lower GDP reduces tax revenue, most importantly revenue from federal income taxes (the largest source of federal revenue). The higher unemployment associated with lower GDP would increase some federal outlays – for example, unemployment compensation.

The fiscal follies of the 1980s rested on a "supply-side" prediction that lower income tax rates would generate sufficient saving, investment, and economic growth to reduce the deficit by slowing the growth of, but not actually cutting, government spending. Moreover, the combination of economic growth, cutting "wasteful" spending on social programs, and shifting programs to states would finance a dramatic increase in military spending. Many economists were skeptical, including such eminent conservatives as the late Professor George J. Stigler who, at a White House press conference following the announcement of his winning the Nobel Prize in Economic Science, gave the president a grade of "incomplete" on economic policy and called supply-side economics more a slogan than a well conceived economic theory before he was hustled off the podium by White House staff. Figure 4.3, above, indicates that this skepticism was justified.

Not only does fiscal policy affect the debt, the debt affects fiscal policies. The rise in the federal debt since 1980 has increased federal net interest payments. Between fiscal years 1976 and 1992, net interest payments rose from $25.1 billion (6.6 percent of federal expenditures) to $198.8 billion (17.2 percent of federal expenditures). This made net interest the fourth largest federal outlay for Fiscal Year 1993 after Social Security ($304.6 billion), national defense ($291 billion), and income security programs ($207.2 billion). Net interest payments in Fiscal Year 1993 exceeded such visible and politically sensitive outlays as Medicare ($130.5 billion), health ($99.4 billion), education ($50 billion), and transportation ($35 billion).

Net interest, like entitlement programs, are "uncontrollable" or non-discretionary outlays. Short of repudiating the debt, there is little discretion over net interest payments. Of the discretionary outlays, the largest is national defense. In spite of the much hailed end of the Cold War and "peace dividend" a good deal of military spending is locally popular in areas with a large defense presence, and hence with many members of Congress.

Unless the government either raised taxes, slashed the shrinking "controllable" or discretionary outlays, or printed enough money to buy up outstanding bonds (with obviously inflationary consequences), the size of the debt and interest payments on the debt constrain the discretion of the federal government in financing other programs – for example, health care reform. This is a possible reason why political and economic conservatives do not view the debt with the disdain or alarm one would expect.

Deficit-cutting fever is one of the negative consequences of a large national debt. Cutting the deficit is popular across a broad spectrum of the American electorate. With tax increases largely precluded by considerations of political survival, this leaves government spending cuts as the most obvious option. Every member of Congress believes that he or she will be able to cut "somebody else's" programs and preserve those that are popular locally.

However, indiscriminate budget cutting without consideration of the types of spending being cut can make the debt problem more difficult to deal with in the long run. In his first budget, President Clinton proposed a combination of cuts in some government programs and increased spending on public investment to reduce unemployment and increase productivity and output. To counter "liberal tax and spend" charges leveled by conservatives and to reduce outlays and the deficit, he withdrew the bulk of his public investment proposals. While the immediate effect was to reduce spending and the deficit, what was left in the budget were largely defense (notwithstanding substantial cuts) and consumption-oriented programs.

Consumption-oriented programs – however socially and politically important many are – do not raise productivity or add to the nation's capacity to produce. Slowing the growth of productivity and the capital stock (including public and human capital) slows the growth of GDP, employment, and income. This will make it more difficult to maintain or lower the debt/GDP ratio without really painful spending cuts and/or raising taxes.

Monetary policy and the debt

Monetary policy affects the debt/GDP ratio in a number of important ways. It largely determines the impact of budget deficits on interest rates, which in turn affects aggregate demand and GDP. Because net interest payments are a substantial component of federal outlays, monetary policies also have an effect on the size of outlays and hence the size of the deficit.

In the extreme, the Federal Reserve could simply buy up the outstanding debt held by the public, or *monetize* the debt. The prices of government securities would soar, real interest rates (nominal interest rates less the rate of inflation) would plummet, the money supply would expand dramatically, and the end result would be extreme inflationary pressures. Fortunately, this is not likely to happen.

In the 1980s, the Federal Reserve attacked inflation with a generally restrictive or "tight" monetary policy in the face of large government budget deficits. This did bring inflation under control in the early 1980s, the cost of which was the worst recession since the 1930s. However, tight monetary policy and loose fiscal policy combined to raise real interest rates, which had two negative consequences for the debt/GDP ratio. By slowing economic activity and the growth of GDP in the face of rapidly growing debt, it contributed to the rapid rise of debt/GDP. High real interest rates also increase federal net interest payments and put additional upward pressure on the deficit, the growth of the debt, and the debt/GDP ratio.

Why doesn't the Fed simply follow an expansionary or "loose" monetary policy that would accommodate the effects of the budget deficits and the debt on interest rates? The Federal Reserve, like most banks, tends to be concerned (critics assert, overly concerned) about inflation. Aggregate demand can't expand indefinitely without generating inflationary pressure unless productive capacity also expands and bottlenecks in the economy that cause inflation to develop before we reach full employment are eliminated.

Although it remains somewhat controversial, most macroeconomists accept the notion of a "natural" output or GDP (the highest level of aggregate output that we can produce without accelerating inflation) and a "natural" unemployment rate (the lowest unemployment rate without accelerating inflation). Accommodating budget deficits with loose monetary policy will accelerate inflation once unemployment falls below the "natural" rate.

It is possible to increase "natural" output and lower the "natural" unemployment rate (they aren't determined by "nature"), but this gets us back to the really basic issues of the effects of the structure of the economy and institutions on the growth of productivity, output, and employment. Increasing net investment, developing new technologies that raise productivity, improving the nation's infrastructure, improving the education and health of the labor force, and reducing labor immobility are examples of the kinds of policies that would do this. These are more difficult and complex than expansionary monetary and fiscal policies and are likely to require greater outlays and deficits in the short run.

Equity considerations

On the surface, one would expect federal spending and taxes to reduce income inequality because "social" programs are seen as benefitting the poor and the federal income tax is progressive (i.e. it taxes high incomes at higher rates than low incomes). However, the effects of the fiscal policies that account for the rapid rise in the federal deficit and debt/GDP ratio since the early 1980s had just the opposite effect on income distribution. Between 1980 and 1991, the average real income in 1991 dollars (after taxes and including tax credits for low incomes, cash transfers, Medicare payments, free school lunches, means tested transfers and returns on home equity) of the richest quintile of households rose – by about 14 percent. Using the same definition of income, the average income of the poorest quintile fell slightly in the same period. Using the same income definition, the ratio of the income of the top quintile to the bottom quintile of households rose from 7.14 in 1980 to 8.37 in 1991.[15] Between 1980 and 1990, the share of aggregate income received by every quintile of households fell except the top quintile, whose share rose from 44.1 percent in 1980 to 46.6 percent in 1990. The Gini coefficient, which measures income inequality (from zero for complete equality to 1 with complete inequality) rose from 0.403 in 1980 to 0.428 in 1990.[16] It is always better to be rich than poor, but the period since 1980 has been a particularly good time to be rich and a particularly bad time to be poor in America.

The "Reagan tax cuts" were in fact tax cuts for corporations and high income households with marginal tax rates above 33 percent under the old system. Social Security taxes were raised to offset some of the revenue loss from the lower income tax rates and to accumulate a surplus in the trust fund to fund pensions after the turn of the century. The Social Security tax is a payroll tax on *wages* below a maximum (currently around $50,000). Thus, the lower income tax and higher Social Security tax shifted more of the tax burden from non-wage income to wages, especially to workers earning wages below the Social Security maximum. Since the recipients of non-wage income from capital and land tend to be high income households, the tax "cuts" made the federal tax system less progressive.

In addition to shifting the tax burden to workers' wages, the Social Security tax (like all payroll taxes) makes labor more expensive relative to capital. This encourages firms to economize on the use of labor and to substitute capital for labor, both of which tend to slow the growth of employment of labor and to increase unemployment.

The federal deficit and debt would have risen even faster in the 1980s and 1990s if programs had not been shifted from the federal to state and local governments. One effect was to reduce public saving by state and local governments. Although federal grants-in-aid to state governments increased from $88.7 billion in 1980 to $186 billion in 1993, the combined surplus in state and local governments fell from $24.8 billion to $2.1 billion in the same period. This also contributed to greater after-tax income inequality because state and local governments derive their revenue from sales, real estate, and income taxes that are less progressive than the federal income tax.

One of the success stories of the past quarter century has been the lowering of the poverty rate of elderly Americans. Between 1966 and 1978, the percentage of Americans 65 years of age and older below the poverty line fell from 28.5 percent to 14 percent; by 1987, it had fallen to 12.2 percent, a 57.2 percent decline since 1966. However, the poverty rate among children under 18 rose by 17 percent and among adults aged 18–64 by 2.9 percent. In real terms, federal expenditure for the elderly increased 52 percent between 1978 and 1987 while federal expenditures for children fell 4 percent.[17]

Nobody wants to return the elderly to poverty – certainly not this ageing author – but the drop in federal expenditures on children,

particularly education spending, is a decline in public human capital
investment. Lower human capital investment means a less productive labor force in the future, and this has negative implications
for future economic growth and the ability to stabilize or lower the
debt/GDP ratio.

(Can, should, will) anything be done about the debt?

The debt is a potentially serious economic problem, and the continuing rise in the debt/GDP ratio and falling national saving and
investment rates are causes for concern. Before deciding what to do
about the national debt it would be useful to know how much of it
finances current operations of the federal government, how much of
it finances public investment and how much of it is externally held.
This sounds simple enough, but it would require major changes in
governmental accounting which is far from an exact science. For
example, simply defining what expenditures are public investment
and public consumption is to some extent arbitrary and politically
loaded. Every member of Congress worth his or her salt will try to get
locally popular programs included as "investment," whether or not
they meet any reasonable economic standard for investment.
Altering national income accounting to account for inter-
generational effects is even more complex.[18]

Massive cuts in federal spending and increases in federal taxes are
not only virtually impossible politically, but also self-defeating as a
means of reducing the debt/GDP ratio. These policies would reduce
aggregate demand, GDP, employment, and income. Lower income
would generate smaller government tax revenue, which would at
least partially offset the effects of reduced government spending on
the deficit and growth of the debt. Cutting public investment and
other expenditures that raise productivity would slow the growth of
capacity, output, and GDP. Even if higher taxes and reduced outlays
slowed the growth of the debt, the ratio of debt to GDP might not
fall because they also slow the growth of GDP.

Dealing with the debt will require increases in government spend-
ing that increases society's stock of physical and human capital.
Public infrastructure investment is essential after a decade of neglect.
Investment in human capital via health, education, and training
programs raise productivity and expand productive capacity.
Increasing federal outlays in these areas may increase total outlays

and the deficit in the short run, but increasing economic growth could lower the debt/GDP ratio in the future.

Current government operations and consumption-oriented spending should be financed out of current tax revenue, which may require higher taxes. One possibility is to restore some of the progressivity of the federal income tax that was lost in the 1980s. Another possibility is a broad-based consumption tax, with a tax credit to reduce its regressivity. Relative to other prices, gasoline was cheaper in the US in 1994 than it was in 1970. Increasing the gasoline tax to bring US gasoline prices in line with those in the rest of the world is an economically sound but politically unpopular way of increasing government tax revenue.

In the contemporary American political climate, it is unlikely that any policies will be undertaken that would reduce the federal deficit and growth of the national debt without increasing unemployment and the inequality of income distribution. President Clinton's early surrender on his public investment program, the unwillingness of the American electorate to accept higher taxes or recognize the productivity of public investment, and the unwillingness of members of Congress to accept cuts that are unpopular in their districts all work against effective policies to deal with the debt.[19]

Notes

1   Charles Schultze, "Of Wolves, Termites, and Pussycats Or, Why We Should Worry about the Budget Deficit," *Brookings Review*, summer 1989, 26–33.

2   Robert Eisner, "The Deficits and Us and Our Grandchildren," in James M. Brock (ed.) *Debt and the Twin Deficits Debate*. Mountain View, CA: Mayfield, 1991, 81–108.

3   Milton Friedman, "Why the Twin Deficits are a Blessing," *Wall Street Journal*, December 14, 1988.

4   Robert Barro, *Macroeconomics*, 2nd edn. New York: Wiley, 349–354; Robert Barro, "The Ricardian Model of Budget Deficits," in James M. Brock (ed.), *Debt and the Twin Deficits Debate*. Mountain View, CA: Mayfield, 1991, 133–148; Michael E. Bradley, "Ricardian Economics," in Frank T. McGill (ed.) *Survey of Social Science: Economics*. Pasadena, CA: Salem Press, 1991, 2030–2037.

5   Schultze, "Of Wolves, Termites and Pussycats."

6   Michael E. Bradley, *Macroeconomics*, 2nd edn. Glenview, IL: Scott,

Foresman, 357–360.

7 Alan S. Blinder, "Is the Federal Debt Really – I Mean *Really* – a Burden?," in James M. Brock (ed.), *Debt and the Twin Deficits Debate*. Mountain View, CA: Mayfield, 1991, 209–225; Robert Eisner, "The Deficits and Us and Our Grandchildren."

8 Adam Smith, *An Inquiry into the Nature and Causes of the Wealth of Nations* (1776). New York: Random House, 1937, 333.

9 Laurence J. Kotlikoff, "Deficit Delusion," *Public Interest* 84: summer 1986, 53–65; Laurence J. Kotlikoff, "The Deficit is Not a Well-Defined Measure of Fiscal Policy," *Science*, 6, 791–795.

10 Kenneth P. Jameson, "Latin America's Burden: The Debt," in James M. Brock (ed.), *Debt and the Twin Deficits Debate*. Mountain View, CA: Mayfield, 1991, 55–77.

11 Robert Eisner, "The Deficits and Us and Our Grandchildren"; Robert Eisner, "Sense and Nonsense About Budget Deficits," *Harvard Business Review*, May–June 1993, 99–111; Robert Heilbroner and Peter Bernstein, *The Debt and the Deficit: False Alarms/Real Possibilities*. New York: Norton, 58–67.

12 Milton Friedman, "Why the Twin Deficits are a Blessing."

13 Benjamin S. Friedman, "US Fiscal Policy in the 1980s: Consequences of Budget Deficits at Full Employment," in James M. Brock (ed.), *Debt and the Twin Deficits Debate*. Mountain View, CA: Mayfield, 1991, 149–172.

14 For example, B. Friedman, "US Fiscal Policy in the 1980s."

15 US Bureau of the Census, *Studies in the Distribution of Income*, Current Population Reports, Series P60–183. Washington, DC: US Government Printing Office, 1992.

16 US Bureau of the Census, *Measuring the Effect of Benefits and Taxes on Income and Poverty*, Current Population Reports, Series P60–182RD. Washington, DC: US Government Printing Office, 1992.

17 Timothy M. Smeeding, "The Debt, the Deficit and Disadvantaged Children: Generational Impacts and Age, Period, and Cohort Effects," in James M. Brock (ed.), *Debt and the Twin Deficits Debate*. Mountain View, CA: Mayfield, 1991, 31–54.

18 Kotlikoff, "Deficit Delusion"; Kotlikoff, The Deficit is Not a Well-Defined Measure of Fiscal Policy."

19 Additional sources: *Economic Report of the President*, published annually. Washington, DC: US Government Printing Office; Robert J. Gordon, *Macroeconomics*, 6th edn. New York: HarperCollins, 1994; Robert Heilbroner and Peter Bernstein, *The Debt and the Deficit: False Alarms/Real Possibilities*, New York: Norton, 1989.

Transforming the East–West relationship

Introduction

No State Department planner in 1975, even if he or she were of the caliber of George Kennan, could have foretold the sort of environment in which the United States would find itself in 1995. The defining relationship in postwar US foreign policy, its rivalry with the Soviet Union, has changed beyond all recognition. The state that preoccupied American attention as the only other superpower on the globe collapsed and its sphere of influence in Eastern Europe imploded. Whilst the two decades preceding 1975 were characterized by continuity and strategic stalemate between East and West, in the period since 1975, American presidents have been forced to confront a much more complex international situation.

The relationship with the Soviet Union has also acted as a framework for America's relationship with its allies, most notably the states of Western Europe. Mutual fear of the USSR originally brought together the North Atlantic Treaty Organization (NATO) partners in 1949 and heralded the start of American political and military leadership on the continent. Following the dramatic revolutions in Eastern Europe in 1989, the United States has been required to rethink its relationship with both its former Western allies, who are less desirous of a tight security embrace, as well as with the former adversary states of the Warsaw Pact.

Each of the four American presidents since 1975 has been challenged to develop new strategies to deal with relations with the Soviet Union and Western European allies. Both Jimmy Carter and Ronald Reagan faced an adversarial Soviet Union, yet each sought differing strategies toward managing the confrontation. Presidents George Bush and Bill Clinton have faced the still harder task of dealing with the transformation of the East–West relationship, from

hostility to cooperation, and with the implications that this has had
for America's allies. This chapter focuses upon the similarities and
differences in the approaches of each of the administrations toward
the problems that they faced. In particular, it seeks to highlight how
the goals of containment and leadership were pursued by successive
presidents, as well as how America has sought to deal with the
process of change in international relations.

Carter versus Reagan

On the face of it, there would appear to be few similarities between
the foreign policy programs of the Carter and Reagan presidencies.
After all, the two men were very different personalities and had come
from different backgrounds. Ideologically, they were from opposing
poles of the political spectrum: Carter, a left of center Democrat
whilst Reagan was a hardline Republican. Reagan even came into
office on the platform that his predecessor had been weak in foreign
affairs and had caused America to lose sight of what Americans saw
as their rightful role in the world.

Yet, when one looks more closely at the progress of the two
presidencies, there are notable parallels between the periods. Both
leaders were seen to represent a break with the old Washington
foreign policy establishment. Carter was a former governor of the
state of Georgia and was seen as representing the South, whilst
Reagan was a governor from California, bringing a West Coast
perspective to bear. Both leaders entered office seeking to break with
the policies of their predecessors. They approached the Soviet Union
and its European allies with the aim of reasserting American strength
and regaining a position of leadership, and both experienced
troubled relationships as a result. Carter and Reagan also held strong
views about the moral superiority of the United States; they sought
to reflect this in their relationships with allies and adversaries alike.
Finally, both administrations experienced significant shifts of policy
during their years in office. Whilst the Carter government hardened
its attitude toward the Soviet Union in the period 1979–1980, the
Reagan government noticeably softened its stance toward its adversary in its second term, between 1986 and 1988.

Perhaps the similarities between the two administrations are not
that surprising after all. For both administrations were attempting to
come to terms, albeit in different ways, with the legacy that had been

left behind from the Vietnam War and the Watergate crisis. These two events had undermined the postwar consensus in the United States on matters of foreign affairs. They had engendered shock and turmoil and had cast doubt upon the nature of America's role in the world. They served to challenge the assumption that had been prevalent since the end of World War II that the country was the legitimate "Defender of Democracy." The withdrawal from Vietnam, which was not completed until 1975, had blighted America's claim to be the leader of the "Free World" and called into question the moral basis of America's foreign policy. It had also shown the limits of American strength, when despite its enormous technological and military sophistication, the US military had been unable to achieve a decisive victory against a poorly developed state in South-East Asia.

Perhaps most importantly of all, Vietnam and then the subsequent Watergate scandal, undermined the trust of the American public in the leadership of their country, both at home and abroad. The war in Asia caused a rupture in the public's willingness to trust the foreign policy decisions of elected officials and the role that they had carved out for the US in world politics. Furthermore, the move to impeach President Nixon cut away public confidence in the office of the presidency itself. Although the power of the chief executive had been growing in foreign affairs, particularly since the Kennedy era, the fall-out from Watergate served to circumscribe the powers of future presidents.

The strategies that the two administrations chose to overcome the legacy of the past were different, but their objectives were the same. Both sought to restore the confidence of the American people in the office of the presidency and in the rightful role of their country as the leading actor on the world stage. Neither Carter nor Reagan questioned the rightness of their cause: both were sure of America's destiny. Their missions were to find ways to restore the support of the domestic audience in the foreign actions of the United States.

Carter sought to achieve his objectives by reordering the foreign policy agenda, with enemies and allies alike. He placed the issue of human rights at the top of his list of priorities and made this one of the most public issues of his presidency. He appointed officials, such as Cyrus Vance to the State Department and Andrew Young to the United Nations (UN), who shared his views and were prepared to act upon the issue. By so doing, the long established issues of the military containment of the Soviet Union and the cohesiveness of the Western

Alliance, were relatively downgraded in importance. The simple bipolar perspective of East–West confrontation was replaced by a more complex view of the world in which issues, such as human rights and economics, rather than just military competition, were central considerations. In the words of Bowker and Williams, the Carter administration was attempting to "transcend containment."[1]

This policy had two important facets. Firstly, by shifting the focus to human rights issues, the US was able to assert its moral superiority over the Soviet Union and the regimes of Eastern Europe. This issue was pursued on a broader front than just the Communist bloc: it was pursued in Latin America and Africa as well. But it was followed most vigorously in East–West relations and offered the US a new and innovative form of leverage. It enabled the US to concentrate attention upon Jews who wished to emigrate and political dissidents in the USSR, as well as supporters of the Conference on Security and Cooperation in Europe (CSCE) in territories of the Warsaw Pact. Human rights also gave the Carter administration a vehicle for rehabilitating America's own international image after Vietnam. Regaining the moral high ground after the revelations of the bombing of Cambodia, and the failure of government officials to be honest with the people about the progress of the war, was considered to be vitally necessary.

Secondly, by demoting the issue of military containment, Carter was attempting to divert attention away from the perception that the United States was losing ground to the Soviet Union. Throughout the Cold War, America had perceived itself to be superior to its adversary and had relied upon this fact to justify its position as leader of its NATO allies. However, following Vietnam and the codification of Soviet nuclear parity in the Strategic Arms Limitation Treaty (SALT) of 1972, the US image as leader was open to question. Carter and his advisers looked to a broader range of issues, such as the Camp David discussions between Israel and Egypt, rather than focusing narrowly on relations with Moscow. By switching attention away from the military index of power and looking to other issues, the administration was both reflecting its belief in the greater complexity of the world and removing the spotlight from the question of declining power.

These changes of priority also served to demonstrate the administration's sensitivity to the needs of its European allies. Amidst a period of detente, in which countries such as the Federal Republic of

Germany had benefitted from an improvement in relations with the Soviet Union, there was less of a desire to look to the United States to act as a military leader. European members of the Alliance were demonstrating greater independence and equality in their relationships with Washington and were less willing to follow American directions. They continued to want reassurances about the American commitment to their security but they also wanted to see a less aggressive and more positivist climate of relations between the US and USSR. Therefore, Carter's demotion of military security issues and his promotion of humanitarian considerations was in keeping with the prevailing transatlantic mood. Human rights provided an issue around which Western European allies could coalesce whilst still preserving the American role of leadership in the West.

Unfortunately for Carter, the tensions within his policies and the hostile external situation in which they had to operate, led to the unraveling of the administration's priorities. At the very heart of his government, there was rivalry between Secretary of State Cyrus Vance's view of the world and the more hawkish perspectives of the powerful National Security Adviser, Zbigniew Brzezinski. The latter was seen to gain an increasingly dominant voice in the government and he came to treat the human rights issue as an ideological crusade against the Soviet Union. Leonid Brezhnev and his Politburo regarded the American pressure on this subject as unwarranted interference in the internal affairs of the Soviet Union and its allies. Both adversaries and American allies alike became unsettled and critical of what Garthoff has called the "zig-zags"[2] in American foreign policy as Carter appeared unable to choose between the advice offered from different parts of his administration.

Furthermore, the international environment in which American policy was enacted came to appear increasingly unfavorable. Soviet adventurism, particularly in Ethiopia/Somalia and Angola, forced regional conflicts between the superpowers back to the top of Washington's agenda. Similarly, the continuing expansion of Soviet nuclear capabilities at the strategic and theater levels raised fears that they were attempting to achieve superiority over the United States and made the achievement of a SALT II treaty very difficult. All these problems added weight to the voices of the domestic critics of the administration on both the right of the Democratic Party as well as the Republicans. The image was projected that Carter had underestimated the perfidy of his opponents and had failed to make

America's allies aware of the dangers. When the Soviets invaded Afghanistan in December 1979, this appeared to bear out the direst warnings of Carter's opponents and the demand for a change in American policies became overwhelming.

The administration responded to calls for change by a major policy swing to hardening its stance towards the Soviet Union. President Carter requested that the SALT II Treaty, which had been signed in Vienna in June 1979, had its ratification delayed by the Senate and instituted sanctions on grain and high technology sales across the Iron Curtain. Carter also declared the establishment of a quick reaction force, with pre-positioned equipment in the Indian Ocean, to be able to intervene in the event of Soviet aggression in the Persian Gulf. Effectively, the hardline approach associated with the Brzezinski wing of the government had triumphed and American policy moved back to outright competition with the USSR. In the words of Garthoff, American policy had moved back to "the Truman–Eisenhower–Kennedy policy of containment."[3]

Ronald Reagan entered office in January 1981 with a message that America had been badly served by the detente policies of the 1970s, the so-called "decade of neglect." His campaign emphasized the weak policies of Carter, epitomized by the tragic failure of the attempt to rescue American hostages held in Iran, after the downfall of the Shah. There were ideologues in the Reagan administration who believed that compromise with the Soviet Union was too dangerous: figures such as Secretary of Defense Caspar Weinberger, Assistant Secretary of Defense Richard Perle, UN ambassador Jeane Kirkpatrick, and CIA director William Casey. They maintained that America had relinquished its leading role in world affairs to the Soviet Union and had been tricked into policies of inactivity. In the meantime, forces opposed to liberal, free market capitalism had continued their activities unabated. Now was the time, argued the Republicans, to rebuild US strength and confront Communism in every corner of the globe with countervailing strength. Only policies such as these could, in the words of Weinberger, "persuade the Soviets that they could not take actions such as they had taken in . . . Angola and Afghanistan and earlier in Cuba, Nicaragua, Ethiopia and elsewhere."[4]

Yet despite Reagan's attempt to distance himself from his predecessor, and the different political hue of his administration, his objectives were basically similar. He desired to reassert America's position of leadership both against its adversaries and amongst its allies. Like Carter, Reagan believed deeply in the moral superiority of the United States, leading to his description of the Soviet Union as an "evil empire" in March 1983. He too believed that the ghost of Vietnam had to be exorcised from American policy so that self-imposed constraints did not prevent the US from fulfilling its sense of global destiny.

What distinguishes the Reagan administration from Carter's were not so much the means that were employed, but rather the order in which those means were applied. Reagan came into office with an agenda of confrontation with the USSR. He embarked at the outset on a deliberate policy of military containment and with an arms control policy that was based on the presupposition that Soviet gains of the past had to be reversed. In contrast, the Carter administration began with a more benign policy towards the USSR, that sought to circumvent its growing power status, but then changed its stance in the latter part of the 1970s. Carter's attitude hardened after what he came to see as the betrayal by Brezhnev over Afghanistan.

As regards NATO allies, Reagan was eager to see a return to the old pattern in which NATO was rallied around an anti-Communist crusade. The Western Europeans were expected once again to follow the American lead. This had proved a satisfactory arrangement in the 1950s when the Europeans were weak and grateful for US protection. It did not, however, prove to be successful amidst a more self-assertive continent. Countries in Western Europe had grown accustomed to the fruits of East–West detente and were less predisposed to regard the Soviet Union as an aggressive and expansionist power. The US administration was expecting the Europeans to forgo the benefits of the rapprochement and return to a Cold War stance. This difference of approach crystallized in 1981 around the subject of the Trans-Siberian Gas Pipeline. American firms such as General Electric were banned from exporting equipment for the completion of the project and the Reagan administration attempted to stop Western European companies fulfilling their orders. European governments refused to support the American position and eventually the US had to back down.

The first Reagan administration set about constructing a set of policies that would restore American preeminence in the West. The centerpiece of this strategy was a build up in conventional and nuclear forces as well as the command and control structures that would enable these forces to prevail in all types of conflict. John Lehman, Secretary of the Navy, established a target for a force of 600 major vessels, with a much enhanced force projection capability. America's nuclear forces saw the reinstatement of the B-1 aircraft project, a new Stealth bomber, and greater priority for the MX and D-5 missile programs. Reagan was able to inherit the increases in military spending that had been undertaken by Carter. Indeed, the whole perception that the Carter years had witnessed reductions in defense spending was erroneous as Harold Brown, the former Defense Secretary, had presided over annual increases. Reagan was responsible merely for increasing this priority, rather than starting a policy afresh. Defense spending increased at the staggering rates of 12.6 percent in 1981 and by 12.2 percent in 1982.[5]

There were two objectives within this policy. The first was to recover a margin of superiority over the Soviet Union that would deter it from policies of adventurism. Consistent with this, the US demonstrated by its intervention in Grenada in 1984 and by its support to the Contra rebels in Nicaragua, that it was prepared to use its military strength to further its foreign policy objectives. As far as allies were concerned, the US could claim to be taking the lead in countering the military strength that the Eastern bloc had amassed in the 1970s.

Secondly, the policy of high defense spending was designed to drive the Soviet Union into a further round of arms competition that it was poorly placed to undertake. Hawks within the administration were eager to pressure the Soviet economy so that it might reach a point of exhaustion. This helps to explain in part the attachment of Reagan to the concept of a layered shield from ballistic missile attack – the Strategic Defense Initiative (SDI), which was announced in March 1983. Such a system, as well as offering a potential escape route from mutual vulnerability, also provided a powerful instrument for squeezing the Soviet economy in the field of high technology research.

In the human rights field, the Reagan administration followed an aggressive policy that sought to highlight abuses that were taking place in the Eastern bloc. This was conducted through the follow up conference of the CSCE in Madrid where the American Secretary of State Shultz and the Soviet Foreign Minister Gromyko openly clashed. The US also chose to focus public attention upon well-known dissidents in the USSR, such as Anatoly Shcharansky and

Andrei Sakharov. Particular attention was drawn to the declaration of martial law in Poland and to the deliberate shooting down of a Korean airliner, Flight KAL 007, which had strayed into Soviet airspace over the island of Sakhalin. The aim of American policy was to embarass the leaders in the Kremlin, rather than to engage in a constructive dialogue that might have secured Soviet concessions.

There can be little doubt that such policies as these proved to be counter-productive in both East–West and West–West relations. The renewed perception of ideologically driven hostility deepened the tension between Washington and Moscow and raised the fear of imminent war. As a consequence, there were no meetings between Reagan and Soviet leaders during the first administration, despite a succession of leaders, Brezhnev, Andropov, and Chernenko. Talks on nuclear arms control were suspended in November 1983, after the deployment of new American Pershing II missiles to Germany, and there was an ice cold stalemate between the two superpowers.

This contributed to sharp antagonisms between the Americans and their NATO allies. The Europeans feared the potential of being the battleground of any US–Soviet conflict and they had been unsettled by discussion amongst American policy-making and academic elites of the concept of a limited nuclear war fought on the continent. This had encouraged the reinvigoration of anti-nuclear protesters. Countries such as the Federal Republic of Germany had the most to lose from a renewed Cold War; they saw relations with East Germany deteriorate and they witnessed the decline in movement of peoples across the inner-German border. From a perception in which they feared abandonment by the United States in the 1970s, the Europeans came to feel that the United States was dragging them down a dead-end path.

But just as the Carter administration's policies changed in the latter part of its term in office, so was the second Reagan administration destined to oversee a substantial departure from the policies previously adopted toward the Soviet Union. The immediate catalyst for this was the arrival of Mikhail Gorbachev as Soviet leader in March 1985. Gorbachev's accession to power ushered in a decade in which the fundamental tenets of postwar US foreign policy were subjected to critical review and change.

The immediate question was how the US should respond to the new leader after so much recent and deep superpower hostility. The US policy of confrontation with the USSR was well entrenched and reflected in military outlays. President Reagan had just received a ringing personal endorsement for his policy of restoring American strength, convincingly winning the 1984 election. In spite of all of this, superpower relations warmed rapidly after 1985. A combination of domestic, Alliance-related, and external factors explain this transformation.

Despite his personal triumph in the presidential election, Reagan faced an increasingly awkward legislature. Over the next few years congressional pressure increased the incentives to follow a more cooperative policy with the Soviet Union. Concern over the twin budget deficits led Congress in 1985 to slash the administration's request for a 7 percent defense spending increase in real terms for Fiscal Year 1986. As a result Reagan was, for the first time in his presidency, forced to accept a real cut in defense expenditure. The passage of the Gramm–Rudman–Hollings Act in December 1985, requiring automatic budget cuts if Congress and the administration could not agree a budget, ended the era of ever rising defense expenditures. With their November 1986 victories in the Senate, the Democrats now controlled both houses of Congress.

Reagan also suffered in his relations with Congress over the "Irangate" scandal. In 1986 it was revealed that the National Security Council had supplied arms to Iran for hostages and had diverted funds to the Nicaraguan Contras in defiance of Congress. Not only was the administration's anti-terrorism policy seriously discredited in the eyes of the allies, but questions were raised over the president's control over White House decision making and his attention to detail. Thus, from both a moral and an efficiency perspective, the administration's claims to Western leadership suffered. Positive developments in the US–Soviet relationship were thus a very useful diversion from the perceived shortcomings of the Reagan administration.

An undeniable element behind the change in American foreign policy stems from the desire of President Reagan not to go down in history as a war-monger, but as a leader who, by standing tall, had convinced the Soviet leadership that the US could not be trifled with. Once that realization of American intent was established, the objective conditions for a radical improvement in East–West relations existed.

Within the White House there had always been a spectrum of opinion between pragmatic figures, such as Secretary of State George

Shultz, and relative hardliners such as Secretary of Defense Caspar Weinberger. Shultz records "an intellectual debate raging."[6] During Reagan's second term, those advocating a more pragmatic approach to the Soviet Union held more sway in the forming of policy. Weinberger and Assistant Secretary of Defense Richard Perle were eventually to leave the administration.

In addition, despite the prevalence of the view that the first Reagan administration's military build-up had confronted Moscow with the futility of any attempt at military hegemony in Europe, a perceptible sense of decline settled over American politics during 1987/1988. Partly spawned by the budget crises, this sense was thrown in to sharp relief by the October 1987 Wall Street crisis. The appearance of Kennedy's *The Rise and Fall of the Great Powers*[7] stimulated an intense, if rather artificial, national debate as to whether the US had overstretched itself with military commitments and, like the British and Soviet empires before it, would now subside into decline. This gave rise to speculation that American policies would henceforth focus on domestic priorities, undermining both American willingness and capacity to lead the Western nations, as well as the acceptance by the Western nations of such leadership.

Certainly a continuation of hardline anti-Soviet policies would have precipitated a transatlantic crisis of the first order. While US allies in NATO were quick to dismiss obvious Soviet attempts to divide the Alliance, such as Gorbachev's offer to freeze Intermediate Nuclear Forces (INF) deployments on the eve of Dutch deployments of INF in April 1985, they were keen to ensure a normalization of relations with the East. Detente did not have the same negative connotations to European leaders, and their publics, as it had in Washington. The priority of NATO in US foreign policy thus made a continuation of rejectionism impossible in the new conditions.[8]

There is thus a range of reasons why the Reagan administration adopted a more cooperative attitude toward the Soviet Union from 1985. Yet undeniably, the largest single factor was the perceptible change in Soviet foreign policy itself. It was this which provided the environment in which the other factors identified could take effect. From 1985, Soviet foreign policy, as determined by Foreign Minister Edvard Shevardnadze and Gorbachev himself, offered the West an increasing amount of opportunities and concessions. The Soviet priority was for a reduction in superpower tensions to allow funds to be diverted from military programs into the efforts to restructure and modernize the ailing Soviet economy.

Arms control takes center stage

The framework around which the improving superpower relationship could be based now needed definition. The first signs of Soviet new thinking came in the area of arms control. In 1985 bilateral arms control negotiations between the US and USSR resumed in Geneva after their complete collapse a year earlier. The resumption occurred despite the US negotiating position not having changed materially from that which had precipitated the Soviet walk-out in 1984. Arms control had always waxed and waned according to the political context in which it operated. The first Reagan administration had held deep reservations over the wisdom of negotiated arms control with the Soviet Union. The record of Soviet compliance with existing treaties was considered to be far from perfect and the treaties were considered to be limiting on American weapons programs. To an extent, these reservations continued into the second term of office. Thus, there were charges of continued Soviet violations of the Anti-Ballistic Missile (ABM) and SALT II treaties. In addition, President Reagan's pursuit of the SDI led his administration to look skeptically at the ABM treaty.

Nevertheless, arms control did come to provide the framework for locking in Soviet concessions and new thinking after 1985. Soviet military power was now to be contained not by an American military build-up, but through negotiated reductions in the arsenals of the superpowers. The second Reagan administration is remarkable for the degree to which arms control discussions, rather than disputes over human rights and regional issues, described the *essence* of superpower relations.

In adapting to an environment where the Soviet Union was now clearly interested in arms reduction, the US leadership had to take account of a number of factors: the US national priorities in terms of the Soviet programs it wished to constrain and those programs of its own which were to be kept out of any arms control regime; distinguishing between genuine Soviet offers and declaratory proposals geared for public consumption; and the need for alliance consultations despite the overwhelmingly bilateral nature of the negotiations. Given the efficiency of the new Soviet team, together with a much greater sensitivity to Western public opinion than had been demonstrated by the gerontocracy that had preceded Gorbachev, the US administration was found to be inadequately prepared and wrong-footed on a number of occasions.

In January 1986 Gorbachev announced a proposal to eliminate nuclear weapons by 1999. In the first stage, the superpowers would cut their strategic nuclear arsenals by 50 percent, eliminate INF in Europe, whilst the UK and France froze their nuclear forces at current levels, i.e. before planned modernizations. Dismissed as utopian in many quarters,[9] this proposal did elicit a response from the US which demonstrated European concerns as much as those of the US administration.[10] Thus, the idea of a zero option for INF was welcomed but it was insisted that this should be global, not limited to Europe, that no commitments could be made with regard to the nuclear forces of the UK and France, and that while the elimination of nuclear weapons remained a goal, it could not be realized until the overwhelming conventional imbalance in Europe favoring the USSR was rectified, with adequate verification. While NATO allies doubted the wisdom of publicly espousing the elimination of nuclear weapons, they contented themselves that NATO's strategy of *flexible response*, by which NATO reserved the right to use nuclear weapons in the event of an attack by Soviet forces in Europe (thereby providing deterrence both against any initial attack and, if necessary, during any war), was safeguarded. US INF deployments in Europe were considered important as a "coupling" factor, extending deterrence by placing Soviet territory at risk from US weapons in response to an attack on Western Europe. Thus, there was a degree of unease over the prospect of a "zero option" for INF among America's allies.[11]

Nevertheless, at the October 1986 Reykjavik Summit, a formula for a "zero option" of INF in Europe, with each side able to retain 100 INF warheads globally was agreed. Deep cuts (50 percent) were also discussed in relation to US and Soviet strategic nuclear weapons, with a move to eliminate all offensive ballistic missiles within ten years. Agreement on both the INF and strategic elements was prevented by Soviet attempts to link these reductions to a ban on the US SDI program. The US allies were clearly shocked by the lack of consultation during these negotiations and the extent of American departures from agreed NATO compromises. The Reykjavik formula on INF was subsequently amended back to a global zero and this formed the basis of the INF Treaty signed in December 1987. US allies drew comfort from the removal of Soviet SS-20s from Europe and the landmark Soviet acceptance of deep asymmetrical cuts accompanied by rigorous on-site inspection.

SDI remained an obstacle to strategic arms control until after the end of Reagan's presidency. Soviet fears centered on the impact of SDI on their ability to retain a second-strike capability in the event of a US first strike. President Reagan was not able to convince allies either of the merits of strategic defenses. Both the UK and French governments feared that if SDI led to the destruction of the ABM Treaty of 1972, the capacity of their nuclear forces to threaten Soviet targets might be jeopardized. European leaders generally saw SDI as a source of concern due to its effects on arms control and on strategic stability.

Beyond the Cold War

At the start of his presidency in 1989, despite SDI, Bush inherited a framework for dealing with the Soviet leadership which had proved very successful. Everywhere Soviet foreign policy appeared to be mellowing. Soviet forces were beginning their withdrawal from Afghanistan. In December of 1988 Gorbachev had overturned years of stalemate in conventional arms control negotiations by announcing deep unilateral cuts and recognizing the West's claim that there was an asymmetry of forces in the Soviet Union's favor in Europe. Together with a publication of Warsaw Pact holdings, Gorbachev appeared to be removing the obstacles to a quick result in the new Conventional Forces in Europe (CFE) negotiations between the 23 members of NATO and the Warsaw Pact. In addition, in July 1989, the Soviet Union delinked agreement on strategic arms control to an agreement on SDI. The way was now clear for a Strategic Arms Reduction Treaty (START) agreement too, subsequently signed in 1991.

Bush had announced at the start of his presidency that he did not intend to preside over major changes in foreign policy. He also said in May that he hoped to "move beyond a policy of containment, integrating the Soviet Union into the family of nations."[12] This would have been a radical statement just a few years before. It came across in 1989 as rather cautious. The attempt to stress continuity inevitably foundered as events over the next few years forced Washington into a fundamental rethink over the American role in the reconstruction of Eastern Europe, its relationship to Germany and the *raison d'être* of the organization that symbolized American leadership in Europe – NATO.

Underlying the substantial Soviet concessions across the broad field of arms control was an urgent domestic imperative to free up resources. The gathering crisis within the Soviet system would soon trigger a profound political change in the European order that would overwhelm formal arms control. Already, in 1988, Gorbachev had sought to strengthen his powers in the face of criticism from radicals and conservatives alike. The contradictions inherent in top-down reform of the Soviet system became apparent as the outer ring of the Soviet Empire, in Eastern and Central Europe, threw off the stranglehold of state Communism in a series of largely peaceful revolutions throughout 1989. By the end of the year, the strategic map of Europe had completely changed. Cold War realities were now history.

President Bush presided over a pragmatic response to these events. Leadership in coordinating aid to the newly emerging democracies was passed over to the EC at the G-7 Summit in June 1989. The EC was undeniably better placed to offer trade concessions but this does offer an interesting commentary on US perceptions of its responsibilities. Similarly, a comparison of the aid given to Poland and Hungary in 1989, with American Marshall Aid to Europe in the immediate postwar years ($80 billion in 1990 dollars),[13] demonstrates the American desire for leadership in European affairs was not as great in the post Cold War environment as it had been in the aftermath of World War II. Thus in 1989, Poland was offered $10 million of immediate economic aid, $15 million for pollution control, a promise that the US would aid in the rescheduling of Polish debts and in the securing of a $325 million credit arrangement from the International Monetary Fund (IMF). Poland was subsequently offered a further $100 million emergency food aid package and $938 million with Hungary over three years by the US Congress.[14] Poland had asked for $10 billion of Western aid.

Bush, along with other Western (and Eastern) leaders felt that the arms control momentum had to be maintained. This would lock in the military gains, made possible by dramatic political change, within enforceable Treaty limitations. The rapidity of the movement in arms control from 1989, until Bush's departure from office, may be explained also by a desire to ensure that progress was made whilst there was still a unified and coherent negotiating partner.[15] This was certainly the case with the 23-nation CFE negotiations.

Given the scale of the Soviet acquiescence in the dramatic changes of 1989/1990, the gains made in arms control and the crucial Soviet support in the UN Security Council during the Gulf crisis of August 1990 to March 1991, it is unsurprising that US policy should swing squarely behind Gorbachev. This involved resisting any encouragement to the centrifugal forces of nationalism within the USSR, especially in the Baltic states. Soviet repression there, in January 1991, was passed over in relative silence. Ukrainian nationalism was criticized by President Bush. This cautious, non-provocative policy also involved not supporting the cause of Boris Yeltsin in any substantial way. The lines of this policy became so entrenched that it was difficult for the US to change tack even after it became apparent that Gorbachev's experiment, and indeed the multinational USSR itself, had failed in the months following the abortive *coup d'état* in August 1991. Thus, US recognition of Baltic independence came after that of most of the other NATO allies.

Clinton's policies toward Russia have shown a similar reliance on a central reforming figure – President Boris Yeltsin. This remained constant, even during the assault on the Soviet Parliament in October 1993. There are no real alternatives, at least within the democratic camp. Nationalism in Russia has become resurgent, partly reflected in a more assertive Russian foreign policy toward parts of its former empire and with respect to the crisis in the former Yugoslavia. Secretary of Defense Les Aspin identified the continuation of reform in Russia as essential for US military and economic security.[16]

For both Bush and Clinton, the gathering crisis and eventual implosion of the Soviet Union posed the question of how to move on from the Cold War policies of containment. The traditional *military* agenda of confronting a heavily armed and ideologically hostile adversary, forward-based in Central Europe, was no longer relevant. A combination of arms control and political change in Eastern Europe had ensured that, even in the unlikely event of any reversion to an aggressive foreign policy by Moscow, the warning times of any attack on Western Europe were now likely to be in the order of months and years, rather than days. Moving beyond containment has meant that US policy has had to embrace a more complex *political* relationship with Russia. Thus it was the political aspects of the US–Soviet/Russian relationship that were crucial in the Gulf and Yugoslav crises, as in the questions surrounding German reunification. The US has had to deal with situations where the Soviet/Russian role has not been primary or even obvious, but where Russian sensitivities to its diminished international influence have needed to be assuaged.

US leadership of the Alliance

Opening up to Eastern Europe?
The new complexities of the US–Russian relationship have also profoundly affected American policies toward the emerging democracies in Eastern Europe. The imperative not to act in any manner that undermines the leadership in Moscow has caused US foreign policy under Bush and Clinton to take a gradualist, incremental approach to security relations with the Eastern states. This, in turn, has had ramifications on the debates over the future direction of NATO in the post Cold War era.

Despite the debate in the West about the rationale for NATO in the post Cold War period, in the former Warsaw Pact states there is a strong enthusiasm for the organization and a desire for membership, stemming from the "strategic vacuum"[17] the states believe themselves to be in. The concerns of these states have been amplified by continuing instability in Moscow and the growing belligerence of Russian nationalism.

Opinion within NATO is divided. Germany would like to see membership opened to the Czech Republic, Hungary, and Poland in a short period, whilst other NATO states fear the consequences of expansion in terms of its effects on operational effectiveness and in extending security guarantees. Anxious too that Russia should not feel itself encircled by an enlarged NATO, yet equally determined that Russian nationalists should not believe they have a veto over NATO's policies in the East, American policy has tried to maintain a delicate balance. This has been complicated by the equally important recognition that NATO needs a new focus. Bush and Clinton have, therefore, moved the Alliance into arrangements that intensify Eastern contacts, thus ameliorating the strategic vacuum, but which do not, yet, offer full membership. NATO's first moves were the establishment of the North Atlantic Cooperation Council (NACC) in December 1991, allowing for regular diplomatic liaison and high level contacts between former Communist and NATO states.

Pressure for membership did not abate, however. In late 1993, President Clinton proposed that NATO further their security dialogue with the Eastern states through the Partnership for Peace (PfP) program. This was adopted at the January 1994 NATO Summit. Whilst postponing any decisions as to expanding NATO,[18] the PfP is a deft diplomatic device that allows those states that are keen to join to demonstrate how their membership will benefit the Alliance. Thus the PfP, open to all NACC and CSCE states, allows for participation in joint military exercises, in joint planning and in creating abilities to operate with NATO forces in peacekeeping and humanitarian operations. The pace of these contacts is determined by each PfP participant, not by NATO. Yet, by opening the PfP to all states, including Russia, NATO has avoided the impression of acting selectively. The NACC states clearly believe the PfP is a "first step" to full membership.[19] Indeed, the PfP is considered an "important step" in the "evolutionary process of NATO expansion" which NATO leaders "expect and welcome."[20] Further, whilst PfP does not give the Eastern states a security guarantee, NATO will "consult" with any participant in the event of a direct threat to its territorial integrity, political independence, or security.

Redefining relations with Western Europe
During the Reagan period, transatlantic tensions were often acute. Congress passed amendments censuring the allies for not carrying their share of NATO's military burden. Trade disputes between the US and the European Community reinforced the impression in Congress that the US was giving a free ride on defense to its economic competitors. The unilateralism of the United States under Reagan was also a source of tension. Yet US leadership, measured in the formulation of arms control policy and in the promulgation of new NATO doctrines (Follow On Forces Attack – FOFA), was not seriously questioned.

For the Bush and Clinton administrations however, a range of factors have served to place questionmarks over the nature and durability of US leadership.

The question of German reunification was an early problem for President Bush. The US approach was one which recognized the maturity of German democracy. The Bush administration thus did not try to assert its authority over the German government but instead worked closely with it during the so-called "2+4" talks. Thus, despite UK and French reservations over a speedy reunification and Soviet opposition to the new Germany being within NATO, the US–German approach triumphed. This may have indicated a willingness on the part of the US to share leadership in Europe with Germany, or may simply have been a recognition of realities. In any case, the reunified Germany will present the US with a different power dynamic among its Western allies in the coming decades.

The 1990–1991 Gulf crisis apparently demonstrated the potency of US global leadership, reinforced now as the solo superpower. Only the USA could have mounted such a military operation as "Desert Storm". Following the triumphal conclusion to the war, President Bush appeared to be signaling an enthusiasm for a US-driven multilateral approach to global problems. Behind the rhetoric of the "New World Order" and despite the fears of a *"Pax Americana,"*[21] the reality is that, beset by economic crisis, the US has had to reduce many of its military commitments. This process, begun by Bush, has accelerated under Clinton. Analysts wonder whether the Clinton administration's emphasis on multilateralism, but with strict constraints on any American involvement, is really a cloak for a substantial US retreat from the burdens of leadership.[22]

This raises fears in Europe, where American troops are seen as the physical expression of the US commitment to defending European security. Aside from the effects on the European states, any reduction in US leadership in Europe is significant because "throughout the Cold War, the US relationship with Europe was the foundation of US global leadership."[23] Alternatively, seeing a retreat from engagement in Europe as a symptom of a global US retreat from leadership may "falsely equate Europe with the world"[24] in the *post* Cold War environment.

A combination of budgetary concerns, arms control and congressional pressure has forced the reduction in US forces in Europe, and worldwide. By the time Reagan left office, the national debt stood at $2.6 trillion with a trade deficit at $170 billion and a budget deficit at $150 billion. Defense expenditure had fallen, in real terms, every year since 1985. By 1990, Bush put forward the first negative growth defense budget for any administration since Carter, envisaging a 2.6 percent cut in real terms for Fiscal Year 1991 and further modest cuts until Fiscal Year 1995. Bush had planned that defense spending would drop from 5 percent of GDP to about 3 percent by Fiscal Year 1995[25] as a result of arms control obligations and the more relaxed international environment generally. The Clinton administration, seeking to divert defense spending in domestic programs and to finance the budget deficit, has targeted a further $88 billion (Fiscal Year 1994–Fiscal Year 1997) cutback in addition to the Bush plans. This will inevitably be accompanied by sharp reductions in force levels.[26]

US force levels in Europe possess a political significance beyond their operational capacities. US manpower figures had been slated to fall from 314,000 to 150,000 by Fiscal Year 1995 due in large part to successful arms control. Nevertheless, Bush had been forced by House amendments in 1992 to cap US forces in Europe at 100,000 by Fiscal Year 1995. Clinton has accepted this 100,000 figure for the "foreseeable future," rather than Bush's plan for 150,000, and gave assurances to this effect at the 1994 NATO Summit in Brussels. Nevertheless, there is a debate as to how low US forces could drop[27] with some advocating a force presence as low as 50,000 or complete withdrawal. Congress faces fewer painful political choices if the economic consequences of American base closures are felt overseas rather than in the US itself. Manpower and base cutbacks have fallen disproportionately on US forces based in Europe.[28] Congressional pressure for cutbacks in Europe has been building due to continuing burdensharing concerns,[29] reinforced by a perception that NATO no longer clearly serves US interests, as demonstrated by its failures over Bosnia.[30]

As part of the effort to find a modern mission for NATO, it was agreed in 1992 that NATO forces could be used in support of peace efforts in the former Yugoslavia, under the authorization of the UN. This has not proved conducive to good transatlantic relations and has also demonstrated a lack of coordination between the UN and NATO authorities. President Clinton has publicly vented his frustrations at NATO allies for not taking firmer action in Bosnia. NATO discussions have been characterized by great dissension between the US on the one hand and the UK and France on the other. US proposals for a lifting of the arms embargo on the Bosnian government and for air strikes against Bosnian Serb positions, were criticized for risking the safety of troops on the ground (of which there are none from the US) through Serb retaliation and for jeopardizing the continuation of the UN Protection Force (UNPROFOR) mission. Nevertheless, under heavy US pressure, NATO aircraft did shoot down four Serbian aircraft violating the UN "No-Fly Zone" in February 1994, the first military action by NATO since its establishment in 1949. In April 1994 NATO aircraft attacked Serb gunners attacking Goradze – a declared UN safe area. The prospect of lifting the arms embargo suggests NATO forces may have to intervene to forcefully evacuate UN personnel, rather than police a peace plan as envisaged. This promises a true crisis in transatlantic relations. From the administration's perspective, the European countries have failed in Bosnia, either to promote a just peace plan (through the European Union) or to apply sufficient military pressures on the Bosnian Serbs (through NATO). From the perspective of European governments, the Bosnian crisis has shown the ambiguities of US leadership in the new environment: neither prepared to truly delegate regional responsibilities nor willing to assume the burdens of leadership.

Restructuring NATO

The case for NATO has to be proven in a world where the principal threat it was created to deter no longer exists. As a military organization, it is ill equipped to deal with the increasingly non-military aspects of security – economic development, migration of refugees, ethnic rights, etc. Conservatism is a strong force, especially as the Alliance worked successfully for forty years and no alternative architecture is yet available to replace it. Eastern European enthusiasm for NATO is a mixed blessing and enthusiasm alone may not overcome the pressures of a budgetary squeeze and a lack of clear mission.

As the primary instrument of US power in Europe, it has fallen to the US administrations of Bush and Clinton to provide the impetus for restructuring NATO. There appear to be four aspects to the American agenda: reconfiguring NATO forces and strategy to take account of arms control and the absence of any discernible Central Front in Europe; developing NATO as a forum for increasing dialogue with the fledgling democracies in the East; reorientating NATO outwards, to deal with security issues affecting American and European security from outside the North Atlantic area and even from outside Europe altogether; and responding to the challenge of a

European Defence Identity. On all these issues, bar the last, there is a high degree of consensus between the Bush and Clinton administrations.

Progress toward the radical restructuring of NATO forces began at the end of 1991 with the decision to emphasize smaller, more flexible, multinational military units within the Strategic Concept. These units would allow national defense ministries some latitude to cut standing armies, prevent a renationalization of defense and simultaneously provide NATO with more options than responding to a frontal attack in Europe. Nevertheless, the US hope that NATO and its infrastructural assets, rather than *ad-hoc* alliances of NATO states (as in the Gulf), could be used to project power or maintain peace outside the NATO area, has not been fully shared by allies. Even the 1992 agreement that NATO could act in support of the UN in Bosnia has not been a happy first experience.

In 1993, Clinton proposed that NATO should support the establishment of Combined Joint Task Forces (CJTFs). These would comprise units from all the services (Combined) and from a variety of nations (Joint), within and outside of the NATO Alliance. Thus, coalitions in support of UN, CSCE, or Western European Union (WEU) mandates could be put together. This would allow the Europeans to act in situations where the US does not feel obliged or capable of so doing, as well as retaining options for the US to build coalitions. The CJTF proposal was accepted at the Brussels Summit of 1994. Taken with the many positive references to a European Security and Defence Identity (ESDI), this greatly reduces the argument over a European Defence Identity which plagued US–European and intra-European relations from 1990.

By contrast to the relaxed attitude of the Clinton administration on this point, the Bush administration approached the attempt to create a European Defence Identity with great caution. Whilst welcoming any European initiative to bear more responsibility for their own defense, administration officials through 1991 warned against any European caucus within the Alliance presenting the US, with *fait accomplis*.[31] The administration actively intervened to influence the deliberations among EC states over the nature of any defense dimension it would seek for itself.[32] In the end, the Maastricht Treaty on European Union created a compromise between French attempts to establish a defense identity for the Union and the concern by others, notably the UK, that any European Defence Identity should act in support of NATO, not seek to replace it. Thus, the Western European Union is described as "an integral part" of the Union but the primacy of NATO is acknowledged on defense matters at several points. What appears to have led to the Clinton administration adopting a more relaxed view is that French policy evolved during 1993, clearly stressing the vitality of the transatlantic link and drawing France once again closer to NATO.[33]

Conclusion

The two decades since 1975 have been characterized by great fluidity in the international environment. American foreign policy has had to take full account of this, especially in Europe where the pace of developments has been greatest after so many years of enforced stability. The two decades have also demonstrated the clear inter-dependence of domestic and foreign policy issues as each super-power has tailored foreign policy to an increasingly difficult economic position.

The policy of containment posed its own dilemmas during this period. After a spell in which the US foreign policy agenda was broadened, containment was aggressively and contentiously restated as the central plank of American policy toward the Soviet Union. Yet, within a few years, containment had been overtaken by drama-tic political change. American foreign policy is still struggling to find a replacement to this relatively simple concept. Given the lack of certainties and the pace of change, the search is likely to be a long one.

The year 1985 witnessed a turning point in US foreign policy as the domestic base for both superpowers necessitated a relaxation of tensions. The mold of postwar US foreign policy was not finally broken, however, until 1989, when the strategic map changed beyond all recognition. The emphasis on Russia, so long the defining element in US foreign policy, substantially diminished. Since then, the sense of change has been palpable, the direction of that change less so. Doubts over American leadership have been a constant, in various ways, throughout the two decades. Yet, since the election of Bill Clinton in 1992, these doubts have taken on a greater mag-nitude.

In part, this is due to the obvious requirement to reduce military expenditure. It is also due to the perception of foreign policy failures under Clinton – Somalia, Haiti, and Bosnia, for example. But in greatest part it stems from an uncertainty over the direction of US foreign policy. There is little enthusiasm for unilateralism, yet no consensus on how to proceed with multilateralism. Clinton has been criticized for spending too little time on foreign policy, for delegating too much decision making to the State Department, and for his inconsistency of approach.[34]

Yet, although Clinton is a president with domestic preoccupations, it is unlikely that his administration will oversee a major shift towards isolationism. The strategy of "enlargement" has been announced to replace containment. This involves strengthening the ties among the major democracies, encouraging free trade, supporting democracy and reform in the former Communist countries, isolating rogue states, and US participation in multilateral operations (but under strict conditions that they are not open-ended and that an exit strategy exists). In addition, the administration has been active over the issue of proliferation of weapons of mass destruction. This issue has been at the forefront of international concerns, particularly with relation to Ukraine and North Korea. With the old certainties of the Cold War removed, America faces a more complex world in which it will have to constantly redefine its relationships with past allies and former enemies.[35]

Notes

1   M. Bowker and P. Williams, *Superpower Detente: A Re-appraisal* (London, Royal Institute of International Affairs/Sage, 1988) p. 171.

2   R. Garthoff, *Detente and Confrontation: American–Soviet Relations From Reagan to Nixon* (Washington, Brookings Institution, 1985) p. 563.

3   Garthoff, *Detente and Confrontation* p. 968.

4   C. Weinberger, *Fighting For Peace* (London, Michael Joseph, 1990) p. 25.

5   A. Cordesman, "The Reagan Administration: Its Past, and Future Impact on the Western Alliance" *Royal United Services Journal*, vol. 31, no. 1, 1986 (London, RUSI, 1986) pp. 36–44.

6   G. Shultz, *Turmoil and Triumph* (New York, Charles Scribner's Sons, 1993) p. 491.

7   P. Kennedy, *The Rise and Fall of the Great Powers* (London, Penguin, 1988).

8   M. Cox, "Whatever Happened to the Second Cold War?" *Review of*

International Studies, vol. 16, no. 2, 1990 (Cambridge University Press, 1990) p. 167.

9 C. Bluth, "American–Russian Strategic Relations" *The World Today*, vol. 49, no. 3, 1993 (London, Royal Institute of International Affairs, 1993) p. 50.

10 T. Risse-Kapen, "The Long-Term Future of European Security" in W. Carlsnaes and S. Smith (eds.) *European Foreign Policy* (London, European Consortium for Political Research/Sage, 1994) p. 57.

11 International Institute for Strategic Studies, *Strategic Survey 1985–1986* (London, IISS, 1986) p. 57.

12 International Institute for Strategic Studies, *Strategic Survey 1989–1990* (London, IISS, 1990) pp. 27–28.

13 International Institute for Strategic Studies, *Strategic Survey 1989–1990* p. 30.

14 International Institute for Strategic Studies, *Strategic Survey 1989–1990* p. 30.

15 F. Chernoff, "Can NATO outlive the USSR?" *International Relations*, vol. 11, no. 1, 1992 (London, David Davies Memorial Institute of International Studies, 1992) p. 11.

16 P. Gebhard, "The United States and European Security" *Adelphi Paper 286* (London, International Institute for Strategic Studies/Brasseys, 1994) p. 11.

17 J. Novotny, "The Czech Republic: An Active Partner with NATO" *NATO Review*, vol. 42, no. 3, 1994 (Brussels, NATO, 1994) p. 20.

18 S. Sloan, "Transatlantic Relations in the Wake of the Brussels Summit" *NATO Review*, vol. 42, no. 2, 1994 (Brussels, NATO, 1994) p. 38.

19 L. Meri, "Estonia, NATO and Peacekeeping" *NATO Review*, vol. 42, no. 2, 1994 (Brussels, NATO, 1994) pp. 7–10.

20 Office of the Press Secretary, The White House *Fact Sheet* March 2 1994 (Washington, DC, White House, 1994) p. 1.

21 See R. Barnet, "Defining the New World Order" and also I. Buruma, "Defining the New World Order" both in *Harper's Magazine* New York, May 1991.

22 T. Hames, "Searching for the New World Order" *International Relations*, vol. 21, no. 1, April 1994 (London, David Davies Memorial Institute of International Studies, 1994) pp. 123–125.

23 Sloan, "Transatlantic Relations in the Wake of the Brussels Summit" p. 38.

24 Gebhard, "The United States and European Security" p. 7.

25   Gebhard, "The United States and European Security" p. 55.

26   Gebhard, "The United States and European Security" p. 56.

27   D. Snyder, "US Military Forces in Europe: How Low Can We Go?" *Survival*, winter 1992/1993 (London, IISS/Brasseys 1993) pp. 24–39.

28   Gebhard, "The United States and European Security" p. 60.

29   Sloan, "Transatlantic Relations in the Wake of the NATO Summit" p. 40.

30   Gebhard, "The United States and European Security" p. 61.

31   W. Nicoll and T. Salmon, *Understanding the New European Community* (Hemel Hempstead, Harvester Wheatsheaf, 1994) p. 262.

32   A. Van Staden, "After Maastricht: Explaining the Movement Towards a Common Defence Policy" in W. Carlsnaes and S. Smith (eds.) *European Foreign Policy* (London, European Consortium for Political Research/Sage, 1994) p. 150.

33   M. Meimeth, "France Gets Closer to NATO" *The World Today*, vol. 50, no. 6, 1994 (London, Royal Institute of International Affairs, 1994) pp. 84–85.

34   Hames, "Searching for The New World Order" pp. 114–115.

35   Additional sources: C. Coker, *Drifting Apart? The Superpowers and their European Allies* (London, Brasseys, 1989); S. Gill (ed.) *Atlantic Relations: Beyond the Reagan Era* (New York, St Martins Press/Harvester Wheatsheaf, 1989); F. Halliday, *The Making of the Second Cold War* (London, Verso, 1983).

Asserting US power

Toward the late 1960s the orthodox consensus that marked the
initial decades of the Cold War policy debates in the United States
was coming to an end. US commitments during the Vietnam War
resulted in massive costs which could not easily be justified. Most
pertinently the loss of 58,123 American lives, but also the opportunity costs of President Johnson's Great Society program for social
restructuring, and the economic costs in the international context
forced a reconsideration of policy priorities. Orthodox "lessons"
suggested the United States could no longer afford to fight such
costly wars, with marginal interests in what was regarded as a
peripheral area of the world.

The initial Cold War strategy was given shape by George Kennan
in his now famous Long Telegram and Mr X. article of 1946 and
1947 respectively. His call for a long-term and patient containment
of Russian expansive tendencies was universalized through the
Truman Doctrine and three years later in 1950 militarized through
the policy document NSC 68.[1] The willingness of the United States
to make open-ended commitments was still apparent at the time of
President John F. Kennedy's inauguration. Kennedy pledged to "pay
any price, bear any burden, meet any hardship, support any friend,
oppose any foes, in order to assure the survival and success of
liberty."[2] Such unlimited promises would not find their way into
subsequent US policy, though at times were reflected in its rhetoric.

While this approach adopted by Truman and Kennedy changed
with the US defeat in Vietnam, it reflected more a change in the
cultural and institutional impact on decision making rather than the
significant changes in the "Third World" where new independent
states, nationalism, and revolutionary movements also challenged

US strategic predominance. Truman's simplistic division of a bipolar world, one based on free and democratic institutions, the other on oppressive totalitarian forces, was incredible. New forces were challenging the dominant superpowers. The reluctance of the United States to admit the plurality and multiplicity of approaches and cultural agendas led to the assumptions and illusions under which policy was made.

Further policy objectives, according to revisionists, sought the maintenance of US standing in the international economic order, access to markets, and to the raw materials of the Third World. Such concerns are revived in recent systemic theories and interpretations of US global preponderance. Pointing out that the United States had 50 percent of the world's wealth with 6.3 percent of its population, Kennan's Policy Planning Staff argued that this "position of disparity" would have to be maintained "without positive detriment to our national security." With the Far East in mind the document suggested the United States should deal in "straight power concepts," not be "hampered by idealistic slogans," and should "cease to talk about vague and . . . unreal objectives such as human rights, the raising of the living standards, and democratization."[3] These goals should not necessarily be seen as mutually exclusive; the presentation of the Soviet threat facilitated the military spending initiated by NSC 68 and the consequent extension of preponderance. That containment, rollback, or preponderance necessitated access to Third World resources was axiomatic in certain cases where the materials in question (uranium, plutonium) were vital to the nascent US nuclear program. Thus the Truman administration found it imperative to keep South Africa in the "Free World" to gain access to uranium deposits indispensable for the development of the hydrogen bomb. Paul Nitze, the head of the Policy Planning Staff in 1950, argued that access "to the minerals of the rest of the world is an absolute requirement of the very life of our nation." The struggle against apartheid was subsumed within the bipolar conflict where "freedom" and "anti-Communism" were culturally synonymous in Washington. In certain cases the links between the colonized world and the colonial powers were strengthened in an attempt to enhance the cohesion of the West under US leadership. With the strategy of US preponderant power, according to Leffler's recent study, "the periphery had to be held or the Eurasian industrial core would be weakened . . . Japan needed Southeast Asia; Western Europe needed the Middle East; and the American rearmament effort required raw materials from throughout the Third World."[4]

Revolutionary or reactionary nationalism, often interpreted through the prism of the bipolar conflict, required Washington to justify its response in terms of a Soviet threat. But even non-Communist nationalism threatened US hegemony. Policies of economic autarky deprived powers access to their country. The size of the nation or the resources within it may be or may not be important, but any successful social progress within even small nations poses the political threat of a potentially "good example." Thus Arevelo's "spiritual socialism" in Guatemala during the 1940s, far from Communist, centered around concepts of *vitalismo*, or a minimum sufficiency may threaten US interests and economic hegemony in a region historically dominated by the United States.[5] Derivations of these policies by the Arbenz government may have contributed to the covert operation against his rule in 1954. The link between the core and the periphery was a vital component in US strategy since 1950. This essay is concerned with US strategy in the subsequent period (1970–1994) of maintaining these interests with new constraints and with the absence of a policy consensus.

In addition, during the period in question US power was changing. After 1968 the so called "Vietnam syndrome" exerted an influence on the will to use power at a time when it was more necessary to do so due to the relative economic decline of the United States. Gabriel Kolko points out the irony that while US military power was relatively weak, it had the greatest need to dominate the "world's poorer nations."[6] Subsequent US provocation of, or intervention in, regional conflicts has been mainly to contain or rollback the perception of, or actual, Soviet power, ensure access to resources, or preserve regional or global stability. With a reduced political will to use troops and the relative decline in economic influence, the various administrations since Nixon have devised methods of pursuing the objectives, ideological and economic, outlined above.

The Nixon administration

Interpretations of US foreign relations derived from Fernand Braudel's "world systems" theory, which argued that as major powers decline and a decentering begins, a recentering of a new configuration of power takes place.[7] Strategies employed by the

Nixon administration can be seen as an attempt to mitigate the relative decline of the United States and prevent the recentering of power elsewhere in the world. In the political context of the end of the Vietnam War it was incumbent on Washington to withdraw its troops and restrain its commitments. The Vietnam War had an adverse effect on the US economy which forced a restructuring of its foreign policy, though the perception of decline may not have been as apparent due to the continuing US military and political capacity. Nevertheless, during the Nixon administration it became increasingly difficult to resort to military solutions.[8]

The 1968 Tet offensive brought the Vietnam War onto the US television screens which, according to popular arguments, detrimentally affected the ability of the United States to stay the course. Arguably, while other influential groups had more influence on the eventual decision to withdraw from the war, in future conflicts media access would be restricted. Nixon's policy of "Vietnamization" centered around the decision to withdraw US troops from the region and bolster the government of South Vietnam with both military and financial assistance. The Vietnamization policy signaled the US retreat from the type of open-ended commitments made by Presidents Truman and Kennedy. The emerging Nixon Doctrine attempted to limit the perception of US decline or retreat. According to Cecil Crabb, it was "designed to refute the idea that, because of the results in Vietnam, the United States no longer had global . . . commitments."[9] The strategies and the assumptions of the Cold War were changing, and President Richard Nixon argued that his program represented a viable way to ensure continued influence in the area.

Even after the decision to leave Vietnam had been made the US suffered the loss of 26,000 troops and perpetuated further conflict in which an estimated two million South-East Asians were killed.[10] With this appalling record in its foreign policy, among the lessons resulting from the war was that a sense of limits should be recovered. The world was no longer as susceptible to US power, and the political will to assert military strengths was partially limited. Economic strength was also reduced. Suggestions that policy strategies should be more defensive rather than a tool to propagate the rhetorical ideals of the United States were made.[11] Nevertheless, the United States had a continued need to gain access to raw materials as their dependency on these increased, hence they could not retreat from the international arena. The "Vietnam syndrome," however, severely limited the ability to use troops in areas that were popularly regarded as of marginal interest. Future administrations inhibited, if not absolutely deterred, from using military force learned not to "pay any price or bear any burden" in open-ended commitments. The new limits of power had to be reconciled with the ongoing imperatives of US strategic interests. Thus in February 1970 Nixon explained:

> the United States will participate in the defense and development of allies and friends, but . . . America cannot – and will not – conceive all plans, design all programs, execute all the decisions, and undertake all the defense of the free nations of the world.[12]

The Nixon Doctrine sought to maintain influence by first withdrawing direct US participation, but bolstering a series of regional "strong countries." Agreements and military aid to select governments would ensure order and stability in the various regions of interest.

According to Thomas McCormick, the Nixon Doctrine was a form of "Sub-Imperialism" which he defines as "the use of substitutes, or proxies, to act on behalf of a given core power." This strategy provided for a minimum of friction in the "periphery" or Third World while at the core or center a period of detente or a relaxation of tension between the superpowers was implemented.[13] Relevant administration objectives were to seek stability in the Third World, maintain core access to their materials, and concurrently pursue diplomacy with Moscow, producing a series of agreements.

An era of multipolarity was emerging, or at least being recognized in Washington, in which Europe, Japan, and China would exert greater influence. The central objectives would remain, but in a new configuration of international power. In early 1971 Nixon reported to Congress that the world was:

> at the end of an era. The postwar order of international relations, the configuration of power that emerged from the Second World War, is gone. With it are gone the conditions which have determined the assumptions and practice of United States foreign policy since 1945.[14]

New parameters of superpower diplomacy found their way into several major agreements that emerged from the May 1972 Moscow Summit centered around political, military, economic, and social issues. Further superpower accord developed through the Helsinki process finally signed in August 1975. The passage of time during these negotiations allowed space in the political process for other significant powers to alter their position. The United States opened, and successfully concluded, diplomatic agreements with the People's Republic of China, and the economic strengths of Europe and Japan were incorporated to a larger degree in a more multipolar world system.

The space created by the superpower agreements may have prompted several challenges to the preponderance of power in the Third World. According to Warren Cohen's recent work on the Cold War period Washington was asking Moscow to recognize the mutual benefit of stability and order in the Third World for both superpowers at a time of economic constraint. The Soviets would find cooperation more beneficial than rivalry in the periphery; the Nixon administration was "asking the Soviets to contain themselves at a time when America's will to hold the line was in doubt."[15]

While the Helsinki Accords recognized the status quo in Europe, the political agreements set out in the Moscow Summit sought to recognize the status quo in the rest of the world. Both superpowers agreed to conduct their relations on the basis of peaceful coexistence, despite the ideological rivalry, and to "recognize that efforts to obtain unilateral advantage at the expense of the other, directly or indirectly, are inconsistent" with the objectives of detente. While the superpowers found temporary agreement, political expectations in the Third World also found temporary expression. In 1970 the people of Chile voted "freely and knowingly" (according to the US ambassador) for a socialist coalition government headed by Salvador Allende Gossens.[16] The Nixon administration could not accept the victory of a leftist or a nationalist government in the Western hemisphere, not only because of extensive US corporate interests and the increased ability to affect the price of copper, due to the Vietnam War induced shortages, but also because the socialist victory would contribute to the perceived inability of the United States to preserve the Western hemisphere from "outside" (in this case ideological) influences. Washington employed tactics short of military force, spending up to $8 million to oppose Allende and make the economy "scream." The government was eventually toppled with US assistance in September 1973. Chile suffered the adverse affects of a brutal regime headed by General Augusto

Pinochet till the late 1980s; the Soviets considered the action a breach of the 1972 agreement; and alienated Latin American countries increased their trade with both Europe and Japan.[17]

In the vital resource area of the Middle East the October 1973 war that erupted when Egypt and Syria attacked Israel in an effort to recapture land lost six years earlier provoked further instability. With the Israeli counteroffensive the superpowers first arranged a limited ceasefire, unsatisfactory to the Soviet Union, they then threatened to intervene to stop the fighting at which point US Secretary of State Henry Kissinger warned them to stay out of the region. Eventually the Israelis won Egyptian recognition of their right to exist by conceding land won through previous conquest. The resulting oil crisis during which the Organization of Petroleum Exporting Countries (OPEC) enforced an "embargo" which demonstrated the vulnerability of increasing Western dependence on Middle Eastern oil. While the price of oil quadrupled the Shah of Iran began supplying the United States at increased prices; but access was restored. Iran thus became an integral part of the Nixon Doctrine. The oil crisis further weakened the structure of detente because despite a tenfold increase in Soviet exports of oil to the United States, Washington felt Moscow should have warned it about the Egyptian attack which it facilitated.[18]

The subsequent Kissinger negotiations focused on restoring a regional balance of power. With a concentration on the political and diplomatic aspects of the conflict and the successful exclusion of the Soviets, Kissinger missed the longer-term threat of a "cumulative economic enfeeblement." The threat of a peripheral area controlling the supplies of oil caused near panic in the West when the "embargo" caused a drop by 14 percent of internationally traded oil. The Nixon administration was perturbed by the potential inability of the United States to gain adequate access at favorable prices to Middle Eastern oil supplies. The United States not only had to concentrate one of its military components in the Gulf region, it also considered plans for the possible invasion of Saudi Arabia.[19]

Concomitant with the further relative decline of the United States and its increasing need to assert power to deal with the emerging nationalistic and economic alternatives in the Third World, the presidency of Richard Nixon, beset by domestic problems including anti-Vietnam demonstrations and Watergate, was losing its political leverage. Congress began to assert some power in the area of foreign policy. Firstly, because it perceived an abuse of legislative powers by the executive it passed the War Powers Act in 1973. Henceforth, conflict would have to be limited to an initial sixty day period if a declaration of war was not congressionally authorized. An extension of thirty days was possible if the military situation, certified by the president, prevented a safe withdrawal. Secondly, as international power seemed to be devolving toward a system based on economic power, the executive saw a reduction in its ability to control foreign policy. Constitutional provisions had given Congress predominant power in this area. More pointedly, US multinational corporations may pursue an agenda not always linked to the national interests of the United States.

The Nixon Doctrine, or the support of strong authoritarian regional countries such as Iran, the Philippines, Brazil, Nicaragua, among others, though vaguely understood, was an attempt to incorporate the lessons of Vietnam into the new configuration of power. A more specific cost–benefit analysis had to be incorporated into the equation, part of which had to account for the Vietnam syndrome.

The Carter administration

The administration of Jimmy Carter not only kept the United States out of most regional conflicts, it tried initially to move away from the traditional East–West division of the world that had shaped the Cold War consensus. While this approach was reflected in his foreign policy staff at the State Department headed by Cyrus Vance, in the latter stages of his administration Carter would return to Cold War paradigms in reaction to events and through the influence of his National Security Adviser, Zbigniew Brzezinski. Carter's departure from the normal approach to regional conflicts was not only a tactical change, but based on a belief that the struggles in the Third World were due to the vast inequalities in the international system. Carter wanted to return the United States to a foreign policy based on the rhetorical ideals of projecting US values to ostensibly benefit the peoples of the world. While the standard pattern of understanding the world from Truman to Ford was based around the East–West axis, Carter wanted to change it to a North–South axis. To this end, he sought to promote human rights in the international arena beyond the minimal political liberties associated with the rhetoric of US foreign policy which he declared the "soul" of his foreign policy.

Alternatively regarded as either naive, if well intentioned, or incompetent in the area of foreign policy, the Carter presidency made some progress toward extricating the United States from overriding Cold War mentality. The point was not that the United States did not have concerns with the Soviet Union, but that not all problems were a result of Soviet behavior, the world was more complex than the bipolar divisions earlier enunciated.

While this approach did not survive the duration of his presidency, the initial policies and actions at minimum kept the United States out of regional conflicts, thus avoiding the use of, and (more pertinently) the death of, US troops. As Nixon had recognized the end of an era, Carter recognized the beginnings of a new period. In May 1977 he stated:

> we are now free of that inordinate fear of communism which once led us to embrace any dictator who joined us in that fear . . . It is a new world that calls for a new American foreign policy – a policy based on constant decency in its values and on optimism in our historical vision.

The new foreign policy, Michael Hunt has pointed out, was a return to a restrained Jeffersonian policy, "confident that the world was becoming an ever more hospitable place for American values."[20]

The new concern with human rights went beyond any previous administration during the Cold War, and was according to the director of the Policy Planning Staff to "include not just the basic rights of due process, together with political freedoms, but also the right of each human being to a just share of the fruits of one country's production." Despite these intentions, a clear policy never emerged and the application of it was mainly concerned with violations in Latin America rather than the more strategically important countries of the Middle East. The right within his administration and the Republican opposition found an easy target for accusations of inconsistency and of undermining authoritarian regimes friendly to the United States.[21]

The divided administration both ignored the human rights violations in Iran because of US dependence on its oil and allowed for some Soviet influence and action in the Middle East and Horn of Africa. Cohen argues Carter was willing to accept this increased Soviet role, giving them a stake in acting "responsibly," and because the Vance faction thought Africa was not worth a superpower conflict. Additionally, the Soviets would learn the Vietnam lesson, that a projection of power in peripheral areas could detrimentally affect their national strength.[22]

Despite Carter's diplomatic successes with the Panama Canal Treaties of 1977 and the Camp David Accords of 1978, the extension of Soviet power, nationalist regimes of the left, or anti-American movements contributed to the rise of the right within his administration and a return to the traditional Cold War assumptions of US foreign policy. A series of events including Cuban and Soviet involvement in Africa, a Communist accession and the Soviet invasion of Afghanistan, Vietnamese victory in Cambodia, the Sandinista revolution in Nicaragua, the deposition of the Shah of Iran, followed later by the hostage crisis, that revived the East–West perspective, brought on a new Cold War, and contributed to the perception of US weakness.

In early 1980, the last year of his presidency, Carter changed policy tactics in what later became known as the Carter Doctrine. He resolved to support US interests in the Middle East stating that:

> Any attempt by any outside force to gain control of the Persian Gulf region will be regarded as an assault on the vital interests of the United States of America, and such an assault will be repelled by any means necessary, including military force.

Still later the return to Cold War assumptions increased military spending initiated through Presidential Directive 59 (PD-59) which allowed for renewed strength and the possibility of winning a limited nuclear war.[23]

Overall, Carter's initial response had been simply to maintain a distance from regional conflicts which he did not perceive as a challenge to US interests, except perhaps in terms of their prestige. The four year period had produced a confused foreign policy exacerbated by internal division and a lack of relevant experience on the part of the president. Cohen lamented the choice but celebrated US democracy, declaring "it was not a job for an amateur; it was not a time for an amateur. But Jimmy Carter was the people's choice."[24]

The Reagan administration

The trend continued, according to LaFeber, who saw Ronald Reagan's election victory as part of his ability to soothe rather than govern.[25] A Cold Warrior had returned to the White House determined to roll back the gains Soviet power had made in the Third World during the Carter tenure. Henceforth, the United States would pursue a strong foreign policy to counter the perceived weakness of the past four years. Regional crises were squarely placed back into the Cold War context despite Carter's attempts to remove the "inordinate" fear of Communism. Reagan took full advantage of the fear and fueled its flames with his hyperbolic rhetoric, identifying the Soviet Union as an "evil empire," which he promised to confine to "the ash heap of history." The Soviets, according to Reagan's misperception, lay behind all the "unrest that is going on. If they weren't engaged in this game of dominoes, there wouldn't be any hot spots in the world."[26]

The United States would respond, though the shape of the new response was quite different. The revival of a sort of Wilsonian internationalism to ostensibly promote freedom from Afghanistan to Nicaragua relied on methods that avoided the Vietnam syndrome. Conflicts involving direct US participation would have to be short and decisive, satisfying the War Powers Act. Longer protracted conflicts would be conducted by proxy warfare through the military and financial support of indigenous groups such as the Contras stationed in Honduras and Costa Rica, and the Mujahedin in Afghanistan, the former fighting the Sandinista government in Nicaragua, the latter fighting the Soviet military.

Reagan's policies in Central America and particularly against Nicaragua, but also against the Frente Farabundo Marti para la Liberacion Nacional (FMLN) in El Salvador were held up to be a test case for US resolve. Soviet involvement in the region was minimal and reactionary. The Cuban response was more extensive, but not part of a concerted effort from Moscow as the Reagan administration alleged; furthermore, the Sandinistas did not operate under the direction of either the Cubans or the Soviets. The revolution in Nicaragua was primarily a result of social and economic inequality.[27] By denying these roots of revolution, Michael Hunt argues, the United States supported unpopular and oppressive groups. US reaction to previous revolutions taught leaders to "anticipate and prepare for an American policy of active hostility." LaFeber points out that one of the lessons drawn by revolutionaries from the Arbenz experience in Guatemala was to ensure that the revolutionary government had its own military.[28] Thus even if the Sandinistas could not resist an invasion, tactically they could inflict enough damage on the invading forces to make the conflict unpopular in the United States. The Vietnam syndrome could be effectively used in tactical considerations.

Substantive negotiations with the Sandinistas were avoided because a diplomatic agreement would leave them in place, and the Reagan administration felt it had to demonstrate US revolve in the region. To do so, Communism had to be seen as a central concern; thus Washington changed the focus of the debate from poverty or Communism as a cause of instability to a question of how much Communism there was in the region. While the situation could not be adequately understood without reference to the extreme poverty and inequality, the Reagan administration tried to do just that. Local realities were subordinated to global perceptions.[29]

Two years after the United States had started its covert proxy war against the Sandinistas, Reagan, seeking further aid for the Contras, addressed a joint session of Congress in April 1983. During his appeal, a part of which extensively quoted from the Truman Doctrine affirming a bipolar division of the world, Reagan asked how NATO allies could be expected to trust the United States if they could not prevail in Central America. Despite the apparent magnitude of the problem, use of US troops was ruled out. Reagan stated, "let me say to those who invoke the memory of Vietnam: There is no thought of sending American combat troops to Central America."[30]

Proxy warfare as part of a strategy called Low Intensity Conflict met the prerequisites of avoiding US casualties. The proxy forces would conduct a number of operations without necessarily engaging the Sandinista military. The operations included a concerted effort to wear down the will of the people in Nicaragua and destroy the infrastructure of the country. The guerrilla warfare, the terrorism of the Contras, and the Sandinista response cost 35,000 Nicaraguans their lives. Further suffering was inflicted through the covert and political war which included the mining of Nicaraguan harbors, an economic embargo, and a "national emergency" in the United States because of the "unusual and extraordinary threat" posed by Nicaragua "to the national security and foreign policy of the United States."[31] The incongruity between the threat and the response remains officially unexplained, though the Sandinistas were removed from office through the democratic elections of February 1990.

The costs in political terms to the Reagan administration were significant. Given the indecisive congressional opposition to his policies Reagan decided to seek funds from private donors and third countries, circumventing the congressional power of the purse. Furthermore, the region may only experience a temporary cessation of conflict as economic and social conditions still deteriorate. James Dunkerley has employed the word "pacification" to suggest the temporality of the situation.[32]

The "threat" posed by the Sandinistas in the form of an "export of revolution" was not credible and this perception was not shared by the European allies. More pertinently, the National Security Council made it clear it did not want to see more "Cuba model" states in the region. The use of US sponsored forces seemed either to demonstrate resolve or prevent a nationalistic government using its resources to improve the conditions within the country. Noam Chomsky argues that the indigenous population is always a problem for the United States because the people have "an unfortunate tendency to succumb to strange and unacceptable ideas about using their resources for their own purposes."[33] World systems theory suggests it is unacceptable for a hegemonic power to allow a country to either remove its economy or its resources from the international trading system. Even if the resources of the country are of little consequence, the threat of the example may pose a sufficient danger to dominant powers that have interests in maintaining open economies. In Nicaragua the improvements in the social conditions centered around health, education, and literacy were dramatic before being eroded by the counterrevolution.

Congress had doubts, as did the public, about the threats the Sandinistas posed to US security. It had no doubts, however, about the veracity of US support for the Mujahedin resisting Soviet aggression in Afghanistan. Congress increased US assistance to the Afghan resistance. The problem with the Reagan Doctrine as applied in Afghanistan, though ultimately successful, was the risks it ran in provoking a direct engagement with the Soviet Union. As the United States increased the levels and sophistication of the weapons supplied to the Mujahedin, it became more likely that the Soviets could take a preemptive strike against points of delivery in Pakistan. The Central Intelligence Agency (CIA) backed groups which could not win militarily, nor could they establish fixed bases; they could, nevertheless, wear the Soviet forces down and aggravate the bleeding wound Gorbachev had recognized. The worst case scenario was that

Soviet "hot pursuit" into Pakistan would necessitate a direct US response.[34] While the Reagan Doctrine in this area adhered to a prevention of US casualties through minimum engagement, the possibilities of escalation, confrontation, and a significant loss of life remained attendant.

From the bipolar perspective the US attack on the "Soviet empire" at the periphery was hailed as a success, part of the effort of winning the Cold War. Orthodox historians could thus argue that part of the intentions of NSC 68 had been fulfilled, the Soviets had been forced to reexamine their internal structure after Reagan's massive increases in the arms race. Unable to compete under prevailing trends Gorbachev's perestroika attempted to restructure the domestic economy, while "new thinking" removed ideology from Soviet foreign policy. In war, even a Cold War, victors sustain heavy costs. The price paid by the United States was an increased debt burden, a declining capacity to compete on economic terms with the European Community or Japan, and a severe erosion of the social infrastructure within the United States. A longer pattern of intervention in the twentieth century has forced the collapse of several reform movements from Progressivism due to World War I, the New Deal due to World War II, and the Great Society due to Vietnam.[35] The economies of Germany and Japan gained leverage in the world order more inclined toward economic power by spending much less of their gross national product on defense.

The Bush administration

Systemic theorists, building on Braudel's premise: "each time decentering occurs, a recentering begins," suggest that since the end of the Vietnam War US power has declined, its hegemony lost in an increasingly polycentric world, and the United States will have to find new ways of defining its role in the world.[36] Cold War paradigms were lost but policy continuities remained. Access to resources remained an objective and methods of asserting power had to be found. Another continuity was the penchant to use force within the constraints of the Vietnam syndrome.

George Bush crafted his own response. Every president since Truman has had a doctrine that has dealt with superpower rivalry in the periphery. Bush had problems identifying his, obviously uncomfortable with the "vision thing" or the "big think thing," he eventually settled on the New World Order, that was neither new nor orderly. Retrospectively, however, the military strategy of "overwhelming power" can be seen as a new form of intervention that achieved basic strategic aims, without the overwhelming loss of US lives.

The strategy proved to be a military success in Panama where only 23 US soldiers were killed, largely by "friendly fire" in the resulting confusion of bombarding not only military installations but also civilian areas with casuality figures ranging between an implausibly low 500 up to 5,000. The outrage voiced in Latin America was not heard sufficiently in the United States where the president's approval ratings increased, prompting the observation that it may be necessary for presidents to bloody their hands to overcome any lingering "wimp" factor. Yet one of the presumptions of overwhelming power must be that the enemy is relatively weak, necessitating what Dunkerley has called "an almost medieval demonization" of the despot "that was as telling as it was unedifying."[37] A year later there was a similar effort to characterize Saddam Hussein as the new Hitler.

After Iraq's brutal invasion of Kuwait in August 1990 a coalition of forces was gathered under the auspices of the United Nations, in this case driven by Washington. While the minimum requirement of the United Nations (UN) was a total Iraqi withdrawal to the August 1990 border, other possibilities emerged in the maximum conditions the United States expected from the crises. Such possibilities included the continued economic embargo against Iraq, the possibility of Saddam Hussein's removal from power, and a dismantling or destruction of Iraq's military and nuclear potential. A reluctance to address these issues through a combination of diplomacy and continued sanctions suggests a further motive for the punitive action countering the original invasion. Chomsky's systemic explanation suggests that the use of overwhelming military force was necessary to assert the primacy of US leadership and mitigate the centrifugal decentering movement toward diplomatic and economic power where major rivals such as a German centered EC and Japan would find added leverage. His argument is given some weight in a Pentagon document leaked and excerpted in the *New York Times* a year after the Gulf conflict. The Defense Planning Guidance for Fiscal Years 1994–1999 posited: "we must account sufficiently for the interests of the advanced industrial nations to discourage them from challenging our leadership or seeking to overturn the established political and economic order." The document further stressed that regional competitors must be deterred "from even aspiring to a larger regional or global role." Critics from another perspective, Tucker and Hendrickson, state there was a "determination to ensure a spectacular defeat for Saddam Hussein . . . due to the vast disparity of power between Iraq and the United States," whose superpower standing relied on the "ability to deliver a crushing blow against those who might forcibly challenge its position." Before the Gulf crisis the Bush administration had suggested the shape of future US responses to conflict in the Third World: "In cases where the US confronts much weaker enemies, our challenge will be not simply to defeat them, but to defeat them decisively and rapidly."[38]

On the eve of the Coalition bombardment of Iraq in January 1991 Bush went on national television to promise that this war would not be "another Vietnam." Never again would American troops be introduced into combat with one hand tied behind their back. It did not matter that the earlier restraint was imposed through public reaction to the television images of wounded and dead troops, constraining the political maneuverability of the Washington decision makers. The theory arose that the Vietnam War was lost on network television, so in the Gulf instead of tying the hands of the troops, the press was restricted; pooled into controllable systems of output. The images of the "smart bombs" were persuasive but unrepresentative of the more common reality; coverage was sanitized. Not that other information was unavailable or inaccessible, but it was not shown on prime time television and therefore did not affect the overwhelming response to the bombing. Smart weapons impressed the public, but awareness that 93.6 percent of bombs dropped according to the US Air Force were unguided suggests that roughly 82,000 tons of bombs were non-precision, and 7,000 tons were "smart", but even a significant proportion of these bombs missed their intended targets.[39] The focus on the sanitary aspects of war manipulated public opinion through complicity with the pool system. The average person saw the successful precision bombing as "a painless Nintendo exercise," as Edward Said described it, and an interpretation of the situation in simplistic Manachaean terms, quite divorced from reality. The estimated Iraqi casualties ranging up to 200,000, will remain estimated because, as Victoria Brittain has observed, "bulldozers scooped the uncounted

bodies . . . into shallow mass graves . . . with a hasty violation of the
First Geneva Convention." Neither Saddam Hussein nor the Coalition forces have any interest in counting them for their own reasons
of power;[40] the former because it would demonstrate his regime's
weakness, the latter because "just war" requirements of a "pro-
portional response" would apparently be violated.

The demonization of Saddam Hussein, justifications for the war
centered around the New World Order and its respect for international law, buoyed public support, which since Vietnam was an
essential aspect for the use of US military force. Even if he underestimated the power of the response Saddam Hussein understood the
prevalent syndrome. Days before the Iraqi aggression in Kuwait,
during his conversation with US Ambassador April Glaspie (during
which she commented that the United States had no opinion on the
border dispute with Kuwait), Hussein stated "yours is a society
which cannot accept 10,000 dead in one battle." Hussein's awareness that he could not defeat the United States did not preclude the
possibility of inflicting substantial casualities, thus threatening to
"achieve a serious bloodying of American power."[41] The deterrent
may have precluded action. Just as Gorbachev had identified
Afghanistan as a "bleeding wound," as Vietnam was earlier, the
Bush administration considered that

> For small countries hostile to us, bleeding our forces in protracted or
> indecisive conflict or embarrassing us by inflicting damage on some
> conspicuous element of our forces may be victory enough, and could
> undercut political support for US efforts against them.[42]

Vietnam and Lebanon (1983) cast long shadows. Given this political
deterrent, if oil or Iraqi power were the main concerns, negotiations
could have explored possible solutions; indeed Article 33, chapter 6
of the UN Charter requires a primary search for a pacific settlement
of disputes. It is, after all, clear from the Glaspie–Hussein transcript
and from the Iraqi economy after its war with Iran that it needed
increased finance through oil revenues to pay its war debts. The
systemic explanations remain pertinent. The crushing victory in the
Gulf prompted President Bush to also declare victory over the
Vietnam syndrome, suggesting that the United States would no
longer be inhibited from using its military force, though he added
that this would not be as necessary in the future.

Indeed, it may be the United States merely overcame the syndrome in the particular configuration of the Gulf situation. In assessing expected future responses, Alexander George indicates that it is unrealistic to expect the same strong action in cases where the United States "does not perceive very important national interests of its own to be at stake."[43] The perception of interests would appear to be a key to understanding the mobilization of popular support for any action. Where short-term interests are not perceived to be threatened, but long-term interests in stability may be, it will be more difficult to gain approval for committing US troops.

The Clinton administration

To date this view has proved essentially correct; US reaction to the internal conflicts in Bosnia and Rwanda has been hesitant and confused. The initial deployment of troops to Somalia was regarded through cynical prisms as an attempt to demonstrate US resolve to counter accusations of policy and leadership drift.

The Clinton presidency opened with a clear statement of intention for the international arena, "when our vital interests are challenged," the president declared during his inauguration "or the will and conscience of the international community is defied, we will act – with peaceful diplomacy whenever possible, with force when necessary." The rhetoric was in part a remnant of campaign attacks on Bush during 1992 when Clinton saw the US role in preventing "mass violence against civilian populations" and providing humanitarian relief where necessary.[44] A year and a half into the administration Clinton's foreign policy drift fell far short of these intentions. Future parameters of involvement focus on the use of, and more crucially the prevention of, US casualties. During the debate on whether the West should intervene to stop the slaughter, war crimes, and abuse of human rights in Bosnia in April 1993, the Department of State issued four essential criteria. Requirements were: a clear military mission; a strong likelihood of success; domestic support; and an exit formula. After a year of criticism the administration put together PDD 25 (Presidential Decision Directive) the main provisions of which were released. Added to the four criteria, a fifth stated that the United States would not get involved unless the crisis involved a threat to the international community. The retreat from the inaugural promises to PDD 25 outlining the restricted involvement in UN peacekeeping can be seen as a result of the death of US personnel in Somalia. While it would be politically unexpedient to ignore Haiti, Somalia, Rwanda, or Bosnia, the Clinton administration has concluded that "marginal interests" only require "marginal involvement."[45] Limited involvement through the use of air strikes whether in Mogadishu, Baghdad, or the NATO mission that shot down Serb planes in April 1994 is more a demonstration of power than an effective use of it.[46]

The administration seemed to be grappling to find or construct a consensus well into its second year in power. Orthodox axioms were shattered during the Vietnam conflict, and further Cold War conceptual approaches were removed grudgingly since 1989. By June 1994 National Security Adviser Anthony Lake pointed out that the waves of criticism overwhelming the Clinton administration were due to the loss of these assumptions; the operative approaches to the making of foreign policy had broken down. No longer was the debate concerned with answering the questions of what methods were most efficacious for containing the Soviet Union, new questions were being asked. Moreover, the administration had to deal with these within a domestic context of a return to isolationism.[47]

Isolationist sentiments may reflect concerns with the domestic economy and a popular desire for a post Cold War "peace dividend." The pursuit of a favorable GATT (General Agreement on Tariffs and Trade) agreement would suggest a continued role as a preponderant power in the international economy (though to date the United States remains the only country not to have signed the agreement, due to congressional ratification delays). Theories derived from the preponderance of power in search of hegemony suggest the unspoken assumptions of policy since World War II, and before, have been an attempt to extend the "liberal internationalist" policies, which included attempts to bring Europe and Japan within the spheres of US influence, containing the Soviet alternative, which ironically contributed to the mobilization of US society and culture during the Cold War. The argument, most recently put forward by Layne and Schwarz, states that US interests are at stake, not so immediately, but within the longer concerns for international order and access to adjacent or regional markets through the pursuit of Open Door theories. Through this interpretation Bosnia may be as important as Vietnam. By June 1994, former Secretary of State James Baker's searing criticism of the Clinton foreign policy rejoined these arguments. The real key to the Balkan situation was

Macedonia: "We have to make it clear that stability in Europe is the key. That should be the new NATO mission, whatever it takes, wherever it is. Because if we do get a wider Balkan war, we'll be back. Forget that reduction of US troops in Europe. We'd be back."[48] The hint at renewed open ended commitments reflects further preponderant intentions.

Preponderance transcends the containment of the Soviet Union, hence the policies in the post Cold War period have not altered that significantly. Yet they face the continued constraints of a declining economic base from which to project power, and in the military sphere, the pervasive Vietnam syndrome. Nonetheless, according to Layne and Schwarz US preponderance may be considered within reach by the foreign policy establishment. US intolerance of instability, uncertainty, mere alternatives, or closed economies points to what they describe as the "apotheosis of American exceptionalism" (perhaps represented in Fukuyama's recent writing) because unlike other great powers which endured political alternatives, the United States risks overstretch and further decline by trying to control all the waves.[49] The international economic, political, and social tensions resultant in part from the strategy of preponderance invites future instability; pacification, as Dunkerley posited, suggests a temporality.

Washington's foreign policy establishment faces a formidable intellectual task in its future attempts to formulate a strategy for a power resolved to lead in the face of relative economic decline and a domestic "check" on the sustained use of its military power.

Notes

1 Mr X., "The Sources of Soviet Conduct," *Foreign Affairs* 25 (July 1947): 566–582. For a critique on the universalization of the policy, see Theodore Draper, "American Hubris: From Truman to the Persian Gulf," *New York Review of Books* 34, no. 12 (July 16, 1987): 41; an excellent concise interpretive introduction to NSC 68 is Ernest R. May (ed.), *American Cold War Strategy: Interpreting NSC 68* (Boston: Bedford Books, 1993). For authoritative histories of the period see John Lewis Gaddis, *The United States and the Origins of the Cold War, 1941–1947* (New York: Columbia University Press, 1972); for more recent interpretations see Melvyn P. Leffler, *A Preponderance of Power: National Security, the Truman Administration, and the Cold War* (Stanford University Press,

1992), and Lloyd C. Gardner, *Spheres of Influence: The Partition of Europe from Munich to Yalta* (London: John Murray, 1993).

2 John F. Kennedy cited by Stephen E. Ambrose, *Rise to Globalism: American Foreign Policy Since 1938* (Harmondsworth: Penguin, 1993), 171.

3 Top Secret Report by the Policy Planning Staff PPS/23, "Review of Current Trends: US Foreign Policy," *Foreign Relations of the United States 1948*, vol. 1, part 2 (Washington, DC: Government Printing Office, 1976), 524–525.

4 Thomas Borstelmann, *Apartheid's Reluctant Uncle: The United States and Southern Africa in the Early Cold War* (New York and Oxford: Oxford University Press, 1993), 196–198; Leffler, *Preponderance*, 18.

5 Thomas J. McCormick, *America's Half-Century: United States Foreign Policy in the Cold War* (Baltimore: Johns Hopkins University Press, 1989), 5; Sheldon B. Liss, *Radical Thought in Central America* (Boulder: Westview Press, 1991), 38.

6 Gabriel Kolko, *Confronting the Third World: United States Foreign Policy, 1945–1980* (New York: Pantheon, 1988), 229.

7 Thomas J. McCormick, "World Systems," in Michael J. Hogan and Thomas G. Paterson (eds.), *Explaining the History of American Foreign Relations* (Cambridge University Press, 1991), 93. Paul Kennedy's *The Rise and Fall of the Great Powers* (London: Fontana, 1988) is a popular argument on US relative decline.

8 Kolko, *Third World*, 236.

9 Cecil V. Crabb, *The Doctrines of American Foreign Policy: Their Meaning, Role, and Future* (Baton Rouge: Louisiana State University, 1982), 280.

10 Walter LaFeber, *The American Age: United States Foreign Policy at Home and Abroad since 1750* (New York: W. W. Norton, 1993), 638.

11 Earl C. Ravenal, *Never Again: Learning from America's Foreign Policy Failures* (Philadelphia: Temple University Press, 1980), 21–32.

12 James M. McCormick, *American Foreign Policy and Process* (Itasca: Peacock Publishers, 1992), 117.

13 McCormick, *America's Half-Century*, 186–187.

14 Saul Landau, *The Dangerous Doctrine: National Security and US Foreign Policy* (Boulder: Westview Press, 1988), 102.

15 Warren I. Cohen, *America in the Age of Soviet Power, 1945–1991* (Cambridge University Press, 1993), 183.

16 McCormick, *American Foreign Policy*, 127; LaFeber, *American Age*, 654–655.

17 LaFeber, *American Age*, 654–656; Kolko, *Third World*, 217–222.

18 LaFeber, *American Age*, 656–660.

19 Martin Walker, *The Cold War* (London: Fourth Estate, 1993), 227–228; Kolko, *Third World*, 230.

20 McCormick, *American Foreign Policy*, 117; Michael H. Hunt, *Ideology and US Foreign Policy* (New Haven: Yale University Press, 1987), 184.

21 David P. Forsythe, *Human Rights and World Politics* (Lincoln: University of Nebraska Press, 1989), 110–112.

22 Cohen, *America*, 208; Walter LaFeber, "From Detente to the Gulf," in Gordon Martel (ed.), *American Foreign Relations Reconsidered, 1890–1993* (London: Routledge, 1994), 154.

23 David Louis Cingranelli, *Ethics, American Foreign Policy, and the Third World* (New York: St Martin's Press, 1993), 184; McCormick, *America's Half-Century*, 212–214.

24 Cohen, *America*, 207.

25 Walter LaFeber, *Inevitable Revolutions: The United States in Central America* (New York: W. W. Norton, 1993), 271.

26 LaFeber, *American Age*, 704.

27 David Ryan, "An Examination of Diplomatic Relations between the United States and Nicaragua during the Reagan Presidency," Ph.D. thesis (Cork: University College, 1992), 1–16.

28 Hunt, *Ideology*, 175; LaFeber, *America, Russia, and the Cold War 1945–1990* (New York: McGraw-Hill, 1991), 160.

29 Lars Schoultz, *National Security and United States Policy towards Latin America* (Princeton University Press, 1987), 10, 63; Ryan, "Diplomatic Relations," 14.

30 Ronald Reagan, "Central America: Defending Our Vital Interests," *Current Policy* 482 (Washington, DC: Department of State, April 27, 1983), 4.

31 Ronald Reagan's Executive Order 12513, May 1, 1985, Document 554, *American Foreign Policy: Current Documents 1985* (Washington, DC: Department of State, 1986), 999.

32 James Dunkerley, *The Pacification of Central America: Political Change in the Isthumus 1987–1993* (London: Verso, 1994), 3.

33 Noam Chomsky, *On Power and Ideology: The Managua Lectures* (Boston: South End Press, 1987), 9.

34 Selig S. Harrison, "Afghanistan: Soviet Intervention, Afghan Resistance, and the American Role," in Michael T. Klare and Peter Kornbluh (eds.), *Low Intensity Warfare: How the USA Fights Wars With-*

out Declaring Them (London: Methuen, 1989), 198–206.

35   Hunt, *Ideology*, 177.

36   McCormick, "World Systems," 93; McCormick, *America's Half-Century*, 1.

37   Lloyd Gardner, comments at the annual Jean Donovan Conference, University College, Cork, Ireland, January 1990. The collected papers are published in Dermot Keogh (ed.), *Beyond the Cold War* (Cork: Hibernian University Press, 1990); Dunkerley, *Pacification*, 30.

38   Noam Chomsky, "On US Gulf Policy," *Open Magazine* (Pamphlet no. 1, 1991), 16; Defense Planning document in *New York Times* March 8, 1992 quoted by Alexander L. George, "Regional Conflicts in the Post-Cold War Era," in Geir Lundestad and Odd Arne Westad (eds.), *Beyond the Cold War: New Dimensions in International Relations* (Oslo: Scandinavian University Press, 1993), 124; Christopher Layne and Benjamin Schwarz, "American Hegemony – Without an Enemy," *Foreign Policy* no. 92 (fall 1993), 10; Robert W. Tucker and David C. Hendrickson, *The Imperial Temptation: The New World Order and America's Purpose* (NewYork: Council on Foreign Relations, 1992), 87; Maureen Dowd, *New York Times*, February 23, 1991.

39   Paul Walker, "The Myth of Surgical Bombing in the Gulf War," in Ramsey Clark et al., *War Crimes* (Washington, DC: Maisonneuve Press, 1992), 87.

40   Edward W. Said, *Culture and Imperialism* (London: Chatto and Windus, 1993), 365; Victoria Brittain, Introduction, in her edited *The Gulf Between Us: The Gulf War and Beyond* (London: Virago Press, 1991), ix.

41   The Glaspie Transcript, July 25, 1990, in Micah L. Sifry and Christopher Cerf, *The Gulf War Reader* (New York: Times Books, 1991), 130, 125; Tucker and Hendrickson, *Imperial Temptation*, 90.

42   Maureen Dowd, *New York Times*, February 23, 1991.

43   George, "Regional Conflicts," 128.

44   Bill Clinton, Inaugural Address, January 21, 1993; Martin Walker, "Withdrawal Symptoms," *The Guardian* (London), May 7, 1994.

45   Martin Walker, "Withdrawal Symptoms," *The Guardian* (London), May 7, 1994.

46   Martin Walker, "Generals Get New Mission Statement," *Guardian Weekly*, April 17, 1994; Patrick Cockburn, "Air Strikes Point to New US Strategy to Save Troops," *Independent* (London), July 14, 1993.

47   Martin Walker, "Clinton Adviser Worried by Isolationist Mood," *The Guardian* (London), June 23, 1994.

48   Layne and Schwarz, *Foreign Policy*, 10–11; Martin Walker inter-

view with James Baker, "Mad as Hell over what they've done to America," *The Guardian* (London), June 25, 1994.

   49   Layne and Schwarz, *Foreign Policy*, 9, 22; Francis Fukuyama, *The End of History and the Last Man* (Harmondsworth: Penguin, 1993).

Part II

Political arenas redefined

Enter women: modest change
in US politics

Over the last twenty-five years, Americans have both acknowledged women's longstanding involvement in politics and now readily accept women as political actors in their own right. Since 1970, United States politics has experienced a trend away from women rarely being public officials to women as a persistent and growing minority of political insiders. A woman's need to conform to feminine stereotypes and modestly mask ambition and competence behind a man has abated in the process. While the furor surrounding Hillary Rodham Clinton reveals the limits of this shift – for a spouse at least, the prominence of Congresswoman Patricia Schroeder, Texas Governor Ann Richards, Supreme Court Justice Sandra Day O'Connor, or Secretary of Health and Human Services Donna Shalala speaks clearly to the emergence of women as political Americans. This move to overt acceptance marks a fundamental trend in US politics over the past quarter century. Nonetheless, when female senators demanded Admiral Frank B. Kelso lose two stars due to his culpability for the Navy's Tailhook scandal, they did not prevail.

Despite the welter of ways that politics has opened for women, and their lot improved, the changes remain modest. The force of women's presence in American politics is eroded by the general difficulty any majority finds in reaching agreement on an issue. Women are as diverse as men in their thinking, so find few forums of widespread agreement even about women's concerns. Only a brief honeymoon of unanimity occurred in the early 1970s before women of color asserted legitimate concerns against a largely white middle class movement. The rise of anti-feminists such as Phyllis Schlafly and Beverly LaHaye demonstrate the complexity of intra-women politics as well.

The chronology detailed in the Appendix to this chapter highlights events important to women in American politics in twenty-five years. Even a quick glance confirms that the changes have been extensive on the policy front and in the emergence of women as political leaders. But then, women began from a greatly curtailed base. While only some events chronicled here are discussed, this overview provides a flavor of the range of change that has occurred. The trend toward change for women, however, is moderated by all that has stayed the same.

Women's entrance into politics is marked by a tension between appearances: little seems to have changed overall, yet enormous and extensive change has occurred from a time when cultural codes dictated that women behave more modestly than men, perhaps especially in politics.

For women, despite the number and range of advances possible to list here, neither the policy claims that launched the National Organization for Women (NOW) in 1966 nor the priorities of the 1977 National Women's Conference have been fully realized. Indisputably though, enormous social and cultural change has led to political change, which in interactive fashion has led to more social and cultural change. Because many articulate and savvy women work in politics today, and most importantly because their prominence has grown, the common past practice of discounting women's political participation becomes more difficult. Nonetheless, the changes that have occurred since 1970 can hardly be seen as transformative, at least not yet.

The way we were

The women's movement was reborn from its suffrage days during the 1960s, but it hardly sprang forth fully grown. By 1970 NOW had celebrated only its fourth birthday and other feminist groups such as the National Women's Political Caucus were yet to be born. A women's policy network was only beginning to emerge from a series of conferences sponsored by the US Women's Bureau during the 1960s.[1] In August 1970, this fledgling network successfully united for the largest mass action for women's rights in the nation's history – the Women's Strike for Equality, spearheaded by NOW. Women held rallies and demonstrations across the country, with housewives going on strike to bring attention to their contributions to society. Earning serious and substantial news coverage, this strike marked the beginning of the widespread trend toward women as political actors in their own right, a trend not seen since the 1920s.

Looking at 1970, we can see the strides American women have made on the policy front. Abortion without restriction was illegal in forty-six of the fifty states. Educational institutions freely discriminated against girls and women. In many states, a married woman was barred from retaining her maiden name, having individual bank accounts or credit ratings, or obtaining loans without her husband's signature. Similarly, being recognized as "head of household" was difficult for a woman, thus affecting a wide swath of financial, legal, or insurance concerns.

In part, this resulted from beliefs about gender roles. Women were overwhelmingly channeled into a mere handful of occupations and often barred from many jobs, especially high-paying "blue collar" ones. If fully employed, she earned only, on average, fifty-nine cents to a man's dollar. Inside the electoral arena, women voted in about the same proportion as men yet only 3 percent of Congress and 5 percent of state legislators were female. In 1970, no state had a woman running for governor, and no woman had ever been one of the "brethren" of the US Supreme Court.

Women's attitudes, on average, still reflected post-World War II domestication, although 1970 marks the brink of change. A Gallup poll in 1969 found 58 percent of men would vote for a qualified woman for president compared to only 49 percent of women. Two years later, in a testament to women's decidedly immodest political awakening, 67 percent of women compared to 65 percent of men responded positively.[2]

From margin to mainstream

Much of what we understand about group politics in the US derives from ethnic groups. If women acted accordingly, they would vote as a bloc, display preferential voting for female candidates, be unified in their support of policies beneficial to women, and support candidates based upon the degree of their support for women's issues.[3] Because women are as diverse as men in their views, however, with self-interests and loyalties other than sex-based ones claiming political consideration, we are not surprised that our understanding of group politics does not well apply to women. In many regards, expecting bloc action in the face of the diversity inherent in a group that constitutes a majority rather than a minority is itself ill-conceived. In 1970, the success of the Women's Equality Strike, the reintroduction of the Equal Rights Amendment (ERA), and the general foment among women, made it possible to overlook this obvious obstacle.

Women in Congress such as Martha Griffiths, Margaret Heckler, Edith Green, and Patsy Mink who had worked across party line to push equity measures during the 1960s contributed to the sense that women could be united during the 1970s. The addition of Shirley Chisholm, the first African-American woman to win election to the House of Representatives, strengthened this feeling through her outspoken feminism. These elected women were aided by the growing feminist movement. NOW recruited prominent black women such as Pauli Murray, Fannie Lou Hamer, and Addie L. Wyatt; and Aileen Hernandez was elected NOW president in 1970.[4]

The Third World Women's Alliance, a black feminist group, participated in the August 1970 mass demonstration. With many women of color helping to found the National Women's Political Caucus (NWPC) in July 1971, the organization deliberately structured itself to represent a broad spectrum of women as well as taking pains to be bipartisan. Fannie Lou Hamer was a keynote speaker, and among those elected to its National Policy Council were Indian rights leader, LaDonna Harris; Dorothy Height, leader of the National Council of Negro Women; from the United Auto Workers, Olga Madar; welfare rights activist Beulah Sanders; and Chicana leader, Lupe Anguiano. Congress began to discuss the ERA in May of 1970. Women, especially feminist women, had reason to ignore their differences.[5]

But the honeymoon of unanimity was short-lived. In a trend that has persisted over time, the diversity of women created its own politics. Despite the early support for the ERA by the National Council of Negro Women, many women of color began to fear that racial unity would be threatened by the anti-male tone of the women's movement. Chicanas resented white feminists' stereotypes of "machismo" dominating their families and communities. Further, many remembered eugenics too well, with birth control used as genocide earlier in the century, so they could not embrace reproductive rights with similar enthusiasm as white middle class women.

Diversity emerged too. Women from forty-three tribes formed the North American Indian Women's Association in 1970; Mexican-American women held the first National Chicana conference in 1971; the Conference of Puerto Rican Women occurred in 1972; and with others, Eleanor Holmes Norton organized the National Black Feminist Organization in 1973.[6]

Another area of diversity within the movement existed between radical or younger feminists and mainstream or older feminists.[7] The radical tactics of leftist groups like Redstockings had influenced NOW in the late 1960s, leaving the widespread but erroneous impression among mainstream Americans that NOW, rather than localized feminist groups across the nation, was the heart of radical feminism. By the mid-1970s, consciousness-raising as a major activity had largely disappeared, and the original feminist left had splintered. With the demise of the feminist left in 1975, innovative movement tactics such as zap actions (outrageous, media-grabbing acts to make a point, by unknown perpetrators), witch hexes (spells), and guerrilla theater demonstrations also disappeared, replaced by the less visible or controversial women's culture public service projects.

However, 1975 was a watershed year for women in American politics for a variety of reasons initiated earlier.[8] Formed to work with and through political parties, the NWPC was called in *Newsweek* a plausible "strategy for a women's political movement where none had existed before."[9] The Women's Rights Project of the American Civil Liberties Union, with Ruth Bader Ginsburg at the helm, became the premier litigator on behalf of women's rights. NOW had incorporated its Legal Defense and Education Fund in 1971 and aggressively pursued cases, but not alone. Feminist litigation was undertaken by at least seven other entities.[10]

The Supreme Court ruled on several cases including *Reed* v. *Reed* in 1971 which held an Idaho law that preferred men over women as executors of wills, violated the equal protection clause; *Frontiero* v. *Richardson* in 1973 in which four justices argued sex classifications should be subject to the same "strict scrutiny" as race; and *Roe* v. *Wade* in 1973 which legalized abortion upon demand in the first trimester. Inside Congress, the ERA was passed; twenty-eight of the needed thirty-eight states ratified it by early 1973 and thirty-four by 1975. Also in 1973, AT&T, the nation's largest employer, lost a $30 million wage discrimination ruling by the Equal Employment

Opportunity Commission (EEOC). In 1974, the Women's Campaign Fund organized as a political action committee (PAC) to support only women for public office. All of this evidenced that feminism was no longer an isolated concept being shoved down the throat of American politics by some ultra-left radical group. But simultaneously, feminism had fostered its own backlash just at a time when the unity of sisterhood was giving way to diversity among women.

Predictably, if feminism was to be taken seriously, serious opposition to feminism emerged, and not just from men. At stake was the contention that feminists could claim to be representatives of all women in US politics. Anti-feminist women along with conservative men now competed for public attention and the claim to speak for "women." In 1973, the National Right to Life flexed its newly formed muscles; Phyllis Schlafly organized STOP ERA; and books based upon feminine virtue became best sellers. By 1974, the Heritage Foundation had been founded by Paul Wyrich, who later helped establish the Moral Majority, both advancing the counterpoints of conservative women.

But majority strategies were also underway inside organized feminism. On one front, traditional women's organizations, such as the American Association of University Women (AAUW) and the National Federation of Business and Professional Women (NFBPW), increased the prominence of feminist issues on their national agendas, thereby dramatically expanding the number of mainstream women who accepted women's rights and equality platforms. Within NOW, a struggle erupted about the structure of the organization; eventually, Eleanor (Ellie) Smeal, leader of the Majority Caucus, prevailed. In 1975, NOW was explicitly moved into the governmental arena. Smeal immediately relocated the national office to Washington, DC, a tactic common to nearly all national women's organizations.[11] But offices were not all that moved.

Despite the prominence of states' sovereignty in law related to women, policy debates also moved to Washington. Two trends regarding policy are obvious during the 1970s which, once established, persisted. Firstly, with the revival of the women's movement, the amount of attention directed toward "women's legislation" increased markedly. Only twice in the twentieth century could legislative effort be compared: the 66th Congress (1919–1921) when women attained suffrage in a constitutional amendment and the 78th Congress (1943–1944: World War II). The entire decade of the 1970s, and the 1980s with a slight decline, witnessed this remarkable level of legislation dealing with women's issues. But while still surpassing any other time in the century, women's legislation still constituted only about 3 percent of the total, reflecting the tension between extensive and modest change.[12]

A second pattern in legislation can be found in the tension between women's political claims for equality because everyone is the same, and women's claims for special treatment because women and men are not similarly situated in society, the polity and the economy. According to Anne Costain, legislation from 1970 to 1974 concentrated exclusively on equality, with the single exception of a non-sex discrimination exemption for the Boy Scouts and the Girl Scouts. Beginning in 1975, both equality and special treatment legislation emerges, a trend that continues since. For example, the 94th Congress of 1975–1976 passed equality legislation to admit women to US military academies, study sex-stereotyping and bias in vocational education, and add sexual non-discrimination clauses to five federal laws. Simultaneously, special needs legislation was passed that would organize a National Women's Conference, encourage proposals to study alcoholism among women, and promote greater participation by women in science.

In other words, by 1975 feminists had discovered the limits of equality. Because policy decisions and prior practice had so systematically treated "man" as the universal human and "woman" as another category, e.g. only men had been included in alcoholism studies, women could not be served without making claims as a special category. Women thus became "special" even though in practice they sought an equal share of the public pie. To confound matters more, if equality meant simply treating women as though they were men, then women's special needs, such as nutrition for pregnant and breast-feeding mothers, would be ignored.

The tension surrounding equality has remained important as the Johnson Controls case of 1991 revealed. The court unanimously ruled that companies cannot establish work patterns that exclude individuals based upon potential harm to a developing fetus – equal treatment.[13]

From mainstream to majority?

Many elements converged to make women and women's concerns move from the margins of American politics to being viewed as mainstream, i.e. ideas not out of the ordinary and appropriate for political consideration. Three areas in particular have laid the foundation for women to take the next step, building a sense that women just might actually be the political majority: the battle surrounding ERA; the struggle concerning reproductive freedoms; and the gender gap in voting and attitudes.

The fight to ratify the ERA galvanized women throughout the US during the late 1970s. As is covered previously, increase in feminist activity in ERA ratification efforts escalated from 1975 to its expiration June 30, 1982. While much more occurred during this time period, and many other issues and groups kept their activities thriving, NOW and the ERA under Ellie Smeal's leadership captured center stage of American women's politics.

ERA also spawned parallel growth among anti-feminists. Phyllis Schlafly had earlier established STOP ERA and initiated her second organization, Eagle Forum, in 1975. Unlike the former group, Eagle Forum carried more of the New Right's broad conservative political agenda than the more narrowly focused STOP ERA. Also showing as a latecomer to the anti-ERA effort was Concerned Women for America (CWA), founded by the wife of a Baptist minister. Beverly LaHaye established her organization with a stronger religious base of "kitchen table lobbyists" than Eagle Forum. She has focused on political initiates, deploying a "write for life" campaign, and has undertaken a litigious strategy to counter the American Civil Liberties Union on behalf of women's freedoms.[14]

In many regards, ERA brought success despite its failure. The surrounding debate provided the impetus for changes in public policy and the roles of women in society. It also mobilized women and markedly shifted the political role of women.[15] Furthermore, polls conducted in the mid- and late-1980s consistently showed increased support for the ERA, a majority of women (56 percent) thinking of themselves as feminists, and 71 percent of respondents believing the women's movement improved women's lives.[16] Women, and their political demands, became demands that warranted attention.

But mainstream and majority politics are not the same. Issues can hold a central place in the mainstream of political discourse and activity without attaining action in a system with minority rights as well as majority rule. No issue for women has illustrated this better, especially in the past decade, than struggles surrounding reproductive rights. Since the landmark court case *Roe* v. *Wade* in 1973, various aspects of abortion and related reproductive rights have persisted as a central issue in US politics. Issues include parental consent or notification for minors, spousal notification, a requirement that doctors inform women of dangers and alternatives to abortions, prohibiting contraceptives to minors, limiting where abortions can be performed, banning publicly-funded abortions, waiting periods, freedom of access to clinics without harassment or threats of violence, and, most recently, attempts to limit coverage under private health insurance and under the proposed health care reform. Women's reproductive policy has birthed interest groups and mass movement activities, moved judicial appointments into "litmus tests" about positions on abortion, left a reluctant Congress in a no-win situation, invoked states' rights arguments, and confounded public opinion polling and political rhetoric.[17] With a boost from the conservative Reagan administration, conservative women gained prominence beyond their numbers.

Like the ERA, politics surrounding abortion rights have proven highly divisive. Also like ERA, proponents and opponents generally attract different types of women. Pro-choice and pro-ERA activists generally are employed, do not belong to a fundamentalist or evangelical religion, and believe in equality between women and men. In contrast, pro-life (anti-abortion) and anti-ERA activists are more likely unemployed, belong to a fundamentalist or evangelical (usually Christian) religion, and believe in separate roles and statuses for women and men. Unlike ERA, the initial abortion rights success with *Roe* v. *Wade* in 1973 did not result from organized action. Although the National Abortion Rights Action League (NARAL) formed in 1969 to end abortion laws in states, litigation rather than grass roots efforts led to the landmark ruling that dramatically changed abortion laws in forty-six states.[18] With the *Roe* decision, other feminist groups which fought to legalize abortion turned their attention to expanding access to abortion, the ERA, employment discrimination, day-care and a host of other related issues.[19]

In contrast, the Court's decision acted as a "bolt" for those who could not believe their government could stand for murder.[20] The anti-abortion activists formed grassroots organizations and employed small-group tactics such as daily protests and blocking abortion clinic doors along with regular lobbying and protesting at state legislatures. Of course, the fact a majority of these female activists were not employed gave them considerable advantage: feminist counter-protesters usually needed to take time from their work. Right wing grassroots tactics occurred with increasing frequency from the mid-1980s onward, but achieved national prominence during the summer of 1988 when Randal Terry took his group, Operation Rescue, to Atlanta to block abortion clinics during the Democratic convention.

As the pro-life camp blocked clinics with mounting frequency, and increasingly violent tactics were deployed by other groups such as the Lambs of Christ, the pro-choice movement awoke. But pro-choice groups had focused their energies mostly in Washington, DC, while the pro-life advocates had concentrated on state legislatures and local governments, thereby gaining early advantage. Pro-choice groups faced another and possibly more significant problem: the Supreme Court no longer supported more than the essence of the reasoning behind the Roe decision.

The election of President Clinton was clearly to pro-choice women's advantage, however. With executive orders, he reversed many of the restrictive measures implemented by Presidents Reagan and Bush. Clinton also appointed Janet Reno as Attorney General who, from her new post, would use the Federal Bureau of Investigation (FBI) to pursue protesters. Ironically, Roe spawned demands to curtail an activist judiciary. It was a conservative, strict constructionist court that approved the use of federal racketeering laws (commonly known as RICO laws) to pursue organized violence among some pro-life activists.[21] The RICO laws were originally written to combat organized crime but are vaguely worded as to their target. Without specific limits, the strict constructionists found the laws applied to organized violence, and a contingent of the anti-abortion movement is both organized and violent. The RICO laws, coupled with the murder of two Florida physicians, precipitated a decline in grass roots protests. The pendulum had swung back toward to pro-choice activists in governmental action with feminist positions gaining ground on the anti-feminists who enjoyed presidential favor under Reagan and Bush.

The struggles surrounding the ERA and reproductive policies

illustrate many of the dynamics of women in politics over the past twenty-five years. They also illustrate divisions among women in US politics. One other important political phenomenon warrants special note as well – the gender gap. In loose application, the term captures widespread, if only marginal, differences in thinking and voting between women and men as political groups.

Women's views are much the same as men's views on basic under-lying political values such as egalitarianism and individualism.[22] Still, and from the earliest days of survey research, persistent sex differences in attitudes about policy related to the use of force and violence and for policies of a compassionate nature can be identified. While hardly astounding in the degree of difference with men as a group, this rather limited form of female unity has been lumped under the rubric "gender gap." The gender gap first took on political significance that propelled women's politics into majority status when NOW activists identified it and planted it with the media during the 1980 presidential election. Women were 8 to 10 points less likely than men to support Ronald Reagan.[23] The term "gender gap" has since been applied to differences in policy and budgetary attitudes, as well as voting habits.

Greater numbers of women than men vote so any difference that drives women away from a candidate can mean the margin of victory. Women's preferences have made a difference in races from the presidential level downward. Although a gender gap of ten points hardly constitutes unity or bloc action, given women's numerical majority as voters, it matters. This represents a marked shift from 1970 when most pundits still believed a woman's vote was heavily influenced by her male partner. For example, George Bush carefully cultivated the women's vote during fall of 1992 after polls showed him far behind among women.

The gender gap has had wide-ranging consequences. For example, Americans discovered a gender gap around the issue of sexual harassment. In 1991, Anita Hill's accusations of sexual harassment coincided with a variety of opportunities leading to an extraordinary number of candidates to step forward for Congress in 1992. Impor-tantly, professional women – women who are most likely to become candidates – reacted strongly to the picture of fourteen men doubting Anita Hill.

Although quite complicated to prove, arguably if women began to doubt their representatives on this issue, representation might also suffer in other areas. And if this doubt left a deep impression, many citizens might shift to a belief that gender balance is preferable to imbalance. Such might be a lasting effect but the evidence will not be in for years. Important for now are the more superficial results in terms of women as candidates.

However, Anita Hill and the gender gap she unearthed was far from the sole reason women candidates stepped forward in 1992. The movement was maturing and its women with it. Women had been preparing to take public posts since the revival of feminism. Most importantly, when the ERA failed in 1982, organized feminism realized with certainty that women could not count upon men to do their legislating for them. Because ERA failed by only a handful of legislators, feminists adopted the goal of electing women to state legislatures before again mobilizing a national effort to pass the ERA. Such a strategy would also help to shape all state laws that control women's lives. For example, in the US federal system, states have overwhelming authority via the myriad of laws governing the practice of abortion and other quality of life policies. On average, more women actively work to ensure women's reproductive rights and broader concerns.

So, to what extent have women entered politics as candidates and officials? Herein lies the long-term possibility of making change less modest.

Women enter politics: candidates and officials

In many regards, efforts directed toward getting more women into public office in the US reflect other developments in politics. Central among them were the initial revival of feminism and its public face as the women's movement, the struggle for the ERA, battles surrounding reproductive rights and later women's health care, and progress on a whole host of issues related to gender roles and expectations in society. The public's memory might focus more on fits and starts in women's political progress related to major media events, e.g. Geraldine Ferraro as vice president nominee in 1984, the Supreme Court confirmation hearings of Clarence Thomas. Yet, women's political progress has been slow and steady over time.

Those who strive to increase the number of women in elective and appointive office have grappled with a fundamental problem since the revival of feminism: an empty "pipeline" of viable female candidates. The problems had interrelated components of the pipeline of lower offices, the viability of women as candidates, and finally surmounting barriers to win elections.

In the 1970s, the viability explanation generally ran thusly: To be qualified to run and win as a candidate for public office, one has to be a viable candidate; to be a viable candidate, one generally must have qualifications acknowledged as relevant for that office; and, at the federal level especially, the candidate must be able to raise campaign funds. Professional and managerial occupations, most notably law and business, have been well suited to prepare individuals for public office, offering both flexibility and skill development such as persuasive speaking.

Most important for viability, however, a candidate needs to be seen as credible. Credibility is itself tricky in that perception rules its granting. It could be derived from having held posts in professional organizations which resulted in a political base or from having held one or more appointive offices on boards or commissions. Of course, professional reputation also contributes to the perception of being desirable on boards and commissions.

Lacking either occupational fit or political experience, those women who did step forward for office often found raising money to run a decent campaign troublesome as well. Gender stereotypes strongly linked politicians with men, and sexism confounded even well-situated women from being perceived as credible candidates.

Basically, because women were excluded from certain kinds of occupations and because political bases were understood as built upon business and professional relationships, women found it difficult to attain lower offices which comprise the pipeline for higher office. If women are unable to attain lower offices, they clearly could not be considered as viable for higher offices. And sufficient campaign funding plagued efforts. The pipeline became the common retort to explain the dearth of women in public office and the desire to fill the pipeline became the long-term struggle. While more women needed to step forward as candidates, they also needed to be seen as viable. Their problem was essentially circular: women lacked elected experience because they had not been elected, and they could not be elected because they lacked experience.

In a landmark study of female candidates during 1976, Susan Carroll identified and debunked much so-called common wisdom surrounding women as candidates in American politics.[24] She noted that incumbents have tremendous reelection advantages and, as so few women were incumbents, women as a group were disadvantaged. Further, the more desirable the seat, because it was either open or more prestigious or selective, the more likely a woman was to face problems as a candidate. This was reflected in the recruitment process where party gatekeepers channeled female candidates as sacrificial lambs into less desirable seats, e.g. challengers for entrenched incumbents, overlooking them for attractive openings.

Carroll also debunked the notion that women, supposedly lacking necessary qualifications and political experience, were not viable candidates. She found that women were well qualified in professional and managerial occupations and well experienced with political parties. In addition, many female candidates reported difficulties with the usual problems in any campaign, e.g. time, people, partisan support, but these were problems of significance for offices beyond state legislatures. Finally, contrary to common wisdom, female candidates did not appear to lose because they were women. Most had androgynous characteristics and few, even those who considered themselves to be feminist, (dared to) emphasize "women's issues." In short, the numbers of women in office would increase if more women stepped forward as candidates.

Table 7.1   *Number of women electoral candidates 1974–1992**

	US Senate	US House	Governor	State legislature
1974	3	44	3	1,125
1976	1	54	2	1,258
1978	2	46	1	1,348
1980	5	52	0	1,426
1982	3	55	2	1,643
1984	10	65	1	1,756
1986	6	64	8	1,813
1988	2	59	2	1,853
1990	8	70	8	2,064
1992	11	108	3	2,375

Source: Data derived entirely from the Center for the American Woman in Politics, National Information Bank on Women in Public Office, Eagleton Institute of Politics, Rutgers University.

Note: * Major party nominees

Table 7.1 shows the number of women who became candidates in the major political parties from 1974 to 1992 for a variety of seats. In the most plentiful category, state legislative seats, the number of candidates has more than doubled since 1974 and was up 15 percent since 1990. The number of female candidates for state legislature has increased each year since the Center for the American Woman in Politics (CAWP) began keeping statistics. At the national level, increases have been far less consistent and proportionally smaller. Clearly 1984 was a benchmark year for women as senatorial candidates, marking both a record high and a high point for the decade. The same can be said for female candidates in House races during 1984. That was the year the Democrats nominated Geraldine Ferraro to be vice president, a year touted at the time as "the year of the woman." While 1990 issued in a new decade and renewed increases in female candidacies, it falls short of the second "year of the woman" in 1992.

For the gubernatorial candidates, we find an inconsistent pattern since 1974 with eight candidates as the highest number in 1986 and again in 1990. Importantly for the entrance of women into politics, gubernatorial candidates seek an executive office rather than a legislative one which magnifies the perceptual credibility problem. Executive offices have been seen as more difficult for women to attain due to stereotypes that project all women as weak in fiscal management and unable to make tough decisions.

States vary widely in the power granted to governors and the condition of their electoral status. Today all states have four-year terms, unlike in 1974, but some have single terms while others have no term limits. Also, election cycles vary, so making consistent sense out of these data is more problematic than for some of the other seats. Of the fifty gubernatorial seats, no more than thirty-six are up for election at one time.

By 1992, the major barrier of the state executive position had been challenged by women but without a major breakthrough. Only three women have served simultaneously as governors. In 1994, however, of the thirty-six up for election, nineteen have women as candidates, and eleven of these candidates are in races for open seats.[25] This constitutes a 238 percent increase over the previous high of eight candidates!

If growth in the rate of female candidates has been inconsistent, the increase of women in elective office has been remarkably steady as Table 7.2 reveals. While the presence of women as public officials can be readily be characterized as modest with about one-fifth of the best cases – statewide elective office and state legislative posts – being held by women, the improvement is significant. No office even approaches parity between males and females, nor even the roughly 44 percent of the overall workforce that is female. Nonetheless, women have more than doubled their presence in public office since 1975, and at the state level some improvements actually approach parity. For example, in 1993 Washington's state legislature boasted a 40 percent female membership with Arizona, Colorado, Vermont, and New Hampshire more than one-third.

Table 7.2   *Percentages of women in elective office 1975–1993*

	US Congress %	Statewide elective %	State legislatures %
1975	4	10	8
1977	4	10	9
1979	3	11	10
1981	4	11	12
1983	4	11	13
1985	5	14	15
1987	5	14	16
1989	5	14	17
1991	6	18	18
1992	6	18	18
1993	10	22	21

Source: Data derived entirely from the Center for the American Woman in Politics, National Information Bank on Women in Public Office, Eagleton Institute of Politics, Rutgers University.

Statewide offices include governors, attorney generals and lieutenant governors but also treasurers, commissioners of agriculture, or superintendents of public instruction (and other weaker remnants of the progressive era and its long ballot). Consistent with Susan Carroll's analysis above, many of these posts have been considered less desirable because they lack much authority or visibility. Yet, women have managed to parlay such statewide seats into qualifications for higher office, so the significance should not be underestimated. Perhaps the best known example is Ann Richards, governor of Texas, who launched her bid from the post of state treasurer.

For statewide offices, much of the growth has occurred since 1985. The US Congress presents the most discouraging picture where the presence of women can barely be called modest. In 1991, the Fund for the Feminist Majority calculated that, at the rate women were entering Congress, the US would not see gender parity in that institution until the year 2333! The much regaled "Year of the Woman" in 1992 moved the number of women senators to seven and members of the house to forty-eight, or to a total of 10 percent of Congress.[26] Even with the near doubling of women in Congress from 6 to 10 percent, NOW calculates gender parity by 2068 if we continue at the 1993 pace. As of June 1994, the NWPC had solid indications that 148 women would run as major party candidates for 122 or 28 percent of 435 seats.[27] In the Senate, eighteen major party female candidates are running for thirteen of thirty-four seats.[28] While NWPC predicts actual gains of only a handful of seats, in part due to the retirement of several female incumbents, the trend still is toward more women in Congress.

Federal judicial appointments are for life, so another important area to consider is the judiciary. Of the nine members of the US Supreme Court, two are now women, the first women to ever serve on the court: Sandra Day O'Connor, appointed in 1981 by President Reagan, and Ruth Bader Ginsburg, a 1994 Clinton appointee. Women have held judgeships in district and appellate federal court; however, their presence has been modest at best.

Table 7.3 provides an indication of numbers of women entering the bench, especially under the current regime, by comparing the four most recent US presidents after their first 16 months of office.[29] This limited time frame enables us to see the immodest changes underway in the Clinton administration. During the initial stages of his presidency, Jimmy Carter made a total of forty-one nominations; of these, three (7 percent) were female. In an equivalent time frame, Ronald Reagan made sixty-six nominations, but mustered only four female nominations (6 percent). Many court watchers proclaimed that Reagan's most lasting legacy would be his judicial appointments as he carefully screened for young conservatives, most of whom were white males. Interestingly, George Bush managed nearly the same number of nominations, sixty-four, at the onset of his administration. The six female nominees constituted 9 percent of his

Table 7.3 *Judicial nominations by sex during the first sixteen months of four presidencies*

	President			
	Carter	Reagan	Bush	Clinton
Sex				
Female	3 (7.3%)	4 (6.1%)	6 (9.4%)	30 (32.9%)
Male	38 (92.7%)	62 (93.9%)	58 (90.6%)	61 (67.1%)
Total	41	66	64	91

Source: Data collected May 24, 1994, provided by the White House, quoted in *Women's Political Times*, vol. 19, summer 1994, p. 8.

nominations. Through May 24, 1994 of his administration, Bill Clinton had made ninety-one nominations. Because many judges appointed by previous Democratic presidents postponed their retirements until another Democratic president was elected and because George Bush bequeathed him many open seats, Clinton had a goodly number of immediate appointments to make. But this time, as the opportunity structure opened in the judiciary, women were poised to take advantage of it. Thirty, or 33 percent of his ninety-one nominations have been females, a remarkable break with previous administrations.

One gains a sense of the scope of this shift by comparing to total appointment records of prior presidents. For example, Carter appointed the most women to the bench, forty or 15.5 percent, of his 258 appointments. Bush appointed thirty-six, or 19.5 percent of his 185 appointments. And Clinton's record to date stands in even starker contrast in comparison to Ronald Reagan, who appointed only twenty-eight women or 7.6 percent of 368 posts. In sixteen months, Clinton has appointed more women than Reagan did in eight years.

Overall then, we find a growing number and proportion of women in public posts. The trend toward the entrance of women into positions of public decision making has been rising steadily over the past twenty-five years, a welcomed trend for those believing representation improves in quality as representatives more closely mirror the citizenry.

But one would be hard pressed to suggest that even this notable progress has resulted in a marked change in US politics. In broad terms, past legacies excluding women from political office, thereby undermining a critical mass, couple with the need to forge majorities in a bipartisan system on an issue-by-issue basis, thus curtailing the effects of obvious change. Whence comes the influence of women on politics and what elements shape and constrain its emergence?

A masculine hold on politics

Although aspects of this association have moderated somewhat since 1970, politics remains heavily immersed in men and masculinity. As Wendy Brown aptly stated, for the Western case at least,

> More than any other kind of human activity, *politics* has historically borne an explicitly masculine identity. It has been more exclusively limited to men than any other realm of endeavor and has been more intensely, self-consciously masculine than most other social practices.[30]

If this is true, then women will find particular challenge gaining influence once inside politics in overcoming, or somehow extending themselves to fit, masculinity. One can point to the change of attitude toward Margaret Thatcher as she toughed, bullied, and braved her way through the Falklands War.

A collection of studies about various US political settings documents the ways in which men and masculinity assert their control and thereby limit women's political influence.[31] For example, in the House of Representatives, reproductive policies prior to 1992 passed through only one committee with a woman member – Patricia Schroeder on, ironically, armed services. As a result, no women had a chance to shape reproductive policies in the crucially important committee phase. But another study of state legislative committees finds that even in committees chaired by a woman and with a substantial proportion of women legislative members, consideration of a bill of particular concern to women and authored by a woman as well, male legislators control the discussion by interrupting, ignoring, insulting, and otherwise verbally dominating the discussion.

Yet another study shows that executive posts in state bureaucracy favor masculine management styles, so women must emulate men if they are to be successful in those posts. Yet, the higher women go in bureaucracy, the more subject they are to sexual harassment.

Further, another study shows disproportionately favorable opportunities and resources flowing to agencies where men predominate, e.g. agriculture and transportation. The very way we think about the agencies as universally beneficial can itself be questioned. For example, millions of dollars for transportation projects are contracted out by men to companies headed by men who overwhelmingly employ men.

The way we think about representation is also important as exemplified by the furor surrounding 1992 as "the year of the woman." In rhetoric at least, women stepped forward to run because the US Senate Judiciary Committee – comprised entirely by men – handled the Clarence Thomas nomination hearings in a manner most women did not expect of their representatives.

As proof that women indeed matter for women's concerns, Karin Tamerius traces a perfect correlation between the amount of effort, reputation, and resources a member of Congress spends on a "women's policy" and sex. Women expend resources on women's concerns; men fall off the expenditure of required personal and office resources. If politics is to fully take women into account so that the majority is no longer viewed as a special interest, then politics must be populated by women. Women must also hold key leadership posts in great enough numbers for a long enough time to have equal access to structural influence.

Ultimately, women have gained tremendously in US politics. They have entered US politics in significant ways: Their numbers have increased in all elective and appointive posts; their votes are courted due to the gender gap; their issues now make the congressional agenda with frequency. But in twenty-five years, the change has been modest. Avenues of influence in politics, steeped in masculine ways, remain largely in the hands of men. Breaking through centuries-old patterns takes more than a mere quarter century.

Appendix: Chronology of key events, 1970–1994

1970
May: (91st Congress) The US Senate subcommittee on Constitutional Amendments holds its first hearings on an ERA since 1955.
August: The ERA passes US House of Representatives 350–15.
August: Women's Strike for Equality, mobilization of women with

demonstrations and strikes across the nation.

1971
July: NWPC forms.
Reed v. *Reed.* The Supreme Court holds that an Idaho law that preferred men over women as executors of wills violated the equal protection clause.
October 12: House passes the ERA 354–23.

1972
Title IX of the Civil Rights Act prohibits sex-based discrimination in educational programs requiring federal funding.
March 22: Senate passes the ERA 84–8. Ratification deadline is set for March 22, 1979.
22 state legislatures (out of thirty-eight necessary) ratify the ERA.

1973
January 22: *Roe* v. *Wade* establishes that the constitutional right to privacy encompasses a woman's decision to terminate a pregnancy.
Doe v. *Bolton*: Supreme Court strikes down restrictions on where abortions could be performed, giving rise to the abortion clinic.
Frontiero v. *Richardson* establishes an "intermediate scrutiny" for the use of sex as a classification.

1974
Women's Campaign Fund organized as the first political action committee to support only women.

1975
Phyllis Schlafly founds Eagle Forum, an anti-feminist organization evolving out of her "STOP ERA" project.
The US Department of Defense (DOD) ends its policy of involuntary discharge for pregnant service members.
June 19–July: UN holds conference (Mexico City) as major event of International Women's Year.

1975–1976
(94th Congress): Congress passes laws admitting women to US military and Coast Guard academies.

1976
Women enter the military academies.
Planned Parenthood v. *Danforth* strikes down a Missouri law requiring a married woman to have husband's consent before an abortion. Court also rules that parents of an unmarried minor cannot give absolute veto to an abortion.

1977
Califano v. *Goldfarb* finds unconstitutional a provision of federal Old Age Survivors and Disability Insurance Benefits program which extends benefits to all widows but not all widowers.
Women working full-time earn 61.9 percent of men's weekly dollar.
Ronnie Alexander, a Yale student, becomes the first student to file a sexual harassment claim under Title IX.
US Army approves integrated basic training.
June 30: *Maher* v. *Roe* affirms right of states to deny women funding for non-therapeutic abortions.
November 18–21: National Women's Conference held in Houston, Texas and established priorities which include:
  full employment with more flexible schedules;
  income transfers labeled as wages, not welfare, for indigent women with dependent children;
  abolition of all gender discrimination in education and employment;
  federally funded child care services for all;
  reproductive freedom;
  revision of criminal and family laws regarding marital support, consensual homosexual activity, and rape;
  government support for battered women and displaced homemakers;
  nonsexist portrayals of women in the media; and
  increased representation of women in elective and appointive public office.

1978
Congress passes Pregnancy Discrimination Act, which provides that women affected by pregnancy, childbirth, and related medical conditions shall be treated the same as other persons not so affected but similar in their ability or inability to work.
City of Los Angeles Dept of Water and Power v. *Manhart.* An

employer may not require women, who tend to live longer than men, to make larger monthly contributions to a pension fund.

Women's Army Corps is abolished; women are integrated into the Army.

June: *Owens* v. *Brown*. Navy women are made eligible for sea duty.

August 15: ERA supporters gain an extension for the ERA until June 30, 1982; 233–189 in the House and 60–36 in the Senate.

By November, 13 additional states have ratified ERA, four states have rescinded ratifications, bringing total to 31.

1979

Andrea Dworkin publishes *Pornography*.

Beverly LaHaye founds CWA, a conservative organization committed to defending women's right to stay at home.

December 19: United Nations General Assembly adopts the Convention on the Elimination of All Forms of Discrimination Against Women.

1979–1980

(96th Congress): Congress passes laws to equalize the treatment and compensation of male and female commissioned officers.

1980

US Army announces a "pause" in its recruitment of women.

The "gender gap" appears in presidential politics. Women vote 46 percent for Ronald Reagan (45 percent for Jimmy Carter, 1976); men vote 54 percent for Reagan (37 percent for Carter).

Betty Friedan publishes *The Second Stage*, a book advocating the women's movement reorient its focus toward "real equality" for men as well as women and the desirability of having children.

Two out of three people living in poverty are women, a doubling in ten years.

A UN report states that women "constitute half of the world's population, perform nearly two-thirds of its work-hours, receive one-tenth of the world's income, and own less than one-one hundredth of the world's property."

June 30: *Harris* v. *McRae* upholds the Hyde Amendment, a federal law prohibiting use of Medicaid funds to pay for abortions for poor women. Poverty is seen as an obstacle not of the government's creation.

July 14–30: UN Decade for Women conference held in Copenhagen, Denmark, continues to address employment, social, education, and political issues.

1981
Male-only selective service registration is reinstituted.

County of Washington v. *Gunther*. Female security guards in county's female jail can be paid less than male guards in the male jail even though the two jobs were substantially equal. Court asserts that the case was not concerned with "the controversial concept of 'comparable worth.' "

The phrase "gender gap" begins to appear in the news media.

Texas v. *Burdine*. Employers cannot be made to "maximize" the number of female or minority employees hired but must have some latitude in personnel decisions.

The "Family Protection Act," one of several introduced into Congress in the early 1980s, fails to pass. Its provisions include eliminating federal laws supporting equal education for women, requiring marriage and motherhood be portrayed as the proper career for girls, repealing laws protecting battered women from their husbands, and banning federally-funded legal aid for women seeking abortion counseling or a divorce.

March 23: *H. L.* v. *Matheson*. A state may require a doctor to inform a teenaged girl's parents before performing an abortion or face criminal penalty.

September 21: Sandra Day O'Connor becomes the first female member of US Supreme Court.

1982
The Army re-segregates basic training.

June 30: The ERA expires, three states short of ratification. Harris survey shows 63 percent of American public favored its passage.

1983
In Minneapolis, an ordinance, on the basis that pornography harms women, classifies pornography as sex discrimination and allows any woman to bring civil suit against makers and distributors of pornography. The ordinance is vetoed by the mayor.

January: The ERA is reintroduced into the House of Representatives and Senate, but fails in November 278–147.

June 15: *City of Akron* v. *Akron Center for Reproductive Health*. Strikes down an Ohio abortion law requiring a twenty-four hour wait following counseling, which includes the statement, "the unborn child is a human life from the moment of conception."

1984
Summer: Geraldine Ferraro, Democrat of New York, is chosen as the Democratic vice presidential candidate, running with Walter Mondale.
November: Women make up 53.5 percent of voters. Women's turnout in the presidential election was 1.5 percent higher than men.

Mid-1980s
90 percent of all abortions occur in the first twenty weeks of pregnancy; 0.01 percent occur after twenty-four weeks.

1985
July 10–19: Forum '85, an NGO conference, is held in Nairobi, Kenya, preceding, rather than paralleling, the UN conference.
July 15–27: The final UN Decade for Women conference is held in Nairobi, Kenya. The United States is able to vote in favor of this conference's document, "The Forward-looking Strategies for the Advancement of Women to the Year 2000," because it did not contain a reference to Zionism as racism.

1987
California Federal Savings v. *Guerra* affirms the right of pregnant women to take unpaid leave although men and nonpregnant women may not. This case is disputed as to being a gain for women or a return to the age of "protective" labor laws.

1988
Women cast ten million more ballots than men.
Women working full-time earn 70.2 percent of men's wages.

1989
July: *Webster* v. *Reproductive Health Services*. Upholds a Missouri law which bans the use of public hospitals and clinics for abortion, "with an analysis that for the first time indicated that the majority of

the Court no longer considered abortion to be a 'fundamental constitutional right.' "

1990

June 18: The Congressional Caucus for Women's Issues releases a report noting the National Institutes of Health (NIH) had not followed its own policy requiring women be included in clinical research trials.

June 25: *Hodgson* v. *Minnesota*. A state law may require notification of both parents before a minor can obtain an abortion, as long as a judicial alternative is present.

September: The Pentagon releases a survey which reports that, of 20,000 worldwide military respondents, 64 percent of women and 17 percent of men claimed that they had been sexually harassed.

1991

Susan Faludi publishes *Backlash*.

Civil Rights Act of 1991 passes. The Act makes illegal all personnel decisions in which sex is a motivating factor.

January: *Robinson* v. *Jacksonville Shipyards*. Finds that the display of pornographic material in the workplace in and of itself constitutes sexual harassment because it sexualizes the workplace atmosphere and has the effect of keeping women out.

March 20: *United Automobile Workers* v. *Johnson Controls, Inc.* Court rules unanimously that companies cannot exclude women from jobs which might harm a developing fetus. On a 5–4 majority, they additionally state that Congress had intended to ban all hiring practices based on a worker's ability to have children.

September–October: During confirmation hearings of Supreme Court nominee Clarence Thomas, allegations made by Anita Hill become public. Hill claims that, while working for the EEOC, she had been sexually harassed by Thomas.

1992

EMILY's (Early Money Is Like Yeast) List, which had 3,500 members and $1.5 million dollars in contributions in 1990, grows to 24,000 members and $6.2 million.

January–March: Questions are raised as to whether 1992 will be the "Year of the Woman."

Spring: US Senator Alan Dixon is defeated in the state primary by

Carol Moseley-Braun, an unknown quantity from Chicago. The race is characterized as "an awesome political defeat in a primary election that, in normal times, he could have won handily." Other woman Senate candidates use the Thomas–Hill issue in winning their primaries.

June: The US Navy expands its inquiry into sexual assaults alleged to have occurred at its Tailhook convention in September 1991. The process initially leads to six assault investigations, fifty-seven investigations for attendance at the scene of the assaults, five for violating Navy standards, and two for impeding the investigation. A Senate panel delays 4,000 Naval promotions until it can be ascertained that the candidates were definitely not involved in the Tailhook assaults.

June 20: Secretary of the Navy Lawrence Garrett resigns after admitting to being nearby during the Tailhook assaults.

June 29: *Planned Parenthood* v. *Casey*. Reaffirms the "essence" of the constitutional right to abortion while permitting new state restrictions including a twenty-four hour waiting period and counseling requirements.

June 30: Female Gulf War veterans report to a Senate panel that they had been sexually assaulted by US military personnel during that war; Senator Cranston postulates that, in a "conservative" estimate, 60,000 out of 1.2 million female veterans have been raped or assaulted.

November: A gender gap appears in the presidential election. 49 percent of women with college degrees, as opposed to 40 percent of men, vote for Clinton; 58 percent of women without a high school diploma and 49 percent of men, vote for him. Four out of eleven women running for Senate are elected. Forty-seven of 106 women running for the House, including twenty-four non-incumbents, are elected.

1993

January 13: *Bray* v. *Alexandria Women's Health Clinic*. The Ku Klux Klan Act of 1871 could not be used to halt blockades of abortion clinics.

February 5: President Clinton signs Family and Medical Leave Act, which had been vetoed by President Bush in 1990 and 1992. The Act allows workers up to twelve weeks of unpaid leave a year but has numerous restrictions.

Spring: The Secretary of Defense changes military policy to increase opportunities for women in the Navy and Air Force.

March: The US Supreme Court declines to hear arguments regarding a Louisiana law, overturned in state court, which would have made abortion illegal in most cases.

June 30: The Texas Supreme Court rules that a ban on anti-abortion protests within 100 feet of an abortion clinic violates the constitutional right to free speech.

August 11: Ruth Bader Ginsburg becomes the second female member of the Supreme Court.

November: *Harris* v. *Forklift Systems*. A plaintiff in a sexual harassment case need not show evidence of psychological harm in order to win the suit.

November 15: US Supreme Court declines to hear an appeal of a decision upholding a 1986 Mississippi law requiring a minor to get the consent of both parents or a judge before being able to obtain an abortion.

1994

January 13: Secretary of Defense changes military policy to allow women into combat in the Army and Marine Corps.

January 24: US Supreme Court rules unanimously that the RICO Act of 1970 applies to anti-abortion demonstrators who block access to abortion clinics.

March: Air Force Lieutenant Jeannie Flynn becomes America's first female fighter pilot.

April: Admiral Frank B. Kelso, a naval officer implicated in the Tailhook scandal, comes up for retirement. Female senators in the US Senate vigorously question if he should be allowed to retire with his full four stars. On a vote of 54–43, Admiral Kelso is allowed to keep his stars; however, Senator Dianne Feinstein (Democrat, California) says, "the days of boys being boys . . . is over."

August: Attorney General Janet Reno uses federal agents to protect abortion clinics after the second murder of a doctor in Pensacola, Florida.

Notes

 1 Georgia Duerst-Lahti, "The Government's Role in Building the Women's Movement," *Political Science Quarterly*, 104:2 (1989), 249–268.
 2 Karen Leigh Beckwith, *American Women and Political Participation:*

The Impacts of Work, Generation, and Feminism (Westport, CT: Greenwood Press, 1986), pp. 17–33, 147–148.

3 David O. Sears and Leonie Huddy, "On the Origins of Political Disunity among Women," in *Women, Politics, and Change*, eds. Louise A. Tilly and Patricia Gurin (New York: Russell Sage Foundation, 1990), p. 249.

4 Susan M. Hartmann, *From Margin To Mainstream: American Women and Politics Since 1960* (Philadelphia: Temple University Press, 1989) pp. 66–71.

5 Hartmann, *Margin to Mainstream*, pp. 74–77.

6 Hartmann, *Margin to Mainstream*, pp. 70–71.

7 Jo Freeman, *The Politics of Women's Liberation* (New York: David McKay Co., 1976).

8 Barbara Ryan, *Feminism and the Women's Movement* (New York: Routledge, 1992), pp. 69–75.

9 Hartmann, *Margin to Mainstream*, p. 77.

10 Hartmann, *Margin to Mainstream*, p. 100.

11 Ryan, *Feminism*, pp. 71–73.

12 Anne N. Costain, "Women's Claims as a Special Interest," in *The Politics of the Gender Gap: The Social Construction of Political Influence*, ed. Carol M. Mueller (Newbury Park, CA: Sage Publications, 1988) pp. 150–172.

13 Interestingly, one aspect also raised by this is the harm to potential fetuses via damaged sperm from men working in toxic environments. Equal treatment for women raises gendered elements for men which are only beginning to be considered.

14 Susan E. Marshall, "Who Speaks for American Women? The future of Antifeminism," *American Feminism: New Issues for a Mature Movement*, The Annals, of the American Academy of Political and Social Science (Newbury Park, CA: Sage Publications, vol. 515, May 1991), pp. 50–62.

15 Janet Boles, "The Equal Rights Amendment as a non-zero-sum game," in *Rights of Passage: The Past and Future of the ERA*, ed. Joan Hoff-Wilson (Bloomington, IN: Indiana University Press, 1986, pp. 54–62), p. 61.

16 Ryan, *Feminism*, p. 109.

17 For a thorough overview see Barbara Hinkson Craig and David M. O'Brien, *Abortion and American Politics* (Chatham, NJ: Chatham House Publishers, 1993).

18 NARAL originally was named the National Association to Repeal Abortion Laws. It changed in 1973 after the Roe decision. In a testament to

the centrality of rhetoric in this movement, it recently changed its name again to the National Abortion and Reproductive Rights Action League (NARRAL).

19   Hickson Craig and O'Brien for most of the information in the section on abortion politics.

20   Kristin Luker, *Abortion and the Politics of Motherhood* (Berkeley: University of California Press, 1984), especially pp. 137–145.

While more men hold leadership posts in the anti-abortion camp than in the pro-choice side, women still predominate in both.

21   Strict constructionists attempt to discern the literal meaning of the constitution and statutes.

22   Sears and Huddy, "Political Disunity among Women."

23   *The Politics of the Gender Gap: The Social Construction of Political Influence*, ed. Carol M. Mueller (Newbury Park, CA: Sage Publications, 1988).

24   Susan Carroll, *Women As Candidates in American Politics* (Bloomington, IN: University of Indiana Press, 1985).

25   According to the NWPC as of June 22, 1994.

26   Senator Kay Bailey Hutchison of Texas joined the Senate through a special election. The number forty-eight includes Eleanor Holmes Norton, a delegate to Congress from Washington, DC. Delegates act as members of Congress but cannot vote.

27   As of June 22, 1994. While not a final list of candidates due to late filing dates in some states, NWPC carefully tracks races so likely has identified all candidates of any note.

28   House terms are for two years and all 435 seats are elected each even year. Senate terms are for six years with one-third of the 100 seats elected each two years.

29   Data as of May 24, 1994 and takes the equivalent time frame for prior administrations. Source, *Women's Political Times*, vol. 19, summer 1994, p. 8 using data provided by the White House.

30   Wendy Brown, *Manhood and Politics* (Totowa, NJ: Rowman & Littlefield Press), p. 4.

31   Georgia Duerst-Lahti and Rita Mae Kelly, *Gender Power, Leadership and Governance* (Ann Arbor, MI: University of Michigan Press, 1995). The studies cited here were conducted by Noelle Norton, Lyn Kathlene, Cheryl King, Rita Mae Kelly, Meredith Newman, Georgia Duerst-Lahti, and Karin Tamerius.

Benign neglect: the realpolitic of race and ethnicity

Thirty years after the passage of the Civil Rights Act and the Voting Rights Act, African-Americans are faced with a new set of questions. While African-American presence in the American political system has grown to a point where several African-Americans are visibly established in American politics, the enthusiastic support in the mass public for the civil rights movement has been transformed to, at best, complacency toward the African-American political agenda. This essay analyzes this most recent phase of the struggle.

After the landmark civil rights legislation of the 1960s, some fairly immediate, if incremental, movement of African-Americans up the political, social, and economic ladders was expected, and in some cases realized. The gains of African-Americans in the United States are usefully characterized by Earl and Merle Black's[1] enhancement of Blumer's[2] notion of "color lines." They explain that the progress of African-Americans in the United States is best understood in terms of breaking outer, intermediate, and inner color lines. They define the "outer color line" as one in which African-Americans are granted voting rights and the right to public accommodations.[3] These accomplishments are encapsulated in the 1964 Civil Rights Act and 1965 Voting Rights Act legislative victories. Barriers to economic, educational and occupational equality constitute the "intermediate color line." This second phase of the move for equality has met with, at best, benign neglect by the American political system and has dominated the African-American political agenda in the years 1970–1995 – the focus years of this essay. The final phase of integration into American society is breaking through the "inner color line," or true interpersonal equality. Although some progress has been made in breaking this barrier, it is not yet the focus of the

African-American agenda in American politics. The distinction
made between outer, intermediate, and inner "color lines" provides
a particularly worthwhile theoretical foundation for this essay
because it helps explain the difficulties of African-American movement in the last twenty-five years.

The civil rights movement and the American Dream

While the fight to win basic civil rights required marches, boycotts
and other forms of protest and civil disobedience, as Black and Black
note, it was clearly the most promising area in which to confront
racism in American society.[4] This outer color line presented a barrier
to African-Americans that could be expressed in a way that confronted the very basic tenets of the American political culture:
African-Americans were not allowed fundamental freedoms basic to
American citizenship. The rhetorical emphasis on equality of opportunity (rather than equality of condition) made the first phase of the
crusade more palatable to the American public.

The spirit of the civil rights movement of the 1960s was best
characterized by Martin Luther King, its consummate spokesman, in
the following:

> I say to you today, my friends, even thought we face the difficulties of
> today and tomorrow, I still have a dream. *It is a dream deeply rooted in
> the American dream* [emphasis added]. I have a dream that one day this
> nation will rise up and live out the true meaning of the American creed:
> "We hold these truths to be self-evident that all men are created
> equal."[5]

Indeed, African-American leaders hit an incredibly responsive chord
with Americans when they asked only for the same treatment that
every other citizen in America was accorded. The theme of equality
of opportunity is one that has been long valued in America. The
democratic enthusiasm that began in the Jacksonian era had been
renewed time and time again during the early part of the twentieth
century: the African-American movement had finally placed itself in
a position to experience some of the fruits of some of this long-term
democratic faith in the ability of the "common man" to play a larger
and larger role in government and take part in the American Dream.

The considerable popularity of the movement (outside of the
white South) was a reflection of the commitment to democracy and

especially the commitment to the individual opportunity to succeed. The American Creed to which King alludes is a creed based in an American obsession with individual liberty. It is an emphasis on the individual rather than on society. Equality is defined in terms of equality of opportunity rather than equality of outcome.[6] Gunnar Myrdal noted several years before the civil rights movement that this creed was widely accepted by African-Americans even though it may have reinforced oppression:

> The American Negroes know that they are a subordinated group experiencing, more than any one else in the nation, the consequences of the fact that the Creed is not lived up to in America. Yet their faith in the Creed is not simply a means of pleading for unfulfilled rights. They, like the whites, are under the spell of the great national suggestion. With one part of themselves they actually believe, as do the whites, that the Creed is ruling America.[7]

The movement gained widespread support because it did not pose a direct threat to the American political system and the dominant way of thinking: it only required that more people be allowed to work within it. The spirit of the African-American movement of the 1960s is characterized by its consistency with the tenets of the American Dream. Indeed, the "freedoms" accorded African-Americans as a result of the successes were almost exclusively ones that did not hinder the well-established freedoms that already existed for the more privileged white population.

African-American political gains were quickly identifiable immediately after the enactment of the major civil rights legislation of the early 1960s. African-American voter registration in almost every Southern state doubled during the course of two or three years. In 1967, Carl Stokes was elected mayor of Cleveland. He was the first African-American to be elected mayor of a major American city. More visible successes followed quickly. African-American needs became an important consideration in the political strategy employed in many areas where African-Americans were voting. Most Americans saw the obvious logic of Martin Luther King's appeal: in a nation where "all men are created equal" African-Americans and whites should be accorded the equal chance to vote. The Voting Rights Act of 1965 had a profound affect on the politics of every Southern state. African-Americans became an important political force in states where African-Americans were accounting for up to one-quarter of the vote (and up to one-third of the population). These political gains were highly consistent with the American Lockean tradition of individual opportunity and the American Dream.

The political progress from the 1960s until today is primarily restricted to getting the vote and electing more public officials. It did not necessarily guarantee any political clout. Indeed, after the initial political success of the movement, America has witnessed a dramatic polarization of the racial vote for candidates all across the nation. Since 1964, the presidential candidate that amassed the overwhelming majority support of African-Americans lost the election five of seven times (Carter in 1976 and Clinton in 1992 were the exceptions). African-American election in a majority white city or congressional jurisdiction is conspicuous and typically merits mention on the national news. There is one African-American in the United States Senate. The 1985 election of an African-American lieutenant governor in Virginia (who subsequently won the governorship) is the first time an African-American was elected to a statewide office in the United States since the Reconstruction years over a century ago. While African-American representation in Congress has held steady in recent times, only one African-American Congressman is elected from a majority white district. White Americans have shown a willingness to allow African-Americans to vote, but have shown a definite unwillingness to vote for African-Americans.

African-Americans are, however, beneficiaries of a much greater willingness of white elected officials to appoint African-Americans to policy making positions. While African-American acceptance within the centers of power may be closely associated with the degree to which an elected candidate sees African-Americans as part of his/her constituency, some are being appointed even by officials who don't see their reelection chances tied to African-American support.

In sum, even though some African-American political progress in the past twenty years has been dramatic and a small number are firmly entrenched in positions of power, African-Americans are not completely integrated into the political system. Until African-Americans are uniformly accepted by whites as legitimate candidates for office, and begin to win significantly more races in majority white jurisdictions, African-Americans will not have achieved political parity in the American system.

Political gains mean little if they do not result in affecting the lives of those who made the gains. These political gains have not translated well into "intermediate color line" gains because African-Americans remain a minority in American politics. Although political freedoms and representation in the government of this racial minority is much greater than it was before the civil rights movement, it remains beholden to an American majority that is not willing to go beyond the American Creed of almost obsessive individualism. The economic, educational and occupational gains made by African-Americans in the United States in this first phase of the civil rights movement (detailed below) can be understood by noting the general consistency between the major civil rights policies and the tenets of the American Dream. African-Americans won the right to join in the American competition for personal material success. Louis Hartz in *The Liberal Tradition in America*[8] accurately names the competition the "Lockean Race" because it is so firmly rooted in the philosophical tradition associated with John Locke. It is a tradition that emphasizes limited government but, more relevant to this discussion, individual property and individual material rewards for individual success. This philosophical tradition associated with the American Dream holds sacred the notion that there should be little government intervention in the economy or in private enterprise. Because of this characteristic of the American ethos, the policies resulting from the civil rights movement that affected the regulation of private enterprise were very different from those affecting government run institutions. In the private sector, the government required only that African-Americans be allowed (and in some cases encouraged) to participate. In private institutions, African-Americans were not given advantages at all commensurate to past disadvantages. The part of the African-American agenda that allowed African-Americans real advantages in the private sector was laid to rest with the 1978 Bakke case and the subsequent widespread acceptance of the idea of "reverse discrimination."[9] As a result, the gains in the private sector were fairly minimal. African-American unemployment and poverty remained high throughout the period from the 1960s legislation until today.

African-American gains were more noticeable in the parts of the economy that the government had established a legitimacy for controlling. In the area of government controlled jobs, African-Americans made direct economic gains as a result of the civil rights movement. The emergence of an African-American middle (income) class is often convincingly attributed to the evidence that African-Americans have become an important part of administration and implementation of public sector services, i.e. African-Americans are holding government jobs. Without confronting the capitalistic, free enterprise tradition in America, African-Americans were able to make economic progress. But this progress was primarily restricted to the public sector.

The progress of the 1960s and 1970s was followed by the "Reagan Revolution" in 1980. President Ronald Reagan's first step into the national political spotlight was in 1964 when he gave the nominating speech for Barry Goldwater at the Republican National Convention. Goldwater had voted against the Civil Rights Act. Goldwater was defeated in a landslide by the successful civil rights movement champion incumbent Lyndon Johnson. Significantly, Goldwater's only success came in his home state of Arizona and five states in the deep South where white reaction to the civil rights policies of Lyndon Johnson were most intense. Republican appeal to conservative white reaction to the civil rights movement was, however, immutably defined in Goldwater's candidacy. As unlikely as it seemed after the crushing Republican defeat in 1964, Reagan's association with that message was politically fortuitous. When the nation began to react to the second stage of the African-American agenda, Reagan had the political lineage to credibly speak out against it. Reagan's message was a classic Lockean response to the redistributive programs necessary to carry out the next phases of the African-American agenda. He plainly wanted government out of the enterprise. It was a message that hit a resounding chord in the American mind. Not only was he elected with stunning support, he carried with him a majority Republican Senate for the first time in over two decades. In 1980 Americans reacted to the poverty programs, the housing programs, the employment programs and the education programs designed to move African-Americans beyond simple freedoms to economic equality with resounding support for an outspoken critic of these programs. By 1980, the momentum of the civil rights movement that began in the 1960s had clearly come to a screeching halt.

Impact of the politics

The impact of the change in direction of American politics had explicit implications for African-Americans as well as other newly integrating ethnic groups. The educational, economic and occupational gains mirror the political trends of the last three decades and deserve careful scrutiny. Following is a discussion of indicators of education, occupation, income, wealth, employment, and poverty as they illuminate the political advances of African-Americans over the last twenty-five years. Following that discussion is a brief parallel discussion of the progress of other ethnic groups.

Education
Movement toward educational equality should be the most palatable part of breaking the "intermediate color line." Providing equal educations for a newly enfranchised group of Americans would not necessarily encroach on the benefits of those already enjoying educational opportunities. Indeed, African-Americans have made vital gains in educational attainment during this century. They have gained both in absolute terms and also relative to whites. In 1992, almost all children (99 percent) between the ages of seven and fifteen were enrolled in school, regardless of race.[10] This is an indication that black–white parity in educational attainment may eventually be reached. This has not yet occurred, although the disparity between the races has narrowed. In 1992, among persons twenty-five years of age and older, 81 percent of whites and 68 percent of African-Americans had completed high school. In 1980 the figure for whites was 69 percent, but for African-Americans it was only 51 percent.[11]

Since 1970 progress has been made by both races, with African-American progress the most striking. A quarter of a century ago only 31 percent of African-Americans twenty-five and older had earned a high school diploma. That statistic has now improved by a dramatic 37 percent.[12] In 1991, the median number of years of school completed by both races is similar (12.8 years for whites and 12.4 years for African-Americans).[13] This is a rare, significant account of success in last twenty-five years.

The division that exists in high school completion rates widens considerably, however, at the college level. One quarter of whites between the ages of twenty-five and thirty-four have completed four or more years of college while this is true of only 12 percent of African-Americans. For African-Americans, this is double the percentage found in 1970. But college completion rates have not seen the steady improvement found in high school graduation rates. There has been no improvement in the percentage of African-Americans completing four or more years of college comparing the present figure with that of 1980. College attendance among African-Americans actually dropped during the 1980s and has only recently begun to rise again.[14]

In sum, there is little question that African-Americans have made major strides in the number of year of school completed, although the disparity among the races at higher levels of schooling, especially at the college level, remains great. These inferior educational rates obviously do not bear well for future employment equality as they will surely translate into inferior economic opportunities.

Occupation

Trends in changes in occupational status of African-Americans historically are similar to those in education. It is clear that real change has occurred in this century. In the early part of this century most African-Americans occupied low-paying agricultural, domestic, or service jobs. After World War II a major shift away from farmwork was underway. In 1940, 32 percent of employed African-Americans worked on farms. This declined to 3 percent by 1970 and down to 2 percent in 1990.[15] About 3 percent of whites are now engaged in farmwork. As with the increases in secondary education, there was a similar trend in white collar occupational gains among African-Americans, from 6 percent in 1940 to 24 percent in 1970 to 44 percent in 1990.[16] While this movement into white collar jobs by African-Americans is clearly positive, unfortunately the similarity to the education trends continues. Concomitant with the lack of movement by African-Americans into college education parity is the evidence that most of the increase in white collar positions among African-Americans was in sales and clerical jobs and not in the high prestige, high-paying professional positions.

In 1994 only a small percentage of employed African-American males (15 percent) held managerial or professional specialty jobs compared to 28 percent of white males. African-American females fared better than African-American males with 20 percent in managerial or professional specialty jobs, compared to 30 percent of white women.[17]

The largest percentage of African-American males (31 percent) is now employed as operators, fabricators, and laborers. Only 19 percent of white males are working in these types of jobs. African-American females are more likely to be found in this job category (11 percent) than white females (7 percent). Females of both races are highly concentrated in technical, sales, and administrative support jobs. White males are slightly more likely than African-American males to be employed in precision production, craft, and repair. Only 2 percent of females of either race do such work.[18] While some of the gains made by African-Americans in occupational status are due to laws forbidding discrimination in hiring and also to changes in racial attitudes toward African-Americans, most are a product of the changing occupational structure in the United States economy. As agriculture mechanized in the early part of this century the demand for agricultural labor declined. At the same time, the economy was expanding and creating more relatively high-paying manufacturing and service sector jobs. This expanded the opportunities of all of those members of society who had previously been trapped in low-paying unskilled jobs and posed no threat to the economic well-being of those established in low- or high-paying jobs.

Unfortunately, the American economy retrenched after the booms associated with World War II, the Korean War, and the Vietnam War. The majority of the new jobs now being created in the United States economy are low-paying service sector jobs. While both African-Americans and whites will suffer from this trend it is likely that African-Americans will endure more hardship than whites. Historically, minorities have been the first to suffer when good jobs become limited.

Income
Educational and occupational trends have produced analogous trends in income, wealth, employment, and poverty. African-Americans began making significant gains in median family income in the aftermath of World War II. The 1960s were a time when these gains were the most pronounced. The following decade also showed some advancement in earnings parity between the races but the improvement began to slow dramatically as the politics changed in the 1980s and early 1990s. Even during the early periods of rapid gain, however, African-American families' earnings relative to whites has remained strikingly low throughout the last half of this century. Since 1950 the median income of African-American

Table 8.1   *Median family income by race and Hispanic origin 1970–1992 (in current dollars)*

	White $	African-American $	Hispanic $
1970	10,236	06,279	N.A.
1975	14,268	08,779	09,551
1976	15,537	09,242	10,259
1977	16,740	09,563	11,421
1978	18,368	10,879	12,566
1979	20,439	11,574	14,169
1980	21,904	12,674	14,716
1981	23,517	13,266	16,401
1982	24,603	13,598	16,227
1983	25,757	14,506	16,956
1984	27,686	15,432	18,833
1985	29,152	16,787	19,027
1986	30,809	17,604	19,995
1987	32,385	18,406	23,300
1988	33,915	19,329	21,769
1989	35,975	20,209	23,446
1990	36,915	21,423	23,431
1991	37,783	21,548	23,895
1992	38,909	21,161	23,903

Source: United States Bureau of the Census, *Statistical Abstract of the United States: 1993* (Washington, DC, US Government Printing Office, 1993) and United States Bureau of the Census, *Money Income of Households, Families, and the Persons in the United States: 1992* Current Population Reports, Series P60–184 (Washington, DC, US Government Printing Office, 1993).

families has only on rare occasions risen to as high as 60 percent of that of white families.[19]

Table 8.1 compares median family income between African-Americans and whites from 1970 to 1992, the time period that is the focus of this essay (figures for Hispanics are discussed in a separate section below). As can be seen, there has been very little change during this period. Progress by African-Americans relative to whites in median family income during the "post civil rights" era has been almost nonexistent. The income gap began to close in the early 1970s and in 1975, African-American family earning had reached 62 percent of that of white families. However, any optimism began to fade when African-Americans began to lose ground relative to whites in the 1980s, a decade when family income grew slowly for both races. Despite early hopes, African-American income as compared to whites is no different today than it was in 1970, or 1950 for that matter.

The result of the last forty years of race policy has been that a small percentage of African-Americans has advanced into the high income brackets. Most, however, remain heavily concentrated in the lowest socioeconomic strata. Currently, over one-quarter (26 percent) of all African-American families earn less than $10,000 per annum compared to 7 percent of white families.[20] While 56 percent of all African-American families exist on an annual income below $25,000, this is true for only 29 percent of white households. At the opposite end of the earning scale, over one-third (34 percent) of white families enjoy an annual income over $50,000. Only 15 percent of African-American families experience such a high standard of living.

Wealth

Although income is the most common way to compare economic conditions of groups of people, wealth is probably a more accurate indicator of economic security than income. Wealth refers to a family's net economic resources – financial assets minus liabilities. Net assets and the additional funds they can bring to a family can be extremely important in times of personal financial crisis or an economic downturn. Those with the most wealth are better able to survive hard times and maintain a comfortable lifestyle. As a result of long-term discrimination, most African-Americans are economically disadvantaged. This impaired position makes it very difficult to accumulate wealth, which in turn leads to further economic vulnerability.

Today, differences between whites and African-Americans on indicators of wealth are even more severe than income differentials. Nearly 30 percent of African-American households in the late 1980s had a net worth of zero or less. Only about 9 percent of white families were in this unfortunate financial situation. Over one-half of African-American households as compared to 22 percent of white households owned less than five thousand dollars of net wealth. Approximately 30 percent of whites and only 5 percent of African-Americans had accumulated economic resources valued at more than $100,000.[21] Further, middle class whites are much more likely than middle class African-Americans to receive earnings from assets such as stock dividends, interest from savings, and rent from property.[22]

Unemployment
One reason for the differing levels of income and wealth is the consistent difference between African-American and white unemployment rates. African-American unemployment is typically twice that of whites. This is true regardless of the state of the economy. In the past two decades African-American unemployment relative to whites was greater than it was in the 1940s and early 1950s.[23] In the 1980s there was a widening of the distance between African-American and white unemployment rates. The black/white ratio hit a high of 2.5 in 1989.[24] In April 1994, unemployment among African-Americans was 11.8 percent compared to 5.6 percent for whites.[25] These figures represent a black/white ratio of 2.1. What is even more dramatic are the extremely high unemployment rates among young African-Americans, especially those sixteen to nineteen years old. The gap in unemployment between young African-Americans and whites is much greater than that of older age groups.[26]

The official unemployment statistics are calculated in such a way that millions of part-time workers who desire full-time work or discouraged workers – individuals who have given up trying to find a job – remain uncounted. It is easy to assume that African-Americans are overrepresented in both of these categories, thus minimizing their actual unemployment figures and the discrepancy that exists between the races. Rates of underemployment, where persons are employed at levels below their training, also point out racial distinctions, with African-Americans again more likely than whites to be underemployed.

Poverty
Finally, after reviewing the educational, occupational, income, wealth, and occupational statistics, it probably comes as no surprise that there are major differences in the poverty rates of the two racial

groups. Today, over one-third of African-Americans live below the official poverty line compared to approximately 11 percent of whites.[27] These figures are very similar to those found in 1970. The poverty rates among both groups rose during the 1980s, and the wide discrepancy was maintained. The divergence that exists between the racial groups in poverty persists at all age levels. In 1970, 42 percent of African-American children lived in poverty. During this same year only 11 percent of white children shared such an unfortunate condition. In 1991, the comparable figures were 46 percent for African-American children and 16 percent for white children.[28] The politics of the 1980s produced an increase in the child poverty rates of both races. Generally, throughout the past twenty-five years the overall poverty rate among African-Americans has been around 20 percent above that of whites.

Other ethnic groups
African-Americans are unlike other ethnic groups in that they carry the burden of a century of slavery and another century of laws designed specifically to discriminate against them. However, other ethnic groups have not been immune from discrimination in the United States in the last twenty-five years. Hispanics comprise the second largest minority group in the United States, representing about 9 percent of the population and, like African-Americans, are easily identifiable as not having been the beneficiaries of years of being part of the established economic and social order. The Hispanic population grew by a remarkable 53 percent between 1980 and 1990 and is expected to continue to grow, eventually passing African Americans as the largest ethnic group in the country.[29] The United States Census Bureau classifies Hispanics and their percentage of the total Hispanic population as follows: Mexican-Americans, 62.6 percent; Puerto Ricans, 11.1 percent; Cubans, 4.9 percent; Central and South Americans, 13.8 percent and others, 7.6 percent.[30] While this ethnic group is diverse, in general, it is socially and economically disadvantaged in comparison to whites and in most cases advantaged in comparison to African-Americans.

In 1992, the median family income of all Hispanics was $23,889 or 61 percent of white family income (see Table 8.1). This represents a more positive position than African-Americans as compared to whites. However, Hispanics have lost ground relative to whites over

the past twenty years. In 1975, Hispanic families earned 67 percent
of white family wages. This rose to 70 percent in 1981. The 1980s
and early 1990s were a time of income decline for Hispanics relative
to whites.

Puerto Ricans account for the lowest median family income
among this ethnic group ($20,595), followed by Mexican-
Americans ($23,019). The median family income of Cubans is
$30,193 which is approximately 77 percent of that of whites.[31]

Hispanics are disproportionately poor with 27 percent of their
population living below the official poverty line. The Puerto Rican
poverty rate of 36 percent is actually higher than that of African-
Americans. Puerto Ricans are followed in poverty by Mexican-
Americans (27 percent) who also have numbers comparable to
African-Americans. The poverty rate of Cubans is the lowest among
all Hispanics at 14 percent.[32]

The April 1994 unemployment rate for Hispanics is 10.8 percent,
one point better than the African-American rate and 5.2 points
worse than white Americans.[33] The jobless rates for Americans of
Mexican and Puerto Rican origins are typically similar with Cuban-
Americans normally significantly lower.

The marginal status of Hispanics in the economy can be explained
in part in terms of their educational attainment. As a group they have
obtained the fewest number of years of education of any ethnic
group. Only 53 percent of Hispanics over the age of twenty-five have
completed four years of high school or more.[34] This compares with
81 percent of whites and 68 percent of African-Americans. The 1970
figures show that Hispanics were slightly ahead of African-
Americans in educational attainment among persons twenty-five
and over. The African-American population is now more educated
in terms of years of schooling completed than Hispanics. One possible reason for the slower progress in educational attainment among
adult Hispanics is the large influx of new undereducated immigrants
into the United States. Mexican-Americans have the lowest high
school completion rate at 45 percent, well below that of Puerto
Ricans (60 percent) and Cubans (62 percent).[35]

The percentage of Hispanics twenty-five years or older who have
completed four years of college or more is less than one-half that of
whites. This ratio has not changed measurably since 1970. Again the
Mexican-American population has the lowest percentage of college
graduates followed by Puerto Ricans and Cubans. The Cuban rate of

college completion is significantly higher than African-Americans and actually somewhat approaches that of whites.[36]

Like African-Americans, Hispanics have made progress over the past twenty-five years. However, they still lag significantly behind whites in terms of key socioeconomic indicators. Historically, Hispanics have not suffered as much harsh, direct discrimination as African-Americans, but more than white, European ethnic groups. As a result they occupy a middle position in American society.

The future

The African-American struggle of the last twenty-five years is a struggle with different goals and different tools than the African-American struggle of the 1950s and 1960s. The freedom to be treated as equal citizens in public places and the freedom to vote are freedoms that are largely won. The shift to governmental policies that promote educational, occupational, and economic equality have met with much less political success. This American neglect of racial and ethnic policy is probably best explained by the relationship between the rhetoric of racial politics and the rhetoric of the American Dream. The attempts to break through the intermediate color line in this second stage of development are more difficult because the political rhetoric associated with this stage is not easily combined with the rhetoric of the dominant American political discourse. Until a politician can champion policies that promote real racial and ethnic gains in the United States by using American individualistic rhetoric or until a majority of Americans are willing to make some real economic changes in order to help the disadvantaged community, only incremental racial and ethnic progress is likely.

Notes

1 E. Black and M. Black, *Politics and Society in the South* (Cambridge, MA, and London, Harvard University Press, 1987).

2 H. Blumer, "The Future of the Color Line," in J. C. McKinney and E. G. Thompson (eds.), *The South in Continuity and Change* (Durham, Duke University Press, 1965).

3 Black and Black, *Politics*, p. 98.

4 Black and Black, *Politics*, p. 98.

5   M. L. King, "I Have A Dream," in *Speeches by the Leaders: The March on Washington for Jobs and Freedom, August 28, 1963* (New York, NAACP, 1963).

6   For excellent discussions of this creed see the following: L. Hartz, *The Liberal Tradition in America* (New York, Brace Jovanovich, 1955), and H. McCloskey and J. Zaller, *The American Ethos: Public Attitudes Toward Capitalism and Democracy* (Cambridge, MA, and London, Harvard University Press, 1984).

7   G. Myrdal, R. Sterner, and A. Rose, *An American Dilemma* (New York, Harper and Row, 1944), p. 4.

8   Hartz, *Liberal Tradition*.

9   *Regents of the University of California* v. *Bakke*, 438 US 265 (1978).

10   United States Bureau of the Census, *School Enrollment: Social and Economic Characteristics of Students: October, 1992*, Current Population Reports, Series P20 474 (Washington, DC, US Government Printing Office, 1993).

11   United States Bureau of the Census, *Statistical Abstract of the United States: 1993* (Washington, DC, US Government Printing Office, 1993).

12   US Census, *Statistical Abstract 1993*.

13   United States Bureau of the Census, *Educational Attainment in the United States: March 1991 and 1990*, Current Population Reports, Series P20 462 (Washington, DC, US Government Printing Office, 1992).

14   "College Enrollment by Racial and Ethnic Group," *Chronicle of Higher Education*, March 18, 1992, p. A35.

15   M. N. Marger, *Race and Ethnic Relations: American and Global Perspectives* (Belmont, CA, Wadsworth, 1994), pp. 255–256.

16   Marger, *Race and Ethnic Relations*, pp. 255–256.

17   United States Department of Labor, *Employment and Earnings, April, 1994*, vol. 41, no. 4 (Washington, DC, US Government Printing Office, 1994).

18   United States Department of Labor, *Employment and Earnings*.

19   United States Bureau of the Census, *Statistical Abstract of the United States: 1981* (Washington, DC, US Government Printing Office, 1981); United States Bureau of the Census, "Race of the Population of the States: 1980," *1980 Census of Population* (Washington, DC, US Government Printing Office, 1980); United States Bureau of the Census, *Money Income of Households, Families, and Persons in the United States: 1992*, Current Population Reports, Series P60 184 (Washington, DC, US Government Printing Office, 1993).

20   United States Bureau of the Census, *The Black Population of the*

United States: March 1992, Current Population Reports, Series P20 404 (Washington, DC, US Government Printing Office, 1993).

21 United States Bureau of the Census, *Household Wealth and Asset Ownership: 1988*, Series P77 22 (Washington, DC, US Government Printing Office, 1990).

22 G. D. Jaynes and R. M. Williams, Jr, *A Common Destiny: Blacks and Society* (Washington, DC, National Academy Press, 1989).

23 J. R. Feagin and C. B. Feagin, *Social Problems: A Critical Power-Conflict Perspective* (Englewood, CA, Prentice-Hall, 1994), p. 118.

24 US Bureau of Census, *Statistical Abstract 1993*.

25 United States Department of Labor, *Employment and Earnings, May, 1994*, vol. 41, no. 5 (Washington, DC, US Government Printing Office, 1994).

26 US Bureau of Census, *Statistical Abstract 1993*.

27 US Bureau of Census, *Statistical Abstract 1993*.

28 US Bureau of Census, *Statistical Abstract 1993*.

29 N. Kanellos, *The Hispanic-American Almanac* (Detroit and London, Gale Research Inc., 1993).

30 US Bureau of Census, *Statistical Abstract 1993*.

31 United States Bureau of the Census, *The Hispanic Population in the United States: March 1992*, Current Population Reports, Series P20 465 (Washington, DC, US Government Printing Office, 1992).

32 US Bureau of Census, *Hispanic Population*.

33 US Bureau of Labor, *Employment and Earnings*.

34 US Bureau of Census, *Hispanic Population*.

35 US Bureau of Census, *Hispanic Population*.

36 US Bureau of Census, *Statistical Abstract 1993*.

Media: becoming an autonomous force

When President Bill Clinton complained to an audience in Providence, Rhode Island in early 1994 that he had been "subject to more assault that any previous president" he was directing his remarks primarily at the media. The media's coverage of politics has become the lament of recent US presidents, other politicians, the general public, and even journalists.

This essay demonstrates that during the period since 1970, the media have become a highly autonomous force in American politics. This development has resulted from changes in media culture and in the media's capability to survey the political environment.

Simultaneously, the American political system has become more dependent on the media to function. This dependence on the press extends to both the electoral process and governance.[1]

Trends in journalism

Two major developments occurred in the media that reshaped their role in American politics. One was the shifting of journalistic attitudes toward their role and the other was technological innovation that enhanced the media's ability to survey their environment.

Attitudinal change of journalists

The consensus among journalists about the nature of journalism began to unravel in the 1960s with the emergence of competing schools of thought. These schools of thought known by terms such as "new journalism" and "adversarial journalism" engendered debates within the journalistic community over the proper role of the press. These schools challenged the traditional role of the journalist as a neutral observer of events, merely a conduit for information.

New journalism   The socioeconomic and educational background
of journalists changed in the 1960s and 1970s. More journalists
were the products of a college education. More than previously were
drawn from ivy league colleges. They also came from other backgrounds such as law. These changes altered journalism and journalistic attitudes toward politicians. The increasing complexity of
events in the 1960s and 1970s (Vietnam, Watergate, the environment movement) lent weight to the argument that the journalist must
be interposed between the facts and the audience to offer necessary
explanation and interpretation. Higher socioeconomic status and
educational level may have contributed to the attitude among journalists that they could fill that role. Journalists saw themselves as
social equals to their authoritative sources.

This first new school of thought, "new journalism," rejected traditional journalism as stultifying and even dishonest. Advocates of
new journalism argued that journalists could not exercise freedom of
expression because they were locked into roles as conduits of official
information. Traditional journalism also was dishonest because its
neutral approach actually aided the authoritative source on which
journalists relied for news. Traditional journalism did not provide
the reader with the journalist's own observations and analysis which
would serve to balance the official statement. Hence, traditional
journalism did not print all the truth.

At the time, Jack Newfield, a new journalism advocate, explained:
"The truth, and even the hard news, usually rests beneath the surface
of any event or social conflict. Yet, reporters rarely question what
they are told by any politician with a title."[2]

According to new journalism, journalists must become more a
part of the story they were telling. Journalists could participate
through offering personal insight, critique, and analysis.[3]

Adversarial journalism   Another byproduct of the new journalism
was a trend termed adversarial journalism. Adversarial journalism
referred to the press's critical stance in relation to political leaders
and institutions, particularly the presidency. The press was to act as
the political opposition, but with a twist. It was not an opposition
with responsibility for offering policy alternatives, but only to

question administration policies and actions.

Adversarial journalism was born of the anti-establishment attitude of many intellectuals during the 1960s and the credibility gap created by the use of lying by the government during peacetime. Events such as the U-2 incident, the Bay of Pigs invasion, the Vietnam War, and Watergate convinced many in the press that government officials were prone to lie to save themselves or the administration politically and that they would attempt to use the press to do so. Hence, press cooperation with administration officials was viewed as a partnership with devious politicians and as a deception of the general public.

Adversarial journalism earned a large following among journalists. Adversarial journalism did have its critics. In 1982, Michael O'Neill, then president of the American Society of Newspaper Editors, criticized the trend:

> We should make peace with the government. We should not be its enemy . . . We are supposed to be the observers, not the participants – not the permanent political opposition. The adversarial culture is a disease attacking the nation's vital organs.[4]

By the early 1980s, journalism and journalists had undergone major transformations most of which enhanced press autonomy. Both the "new journalism" and "adversarial journalism" raised the consciousness of journalists and gave birth to a generation within journalism that perceived its role in terms of distance from, equality with, and (in some cases) even superiority over those they reported on. These developments within journalism helped the press possess firmer control than ever before as gatekeepers of the media. The press also acquired a greater desire and capability to scrutinize political activities independent of politicians.

Technology

The United States is now part of a global village becoming increasingly more intertwined. The cause, quite simply, is a communications revolution spurred by innovations in technology. With the assistance of this technology, MTV and CNN now span the globe. Meanwhile, Americans with satellite dishes now watch broadcasts from other nations. One dramatic example of this technological wonder was the worldwide news conference conducted by the president of the United States in May 1994. President Bill Clinton answered questions on a CNN program beamed to more than 200 nations. He took questions from journalists in Bosnia, South Korea, Poland, and other nations.[5]

The cause of this communications revolution is the introduction of new technologies which have significantly altered the mass media, particularly the broadcast media. Several new technologies or variations of existing technology have emerged and/or have been implemented in the past twenty-five years. We will discuss two: cable and satellite. Their appearance has had, and will yet have, an effect on the role of the news media in American politics.

Cable Although initiated in the late 1940s as a response to a limitation by the Federal Communications Commission on licensing of new stations, cable mushroomed in the 1970s and 1980s with the deregulation of the industry. In 1975 there were 3,300 cable systems in the US. Today there are over 11,000.[6] As of 1992, over 55 million households had cable.[7] That represented 60 percent of all homes with television sets.

Cable has become popular to Americans because it offers consumers a wider range of program options than ever before. Cable systems usually now offer 50 to 60 channels and are potentially capable of carrying up to 100 program alternatives.

Cable viewing also has been increasing. Between 1987 and 1988 alone, audience viewing of cable programming increased 33 percent. Cable programs, superstations such as WTBS (Atlanta) and WGN (Chicago), and pay services such as HBO and Disney Channel combined accounted for more than one-third of prime time audience viewing. In 1980, such programs constituted only 12 percent of prime time audience viewing.[8] CNN alone is now available in more than two-thirds of American homes.[9]

One characteristic of cable not shared by other mass media is its interactive capability. Several experiments in interactive cable have been conducted in cable-connected cities; the best known and the prototype has been the QUBE system developed by Warner-Amex Corporation in Columbus, Ohio. The system can be used for such actions as selecting entertainment services, transacting personal financial affairs, and shopping at home.[10]

Cable has increased the number of news media sources available to the average citizen. It also has fostered the growth of primarily political channels such as CNN and C-SPAN, which offers unedited

coverage of interviews, news conferences, speeches, and seminars.
The two C-SPAN channels offer live coverage of floor proceedings of
the two houses of Congress.

Satellite   An ideal companion for the growth of cable has been the
use of commercial satellites for transmitting television programming. Satellites are equipped with transponders or channels
which allow up to fifty-four programming options from as many
different locations to be received and then beamed back to earth
stations.

Satellites have been used by cable systems for programming
options since HBO became the first satellite programming service in
1975. Superstation WTBS in Atlanta joined HBO by offering its
signal via satellite one year later. A large number of satellite programming services now compete, greatly expanding the offering of
local cable systems beyond local over-the-air stations and superstations.

Satellite programming has made possible the proliferation of political channels as well. Also, political satellite programming beams
across national borders as demonstrated with the presidential press
conference mentioned above. For news in particular, these new
technologies have enhanced the surveillance capability of the press.
Satellites allow for almost immediate transmission of news from
bureaus, as well as live transmissions from remote areas. This
surveillance capability has been particularly salient for those
intensely interested in politics.

The effects on media role

Changes in journalistic attitudes in American politics and new technology have enhanced the role of the media in American politics. The
former has done so by fostering a sense of ability and even social
responsibility to critique politicians and politics rather than just
report on them. The latter has provided increased technical
capability to survey politics and, while doing so, carry in tow a far
larger audience than before.

Now let us turn to that role as it applies to two aspects of American
politics: elections and governance.

Media role in American politics

Media electoral role

The mode of selecting presidents underwent a major transformation during the 1960s and 1970s which has impacted since on American national politics and the role of the press. The nomination process experienced the most radical change. The two major parties adopted major reforms designed to democratize the selection process. These included primaries for nominating party candidates, greater representation of minority groups in the delegate selection process, and continued openness throughout the entire process. The party's leadership role in the nomination process was severely hampered by these reforms.

These changes left a vacuum that the media came to fill. During this quarter century period, the electoral system became more dependent on the press for the conduct of campaigns and elections. Some entity needed to organize electoral campaigns. As the parties withdrew from the process, the media became the force to be relied upon to play that role.

As a result of this increasing reliance on mass media, the role of the press as the gatekeepers for news coverage in campaigns has grown. With the assistance of satellite technology, more news organizations – including metropolitan newspapers and local broadcast stations – cover presidential campaigns. More reporters seek interviews with the candidates. More debates are scheduled by news organizations. More journalists serve as moderators or panelists for these debates. More journalists follow the candidates. During the pre-primary stage in 1988, about 35 news organizations regularly followed George Bush alone.[11] By contrast, in 1976, during the pre-primary period, Jimmy Carter had a media entourage of two journalists.[12] Today, voters, candidates, and the entire electoral process are affected by the role of the media.

The press today performs roles which affect the nature of the campaign, particularly at the primary stages. Some roles were previously performed by others, particularly the political party and its leadership. Also, some roles, such as mentioner, are far more important in the primary season than in the general election campaign. The roles the press now plays are mentioner, categorizer, and agenda-setter. Through these roles, the press becomes a significant winnower of presidential candidates.

The mentioner role is critical for candidates seeking to communicate with voters. Candidates are enhanced or diminished by the press simply as a result of the amount of coverage devoted to their campaigns. Since there is only one national election in the US and since presidential candidates often enter the race with little national name recognition and low voter awareness, the press is critical in introducing the current crop of presidential contenders to the electorate.

Journalists cover some candidacies more extensively than others. This role is especially important in the pre-primary stages of the campaign, when no primary or caucus results exist. The effect can be substantial coverage for certain candidates and near obscurity for others. For example, in 1988, before the Iowa caucus, then vice president George Bush and Senator Bob Dole together received well over half of the coverage of the Republican race. This occurred even though they constituted only one-third of the Republican field.[13]

The press also categorizes candidates – presenting images of candidates to the voters. These images usually are not those carefully crafted by the candidate; rather they fit press needs for simple, handy identification of candidates. The press attaches labels to candidates in order to simplify the process of describing them to the audience, and to remove "image making" from the hands of the candidates' media consultants.

These press labels may be derived from the candidate's personal or professional background, issue positions, coalitions of support, or personal style. During the 1992 presidential campaigns, there were several examples of media labeling: former Massachusetts senator Paul Tsongas, the Northeastern liberal; Nebraska senator Bob Kerrey, the Vietnam war hero; Iowa senator Tom Harkin, the prairie populist; and Virginia governor Douglas Wilder, the black candidate. Labels can be damaging to campaigns. Candidates are stereotyped and catalogued in ways that make it difficult to make broad appeals to the electorate if their label restricts them to certain issues or groups of supporters.

Still another role is that of agenda-setter. The press and candidates engage in a daily struggle for control of the campaign agenda. Candidates seek to transmit messages to voters which identify the candidate's record, personal characteristics, and stances on policy. Journalists, on the other hand, possess a contrasting agenda. They seek news – change in a candidate's position, conflict between the candidates, a revelation of an indiscretion, some indication of candidate disingenuousness, or candidate responses to journalists' queries about issues high on press agendas.

There is evidence that the press wins the battle most of the time. Several studies of news media coverage of presidential campaigns have concluded that press coverage is preoccupied with aspects of interest to reporters – the "hoopla" and "horse race" of the campaign, "winners and losers," campaign strategy, poll results, and campaign appearances.[14] In 1988, one study of network news coverage during the primaries concluded 40 percent of the election stories were about the horse race.[15]

Such coverage displaces reporting of policy issues. In the 1988 primary season, news media discussion of campaign issues far outweighed discussion of policy issues, and the fall general election campaign was not substantially more policy-oriented than the primary season.[16] However, even when policy issues are discussed, they may not be those issues stressed by the candidates. The press favors certain types of policy issues, particularly those which are clear-cut and neatly divide the candidates.[17] These are issues that can be expressed simply and involve high emotion and conflict. Examples from recent campaigns include abortion, the death penalty, gun control, and tax increases.

Journalists favor issues of interest to them since such control over the agenda enhances their autonomy in reporting on the campaign. The press gain more control over the campaign agenda. Candidates are thrown off their carefully managed speeches and themes when press queries focus on a single unexpected issue. The candidates are forced to fit their own campaign priorities to those of the press. The press agenda dominates news coverage of the campaign, and the messages that candidates wish to send to voters, especially those concerning general policy direction and specific policy issues, are rarely included in campaign news coverage.

Today, voters' perceptions of candidates and the campaign are affected by the media's portrayal. When the voter seeks information about the campaign, the media content is the major, if not the sole, source of that information. Campaigns have become oriented toward media coverage.

In turn, candidates gear their presentation of themselves to the media, with the presumption that the media will transmit that presentation to the voters. As noted above, that often does not occur.

The media's role in campaigns has not radically altered the image making process which has always been a part of American presidential campaigns, but candidates have learned to adjust to a new environment which places emphasis on different skills than in the past. Television, particularly, creates the dangerous illusion that voters can personally know the candidates.

Aware of the media's role in shaping voters' perceptions and lacking any other vehicle with the same reach, candidates have come to rely on the media in crafting an image of themselves. Although paid political advertising is widely viewed as the main vehicle for image making (and does play a larger role in the general election campaign than in the primaries), candidates view news coverage as the most important factor in communicating with voters.

The role of the media and the biases toward image making have raised fears that candidates with media skills and backgrounds will be unfairly advantaged in American electoral politics. In the 1980s and 1990s, the success of Ronald Reagan, a former actor, and the entrance into presidential electoral politics of Pat Robertson, former televangelist, and Pat Buchanan, a television commentator and syndicated newspaper columnist, was viewed as evidence of this trend.

However, such fears are overstated. Losers in recent presidential campaigns have included Paul Simon and Al Gore, former journalists. Although Gore later was elected vice president on the ticket with President Bill Clinton, instead of being praised for his media skills, he was criticized for his "wooden" style of speaking.

Clearly the media perform roles in American national elections that were carried out by others in the past, particularly the party. The party's weakness resulted in a media-filled vacuum. However, this role-switching presents serious problems for the American electoral process. The political parties presented competing platforms, placed forward candidates with the intent of accumulating majority support, and acquired some responsibility for the success or failure of their candidates in the area of national governance. Failure resulted in the candidates and the party being repudiated at the polls in the next election.

But the media are very different. Their capabilities do not lie in the areas of organizing elections. The media are for-profit enterprises far more interested in what sells newspapers or boosts ratings than in the consequences of the voters' choices in November. The media as media do not care about the outcome of elections, except as they may touch on First Amendment issues. Whether Democrats or Republicans, liberals or conservatives win an election is of little consequence since either or both will become the objects of media scrutiny and criticism.

Hence, American electoral politics faces an acute dilemma: how to move from a national electoral system heavily influenced by a political force, the media, which is fundamentally disinterested in the outcome of the election but highly attuned to its own commercial benefit and the maintenance of autonomy, back to a system where political forces with a stake in the outcome use policy issues to compete for the voter's loyalty.

Media and governance

The press has also acquired a larger role in governance. This section analyzes briefly the relationship of the press with three national political institutions – the presidency, the Congress, and the Supreme Court.

Presidency

Presidents needed the media by 1995 more than they had in 1970. Expectations of presidential leadership had risen, but the actual power of the president over the legislative process remained unchanged during this period. In fact, it could be argued it was somewhat diminished. The Congress has been more assertive in areas such as foreign, defense, and budgetary policy, thus limiting the president's power to lead in public policy.

Given the complexity of the president's situation, incumbent presidents have turned to the media as a tool for informing and persuading the American public and the Congress of the president's policy objectives. Presidents from Nixon to Clinton attempted to employ the media, particularly television, to gain public support and forestall congressional opposition regarding the president's public policy decisions.

The press's relationship with the president changed dramatically during this period. At the beginning of the period, there had been no Watergate. By 1995, presidents faced a far more active press with greater suspicion of the motives of the president. Influenced by adversarial journalism, the White House press corps was more likely to question the words and actions of the president.

Moreover, the press's increasing autonomy meant that the messages presidents wished to convey to the public were not automatically transmitted. Soundbites by politicians were reduced while reporters' analysis constituted a larger portion of the news story. The average soundbite in 1992 was only 7.3 seconds from 42 seconds in 1968.[18] One option for presidents, the televised address to the nation, was also endangered. Whereas prior to 1970, denial of time to the president by the three major networks was rare, that refusal has occurred more frequently since.

As a consequence, presidents have become more sophisticated in their use of the press and have devised a variety of methods to attempt to manage the news. Timing of news conferences, scheduling of photo opportunities, and planned release of information is designed to heighten or diminish the likelihood of press coverage of White House news. However, they still must compete with other players in national politics. Sometimes presidents are overshadowed by other players. For example, in late 1993 and early 1994, President Clinton found news emphasis on his health care plan temporarily displaced by attention to a more moderate plan of a junior Democratic member of Congress. They cannot take for granted that the press will always offer them all the coverage they feel they need.

Due to the increased autonomy of the press, the public spotlight for the president often means bad news descends on the White House first. The blame for national problems is routinely laid at the president's doorstep by the press. Managing the news is an attempt to lessen the damage of that bad news.

Despite press accusations that the White House creates news content and White House claims that the press completely controls the president's image, the battle continues. Neither player can dominate the other. The very persistence of the struggle indicates, however, that the press has become increasingly autonomous in its relations with the White House, while the president has become ever more dependent on the press for help in governing, and both sides are fully aware of it.

Congress
Although the presidency's changing relationship with the news media has received greater notice from scholars, the Congress also

has been affected by the media. In the late 1970s, a political consultant summed up the widespread consensus on the media effects on Congress in describing the current typical congressional candidate and members of Congress:

> Guys with the blow-dried hair who read the script well. That's not the kind of guy who'd been elected to the Congress or Senate ten years ago. You've got a guy who is not concerned with issues; who isn't concerned about the mechanics of government; who doesn't attend committee meetings; who avoids taking positions at any opportunity and who yet is a master at getting his face in the newspapers and on television . . . You get the modern media candidate.[19]

However, the presence of the media has not accomplished the radical overhaul implied in the consultant's assessment. Although members of Congress are accused of using the national media to accomplish legislative and electoral objectives, such usage usually is not even attempted.

Actually, press coverage of Congress is a process of members of Congress offering a wide variety of potential stories to choose from, while reporters select those which fit what they value as news. As in any similar buyer's market, members of Congress must tailor their offerings to national news media along the lines of news values. Viewing realistically the chances of success, many members, particularly those in the House, do not even bother to actively court national media attention. Their press operations are geared to their own constituency.

Hence, the real competition exists among a much smaller group of members who attempt to establish reputations through the national press for future leadership bids, presidential races, or legislative prowess.

Given the wide array of possible stories, it is not surprising that the press turns to the leadership who have proven expertise, power, and, in most cases, widespread visibility. They constitute the stable lead players in a congressional cast of hundreds.

But journalistic imperatives are still important. The other members who gain press notice are those who meet news imperatives. This has been a source of criticism since many members who would not receive notice in the 1950s and 1960s now do.

The problem of journalistic freedom in coverage of Congress was more acute in the 1970s. The 1970s was a period of weak House leadership and intense fragmentation of power in the House. The rise of subcommittees designed to spread power to more junior members also meant more chaos within the chamber.

However, the House moved to limit the problem by enhancing the role of the leadership. Tip O'Neill, Jim Wright, and Newt Gingrich were more powerful leaders and provided more centralization of authority. Although it is obvious that the media may cover whomever they wish, as the leaders have become more powerful, the media have followed that path of power to the leaders.

Unlike in the electoral process, the House has reformed itself somewhat in order to organize its own agenda rather than face the prospect of the media filling that vacuum.

The Supreme Court

Viewed as the most aloof of institutions, the Supreme Court seems a world away from the influence of the media. But during the 1980s and 1990s this distance began to shrink.

One of the issues surrounding the Supreme Court was the right of the public to see its proceedings through television. During the 1980s and 1990s cameras began to inch their way into courtrooms. In 1990 the Judicial Conference of the United States, the administrative organization of federal courts, initiated an experiment of cameras in federal courts. The Supreme Court did not join the experiment. But pressure was placed on the Court to accede to the broadcast media's demands for inclusion, although the justices shrank from the prospect, especially following the highly publicized Robert Bork and Clarence Thomas hearings.

The justices did become more public in the 1980s and 1990s than they had been previously. Several justices sat for television and print interviews, a rarity in the past. All of the justices appeared on a public television documentary on the Court. The justices' speeches and participation in symposia became news.

Part of this more public stance stems from the appointment of justices who are younger and more familiar with the television generation. Also, the norms have changed somewhat with such activity more countenanced by the other justices than was true in the past. Also, the range of media coverage has been enlarged. With the addition of C-SPAN, the speeches by justices are more likely to be televised nationally and therefore receive some attention from the media.

The profile of the Court also was greatly heightened by the contentious appointment process for several nominees in the 1980s and 1990s. The nomination of William Rehnquist as chief justice in 1986 and the nominations as associate justices of Robert Bork, Douglas Ginsburg, and Anthony Kennedy, all in 1987, were the subject of extensive news coverage. Saturation television coverage was devoted to the nomination of Clarence Thomas following Anita Hill's charges of sexual harassment. The Supreme Court became a major topic of news interest during the late 1980s and early 1990s.

Whether this publicity seriously impacted on the Court's decision making process is unknown. It did affect the behavior of individual justices. The reactions were not uniform. While one justice, Ruth Bader Ginsburg, granted interviews and gave media appearances to further her role as a female role model, another justice, Clarence Thomas, shunned press interaction and even public interaction with the exception of talking to conservative groups.

But the Court's interaction with the media during this period indicates that even the most remote of American political institutions has not been untouched by the media.[20]

Conclusion: the future

The political role of the media has undergone dramatic change during the period 1970–1995. The journalistic self-conception of role has been transformed. New technologies have increased the media's ability to play a salient role.

In the future, the media's role will likely increase. It is unlikely there will be a return in journalistic attitudes to greater comfort with politicians. Widespread negative public reaction to the media's critic role would have to occur. Although there are periodic complaints of media negativism, such wholesale rejection of that role is unlikely. In fact, in periods when political leaders or administrations are unpopular, it is sure to intensify.

The new communications technologies will have real consequences for the political system. One political consequence is the potential fragmentation of the body politic. With the increasing availability of broadcast channels which appeal primarily to specialized audiences, will subcultures be encouraged to flourish and to foster separate political cultures?

There is also debate over whether the new technologies will

produce the evolution of direct democracy. It is conceivable that future voting could occur in the privacy of the home with the touch of a button. Even short of actual voting, the interactive capabilities of new technologies can potentially facilitate communication of public views on policy proposals, pending legislation, and executive decisions. The general public could register an immediate response to governmental action or even any proposed action. This response also could be made without a single new interactive technology if two existing technologies – television and touchtone telephone – were combined.[21] The use of interactive cable has been encouraged by some scholars as a means to make democracy work better – a kind of electronic complaint box.[22]

But fears also have been expressed that the availability and use of such technology would pose serious problems for American politics.[23] The immediate interactive capability might make possible a direct democracy, where citizens would make decisions and strongly influence policy making. The filter of representatives acting in a slower, more deliberate manner might be lost.

One scholar dismisses such concerns as unrealistic:

> One science-fiction fantasy has the public engaged in a national town meeting on cable TV with various issues being debated and then decided by a push-button vote. War could be declared on Monday, canceled on Tuesday, and declared again on Wednesday.[24]

Experience suggests that, instead, new technologies will simply augment those processes already in place. The new technology may well facilitate greater understanding of issues, but mediating institutions would still be necessary to avoid an overload of issue concentration and to offer a "cooling off" period between public response to issues and events and public policy.[25]

The media will continue to affect American elections unless the parties, the candidates, and/or the Congress take steps to hand power over the electoral process back to the political parties. Their influence over governance may well increase. Presidents will continue to seek to use the media as a source for mobilizing public support for their policy initiatives. Some members of Congress, particularly the leaders, will attempt to employ the media to blunt the president or set their own agendas for national policy debate. Finally, the Court may find it difficult to resist the pressure to make itself more accessible to the media.

The media will likely become no less autonomous from political leaders and institutions, but the political system may become more dependent on the media.[26]

Notes

1   Throughout this chapter, the terms "media" and "press" are used interchangeably to refer to the news organizations that serve as regular general news sources for Americans.

2   Jack Newfield, "Journalism, Old, New, and Corporate," in Ronald Weber (ed.), *The Reporter as Artist: A Look at the New Journalism Controversy*, New York, Hastings House, 1974, p. 59.

3   For a compilation of views on new journalism, see Ronald Weber (ed.), *The Reporter as Artist: A Look at the New Journalism Controversy*, New York, Hastings House, 1974; Michael L. Johnson, *The New Journalism*, Lawrence, KS, University of Kansas Press, 1971; and Paul H. Weaver, "The New Journalism and the Old-Thoughts after Watergate," *The Public Interest* (spring 1974), pp. 67–88.

4   Quoted in James Boylan, "Declarations of Independence," *Columbia Journalism Review* (November/December 1986), 44.

5   Gwen Ifill, "Clinton Defends Foreign Policy Record," *New York Times*, May 4, 1994, p. A4.

6   *Television & Video Almanac 1993*, p. 21A.

7   *Television & Video Almanac 1993*, p. 19A.

8   Jeremy Gerard, "Even with 'Remembrance,' a Ratings Month to Forget," *New York Times*, December 5, 1988; and Watson James, *Transition in Television*, Chicago, Crain Books, 1983, pp. 1–3.

9   "TBS Posts Net Income of $78 Million," *Business Wire*, February 18, 1993.

10   For an extensive discussion of the future of cable in the United States and elsewhere, see Ralph M. Negrine (ed.), *Cable Television and the Future of Broadcasting*, New York, St Martin's Press, 1985.

11   Dom Bonafede, "Hey, Look Me Over," *National Journal*, November 21, 1987, p. 2968.

12   F. Christopher Arterton, "The Media Politics of Campaigns," in James David Barber (ed.), *Race for the Presidency*, Englewood Cliffs, NJ, Prentice-Hall, 1978, pp. 32–33.

13   S. Robert Lichter, Daniel Amundson, and Richard Noyes, *The Video Campaign: Network Coverage of the 1988 Primaries*, Washington, AEI, 1989, p. 53.

14 See Thomas E. Patterson, *The Mass Media Election*, New York, Praeger, 1980, pp. 21–30; and Michael J. Robinson and Margaret Sheehan, *Over the Wire and on TV*, New York, Russell Sage, 1983, pp. 144–166.

15 Lichter et al., *Video Campaign*, pp. 14–15.

16 Lichter et al., *Video Campaign*, p. 15; and Marjorie Randon Hershey, "The Campaign and the Media," in Gerald M. Pomper et al. (eds.), *The Election of 1988*, Chatham, NJ, Chatham House, 1989, pp. 97–98.

17 Colin Seymour-Ure, *The Political Impact of the Mass Media*, Beverly Hills, CA, Sage, 1974, p. 223.

18 Paul Taylor, "Political Coverage in the 1990s: Teaching the Old News New Tricks," in *The New News v. The Olds News: The Press and Politics in the 1990s* (Washington, DC, The Twentieth Century Fund, 1992), pp. 40–41.

19 Quoted in Michael J. Robinson, "Three Faces of Congressional Media," in Thomas E. Mann and Norman Ornstein (eds.), *The New Congress*, Washington, AEI, 1981, p. 94.

20 For more discussion of the relationship between the US Supreme Court and the press, see Richard Davis, *Decisions and Images: The Supreme Court and the Press*, Englewood Cliffs, NJ, Prentice Hall, 1994.

21 Frederick Williams, *The Communications Revolution*, Beverly Hills, CA, Sage, 1982, p. 193.

22 Ithiel de Sola Pool (ed.), *Talking Back*, Cambridge, MA, MIT Press, 1973, pp. 237–246.

23 Edward V. Dolan, *TV or CATV? A Struggle for Power*, Port Washington, New York, National University Publications Associated Faculty Press, Inc., 1984, pp. 69–71; and Vernone Sparkes, "Cable Television in the United States," in Ralph M. Negrine (ed.), *Cable Television and the Future of Broadcasting*, New York, St Martin's Press, 1985, pp. 41–42.

24 Pool, *Talking Back*, p. 237.

25 Pool, *Talking Back*, p. 244.

26 Recommended further reading: Timothy E. Cook, *Making Laws and Making News: Media Strategies in the US House of Representatives*, Washington, DC, Brookings Institution, 1990; Richard Davis, *The Press and American Politics: The New Mediator*, New York, Longman, 1992; Samuel Kernell, *Going Public: New Strategies of Presidential Leadership*, 2nd edn, Washington, DC, CQ Press, 1993; S. Robert Lichter, Stanley Rothman, and Linda Lichter, *The Media Elite*, Bethesda, MD, Adler & Adler, 1986; Mathew D. McCubbins (ed.), *Under the Watchful Eye: Managing Presidential Campaigns in the Television Era*, Washington, DC, CQ Press, 1992; Thomas E. Patterson, *Out of Order*, New York, Alfred A. Knopf, 1993.

Campaign spending and public mistrust: the limited impact of reform

A vague feeling of "alienation"

Toward the end of *The Making of the President, 1972* Theodore H. White observed that the most bleak message of that year's election was "its shrivelled size . . . Only 55.7 percent of all Americans old enough to be eligible to vote bothered to cast a vote for President . . . Something in this turn of time had made Americans feel that their votes were unconnected with the control they should have over their own lives." "Alienation" was the fashionable word for the vague feeling."[1] The context within which this "vague feeling" had developed was one of policy conflict, program failure, and social division. The foundation for electoral diffidence did not spring, full grown, from the loins of the 1972 election. The divisions had arisen angrily during the campaigns of four years earlier, and the issues were emerging before that.

The presidential campaigns that bracket 1970 set the context for the development of a new rhetoric engaging with ideas about restoring the link between electorate and elected. In the 1968 and 1972 campaigns the public had seen the party political structure that had seemed solid since the presidential victories of Franklin Roosevelt shaken to its roots. Traditional alliances proved unreliable when confronted with new policy questions that did not fit comfortably with established group cleavages. Newly active groups using non-traditional methods did not necessarily slot into the existing shape of party political debate. The preexisting national political coalitions appeared to be outliving their time. There is a comfort in the concreteness of well-known and well-established political patterns, however anachronistic; their erosion, however timely, must be a source of anxiety for citizens. In particular the weakening of commonly accepted patterns of political cause and effect confuses the issue for those who wish to understand the impact that their vote will have.

Suspicion among the electorate that all was not well in the connection between their votes and their government's responses was not new. The "paranoid style" that Richard Hofstadter detects in American political history is as likely to give credence to malign intent by office holders as against them.[2] "Politics" has never achieved a great deal of professional credibility in the United States, and "politics as usual" is a self-referential epithet to indicate the lowest of low practice, which can nonetheless only be expected and taken on sufferance. Wartime nationalism and apparently successful postwar recovery had underpinned a period of relatively consistent political patterns and accepted political practices. While both specific and broad political concerns existed, the impact of these had generally been limited to particular election campaigns, within particular regions, or had not appeared on the campaign agenda at all. At a time of sharp political change, however, the agenda becomes more open, and any of the debates that have previously been contained may gain temporary or long-term significance as the political subsoil shifts.

The end of reliable democracy

It was the Democratic Party's relationship with its traditional electoral coalition that suffered especially during the 1968 presidential election. The party of the incumbent president was used to approaching elections with a sense of political advantage, but in 1968 Democratic President Lyndon Johnson was beleaguered in the White House, faced by failing policies at home and abroad. Entanglement in Vietnam had increasingly become an ambivalent domestic issue; US armed forces deployment of personnel had increased during Johnson's term from a few thousand to over half a million. A patriotic willingness to support the country's foreign ventures was curdled by the loss of American lives in a dispute where the national interest was not well understood. The country as a whole was not anti-war, but it was a unique and anxious experience for the United States to be conducting a war in the face of considerable vocal and controversial disquiet among both the public and those drafted into the forces.[3]

The immense cost of the war in South East Asia helped subvert the

administration's ability to deliver on expensive domestic policy commitments. President John F. Kennedy's New Frontier approach had
stimulated new hopes and new approaches in US government.
Building further, Johnson's Great Society program was promoted as
an interventionist, progressive, problem-solving wave of domestic
initiatives to tackle deprivation, discrimination, and poverty in the
nation. Urban areas were especially targeted by these programs. But
support was not universal for these policies. Some felt that the
programs were aimed to benefit African-American-populated urban
areas in blighted cities with high crime rates. Such a perception could
easily amalgamate civil rights protesters, urban rioters, and
criminals into an unholy special interest. Traditional blue collar
Democrats were disturbed. Any range of initiatives as substantial as
the Great Society is expensive, prone to start-up problems, and have
a substantial experimental element. When cuts began to bite, critics
claimed that the administration had wasted tax dollars on a failed,
overblown experiment, while beneficiaries worried that their gains
would not survive.

In the face of these strains, conservative former Democrat George
Wallace launched the American Independent Party, while a group
led by Allard Loewenstein and Curtis Gans, looking for a liberal
alternative, supported the apparently quixotic campaign of anti-war
Democratic Senator Eugene McCarthy. After President Johnson
made an unexpectedly poor showing in the New Hampshire primary, Senator Robert Kennedy announced his candidacy; soon after
the president withdrew from the campaign, leaving the way open for
Vice President Hubert Humphrey to enter the lists. As if this was not
chaos enough, Robert Kennedy was assassinated at a California
primary victory celebration in June 1968, adding to the national
shock following the assassination of civil rights leader Martin Luther
King only weeks earlier.

The urban and campus unrest of this period sprang from a variety
of stimuli, but they all fired the feeling of national social disorder. On
the one hand, the traditional leaders of the Democratic Party seemed
unable to establish a bridge to the dissenting forces in their ranks. On
the other, many dissenters felt that their opinions were being ignored
by the political system, especially as it seemed that, even after a
vigorous primary campaign, Hubert Humphrey – a candidate who
had played no substantial part in the primary elections – would be
nominated. Humphrey was nominated at the Chicago convention,

while outside, rioting police attacked the thousands of demonstrators who had assembled in the city. Television viewers across the nation saw Democrats protesting in the streets, against Democrats in office, in a Democrat-controlled city. Chicago appeared to provide evidence that Democrats could be blamed for failed policies, for the dissent, and for the inability to maintain law and order. Humphrey was never able to shake off the disadvantage of these visible fractures within the party coalition, and Richard Nixon was able to win the presidency while avoiding making firm policy commitments of his own.

Into the breach

The time was ripe for a period of principled, responsive leadership. The Republicans under Nixon were not able to provide this. Having won the election almost by default in the face of the Democratic Party's self-destruction, the Republican campaign had done little to define the policy agenda. It was in spite of this a notable campaign. Not a naturally charismatic person, Nixon's campaign was nonetheless a personally focused, centralized challenge bringing together advertising skills and political logistics in a way not seen before. The campaign team, accustomed to the heightened atmosphere of California electoral politics, designed an entrepreneurial, individualized campaign geared to the use and direction of the latest available media and technology. A new standard for campaigning was set by the Nixon team, and the lessons learned were soon having an impact at all levels.[4]

Acting well within the tradition of successive administrations, Nixon was looking more toward Republican moderation of domestic policy than to any rapid or considerable changes. Nixon's victory brought no real electoral gains to the Republicans at other levels. His conduct of the presidency continued to be personal, even his policy successes appearing to bring little added strength to his party. His attempts to contribute personal glamor to the office he held were not notably successful either. The introduction of Ruritanian special uniforms for White House staff was a public relations failure, bringing comic opera style to the executive. The operation of the White House as a sandbagged fiefdom, with staff identifying lists of Nixon's enemies, then using the full force of government to attack them, did not come fully to light until later, but contributed to an atmosphere of suspicion and growing antagonism in Washington.[5]

At the same time, the potential for effective political linkage between leaders and followers was being reduced by political changes. Many groups within national politics were acting on the powerful lessons of the civil rights movement. The women's movement, the youth movement, the anti-war movement, and the ecology movement emerged, along with a wide range of issue groups and ideological groups, and some existing interest groups adopted new techniques and forms. Some of these declined quickly, others became part of the political landscape. An already fragmented system became increasingly diverse. The parties lost more loyalists as the politically active found alternative routes to express their wishes. These developments enhanced choice of political activity, but carried with them no certainty of impact in the political marketplace.

The policy excesses and extreme personalization of the Johnson and Nixon administrations led to accusations that an "imperial presidency" had developed. Former White House operatives, as well as contemporary journalists, painted a picture of an executive led with energy, acting assertively, but isolated within a cocoon of uncritically loyalist staff.[6]

Questioning the expense

The feeling of electoral disconnection that White identified among citizens may be attributable to many separate changes in the texture of political life. The emergence of newly active groups, the development of new methods of political activity and communication, the rise of particularly difficult policy challenges, and the reaction to these of contemporary office holders were all part of the pattern.

Both the public and the office holders were unnerved. The emergence of new groups into the field, and fresh demands for benefits from groups new and old, can threaten the policy gains of existing groups without going far enough to satisfy new ones. In these cases many elements of the electorate may feel their government is being unresponsive, and that the connection between government and the governed should be reviewed. It is logical that election practice would be considered as an area where the connection could be improved. With Democrats taking the lead, both political parties initiated examination and reform of candidate selection processes. Additionally, contemporary anxieties allowed underlying concerns about campaign financing onto the agenda.

The campaign finance laws in existence at the time were easily avoided and generally not enforced. Public disquiet was also evident concerning the extent of economic power in election campaigns. Campaigning was becoming increasingly expensive, and wealthy supporters were in the habit of making very large contributions to the campaigns of candidates for major office. Some felt that this too might be contributing to a perceived unresponsiveness to "ordinary people," regardless of the fact that American election campaigns had in fact been expensive for some time. Over a century ago, in 1880, Republican James A. Garfield ran the first million-dollar presidential campaign. Expenditure had been in the millions ever since, but, with the exception of occasional high-spending elections, spending had risen only gradually until after World War II. In 1948 the Republican and Democratic campaigns together had spent less than $5 million, but spending doubled by 1952, and doubled again by 1960, when the Kennedy and Nixon campaigns had spent about $10 million each. When Nixon ran again, in 1968, his campaign cost $25 million. Campaign inflation was driven in part by new and expensive election technology, particularly the use of paid television advertising, and fed by the loosely regulated donations of wealthy individuals and organized interests.

A growing consensus for reform

There was some recognition of this concern about the escalating costs of campaigns in the commissioning by President Kennedy of a report, published in 1962, which introduced the idea of partial public funding of campaigns. In 1966 reform suggestions from President Johnson coincided with a growing feeling in Congress that something had to be done to defuse criticism. Public confidence in the system was eroding, and an image developed of political decisions being made by self-serving politicians and their affluent supporters.[7]

These suspicions were not improved by the conduct of the 1968 campaign. The vigorous and often nasty contest within the Democratic Party resulted in the selection of Hubert Humphrey, a candidate who had entered none of the primary contests, as the party's presidential nominee. Even many activists saw this as evidence that political leaders were willing to ignore widespread public tumult. On the Republican side, Chicago newspaper proprietor W. Clement Stone donated $2.8 million to the Nixon campaign, thereby underwriting more than 11 percent of the total cost of the Republican presidential election campaign. Candidates at all levels needed only a few contributions approaching this size on which to base major election campaigns. Suspicions strengthened that large contributors were gaining unfair political advantage, and buying personal advancement, at the same time as interfering with and disconnecting the link between the public and their elected representatives.

In addition many candidates for federal office were growing worried. Not all felt that they had the capacity to raise the campaign cash that would be needed in such an inflationary world. Democrats were worried that in presidential races their own nominees might be overwhelmed by heavily backed Republicans. These considerations brought powerful pressures to bear on the Democrat-controlled Congress. It could be argued that some form of campaign finance reform would have a partisan benefit. At the same time, if White is correct, the sense of political efficacy held by citizens had declined in the face of the social and political challenges in 1970s America. Congress could appear to respond to these concerns while the majority party simultaneously addressed some concerns of its own.

The 1971 passage of the Revenue Act, and the Federal Election Campaign Act (FECA) initiated the era – which stretches to the present day – of campaign regulation. While they responded to the concerns of the day, this legislation was not a reaction to the Watergate scandal, or to the conduct of the 1972 election. Indeed it may be that any causal link operated at least to a small extent the other way around.

The legislation of 1971

The 1971 FECA tackled the questions of disclosure of political contributions; limitation of campaign spending on media advertising; and limitation of the use of personal fortunes for campaign spending. Additionally the Revenue Act of the same year introduced tax deductions for small political contributions, and a "check off " provision whereby tax payers could divert $1 per person to a fund to underwrite the public funding of presidential election campaigns. Much of the legislation was later superseded; some of its provisions were struck down by the courts, and others were altered even before

they were put into action. Nevertheless these Acts, however vestigial
their remnants, set the agenda for campaign regulation over the past
quarter century. The issues of prompt financial disclosure, limited
campaign contributions, campaign spending ceilings, and public
funding of election campaigns were repeatedly addressed in legal
challenges to the legislation, and in subsequent legislative
adjustments to the regulations. The 1971 legislation formed the
foundation of the later, more lasting amendments that make up
current campaign law.

Full implementation of this legislation was delayed. President
Nixon's signature was appended on condition that the major limitations would not apply to 1972, which was to be his own final election
campaign. The one element that would apply was to be the disclosure rule, which came into effect on April 7th, 1972. Fundraisers
within the Committee to Re-elect the President used the window of
opportunity immediately before this date to solicit millions of dollars
with the promise of complete confidentiality. Later investigation
showed that much of this money was mishandled, but at the time it
was the cream of a campaign that was "awash with money, enough
to overfertilize the imagination and ambitions of the most balanced
minds."[8]

Expenditure leapt in 1972. The Democrats spent $30 million on
the McGovern campaign, but the Nixon campaign more than
doubled the previous spending record to exceed $60 million. The
rich continued to feature. W. Clement Stone followed up his 1968
largesse with another $2 million donation in 1972, and a total of
$51.3 million was collected from only 1,254 persons.[9] Furthermore,
the fertile imaginations of some operatives in the system were stimulated to use part of this money for a campaign of misinformation and
psuedo-intelligence operations that included surreptitious
disruption of opponents' campaigns, and famously, the Watergate
break-in. The subsequent investigation, helped by the new disclosure
laws, exposed the campaign finance system to further public attention, confirmed the worst impressions of politicians as unaccountable and out of control, and led to the only presidential resignation in
American history. When Nixon went, his elected vice-president was
no longer there to take over. Spiro Agnew had already resigned in the
light of allegations about earlier financial irregularities during his
governorship of Maryland. It is not unreasonable to say that the
conduct of their political leaders robbed Americans of a fair election

in 1972. If there was a vague feeling of disconnection at the close of the election, this can only have been exacerbated by the disclosures that came with the post mortem.

The finance structure takes shape

In this atmosphere the 1974 amendments expanding the coverage of the FECA were passed even before many of the clauses of the original Act had taken effect. The adaptations did not finish there. Challenges to the laws have come before the courts, and have altered their effect, especially the landmark case in 1976 of *Buckley* v. *Valeo*. Laws in action do not always have the effects intended by the legislators, and such considerations led to more amendments being passed in 1976, and again in 1979. The effects of these reforms, and the possibility of further changes, continue to be a source of controversy, but the operation of the laws may still be considered under the categories where an impact was expected: disclosure of the origins of donations, limitation of individual donations, regulation of expenditure, and introduction of public funding.

Disclosure

It is perhaps the law on disclosure of campaign contributions that has survived most intact from the original legislation. The demand for public accountability by making political actions widely visible sounds eminently reasonable in a political system often praised by self-congratulatory participants for its pluralist characteristics. The pressure for disclosure of campaign contributions fits easily into this general concern that political participants and organizations be open to public examination.

The 1971 Campaign Act required candidates for House and Senate, their campaign committees, and active political committees, to file reports disclosing expenditures and donations. Presidential candidates had to make regular reports on contributions received during the course of their campaign, and political parties were required to disclose the accounts of presidential convention costs. Reports by political committees and candidates had to identify the donors of all contributions or loans exceeding $100 per annum (raised to $200 by the 1979 amendments). The amendments of 1974 simplified oversight with the establishment of a single Federal

Elections Commission (FEC).

The fate of the Commission exemplifies the many ways law as written is forced to adapt in operation. The attempt to regulate campaign finances was not met with blanket approval, and a coalition of those opposed to various aspects of the law challenged its operation in the *Buckley* v. *Valeo* court case. In January 1976 the Supreme Court upheld the plaintiffs' case in part, including the claim that the FEC was improperly constituted. The Commission had only been in operation for a year, but this Supreme Court decision forced Congress to amend the law once again in order to maintain campaign finance regulation. After a hiatus of some months, the Commission was reconstituted in a constitutionally satisfactory way as part of the 1976 FECA amendments.

The decade ended with further changes in 1979, based on experience of the system in action. Campaigns were diverting considerable time, skill, and expense into filing reports, when they needed to be campaigning for electoral victory. In response the number of reports to be filed was reduced for congressional candidates and thresholds for disclosure were raised modestly.

Though the disclosure parameters have been changed, and the FEC reconstituted, the original intent on disclosure of the early regulations seems not fundamentally to have altered. In so far as the new campaign law was supposed to disperse the shadows around candidate funding and spending, the mechanisms are still there. All those pursuing federal office have to file their reports accordingly. The details are available to anyone, and the possibility that an inquisitive reporter, or opponent, will examine the returns for evidence of any campaign finance indiscretion complements the other regulations of the 1970s' laws.

Regulating donations

One of the concerns of the reformers was the potentially undemocratic effect of very large campaign contributions by rich individuals or organizations. The 1971 FECA limited campaign spending out of the personal wealth of the candidate and his or her close family. Additionally the 1971 Revenue Act included new provisions making some small political contributions tax deductible – a measure aimed at extending the financial base of candidates' campaigns by encouraging a broader sector of the electorate to make contributions.

Public anger and political revenge after Watergate gave reformers the opportunity to curtail the obvious exercise of financial clout. 1974 saw the introduction of a limit on individuals' political donations of $1,000 per candidate per election. Any citizen could donate both to primary and general election campaigns, and to more than one candidate for election, but however many candidates in elections at different levels and in different constituencies were covered, the total donated in any one year by any one person could not exceed $25,000. The law also introduced separate regulations covering Political Action Committees (PACs), formed by a wide variety of labor, business, ideological, and lobbying organizations, and charged with the responsibility of disbursing funds in pursuance of the political objectives of the parent organization. PAC contributions were limited to $5,000 per candidate per election, with no ceiling on overall campaign contributions.

The regulation of donations also suffered from the attentions of the Supreme Court in 1976, when, as part of the *Buckley* v. *Valeo* decision, the blanket limitation on donations to a candidate's own campaign by the candidate and his or her immediate family were declared unconstitutional infringements of free speech. While there appeared little possibility of revising the law to reimpose such limits without again falling foul of the Constitution, there were other regulations covering contributions which were introduced in 1976, particularly covering the growing participation of political committees.

In an effort simultaneously to simplify donations and to channel more money through the political parties, limits on contributions to national party committees were set at $20,000 per annum for individuals and $15,000 for PACs. Both Democratic and Republican parties have National Committees as well as separate House and Senate Campaign Committees which may make direct donations to the campaigns of candidates for federal office (up to $10,000 per candidate from the House Committee; $10,000 to House candidates, $17,500 to Senate candidates from the other two committees). Individuals were also allowed to donate up to $5,000 annually to political committees.

The limitations on donations were intended to broaden political participation, and, by removing large contributors from the scene, to reduce the real or apparent debt that some candidates might otherwise owe to particularly generous supporters. The pattern established by the beginning of the 1980s, and still in force today, retains the limits on individual donations and PAC contributions, but the law found no way of restricting the use of personal wealth by candidates, however immense. Also some supporters, rather than contributing to a campaign, might choose to exercise their support in spending parallel with the campaign. This is a "donation" of kinds, but being not directly controlled by the campaign organization it has to be regulated by attempted limits on political spending.

Regulating expenditure

The Supreme Court decision in *Buckley* v. *Valeo* affected all aspects of campaign law, but possibly influenced expenditure regulation more than anything else. The 1971 law addressed the most inflationary, and what was considered the most manipulative, area of campaign spending by putting limits on candidate spending on media advertising. By 1974 congressional resolve to limit spending had been further strengthened, and overall spending limits were imposed for all candidates for federal office. Furthermore, independent spending – money spent by individuals independent of the official election campaign, but in an attempt to influence the outcome – was limited to $1,000. Every one of these regulations was struck down by the Supreme Court.

The loss of the particular regulations is not so significant as the general reasoning behind the legal decision which makes an apparent equation between freedom to spend on getting a message across and freedom of speech. As Frank Sorauf says, " 'Money talks' was elevated from popular saying to constitutional principle."[10] This makes spending limits very difficult to compose without falling foul of the First Amendment to the Constitution of the United States. The echoes of this decision continue to be heard. Herbert Alexander, reviewing attempts to construct further campaign finance regulation in 1993 commented that "Most Democrats continue to insist the only meaningful reforms are controls on spending . . . ignor(ing) the fact that option has been precluded by the Supreme Court."[11]

Little remains of the attempt to limit campaign spending for election to all federal offices. Only in cases of presidential candidates accepting public funds have spending limits been maintained. If the official campaign organization of a presidential candidate accepts public funds, the Supreme Court takes the position that the campaign is entering into a contract. As such, it is legitimate for the government to include spending limits as a condition of the grant. These limits can still only be imposed on the official campaign. Independent expenditure aimed at influencing the presidential election remains outside this remit.

The maximum amounts which the political parties could spend in support of any candidates for federal office, called coordinated contributions, were regulated by the 1974 amendments. Index-linked, these figures had by 1992 reached $27,620 for House seats (double in states with only one seat). At Senate level a formula depending in part on the size of the constituency is used producing 1992 limits ranging from $55,240 to in excess of $1.2 million according to the size of the state. At the presidential level in 1992 the parties each disclosed $10.2 million in coordinated spending. Total coordinated spending on all races in the 1992 election cycle was $27 million by the Democrats, and $32.9 million by the Republicans.[12]

The most notable action on spending in the 1979 amendments appears to have eased dramatically the limits that exist by creating an alternative and less restricted route for the funds. The earlier finance regulations appeared to be in danger of accelerating the decline of political parties by favoring a funding system focused on candidate campaigns and political committees. In response, state and local parties were given new freedoms in the name of party-building and get-out-the-vote efforts. Unlimited spending is allowed at this level on the traditional campaign materials used in volunteer activities (e.g. leaflets and stickers), and on efforts to register voters and encourage them to exercise their franchise. This channel was shortly to be a conduit for a huge amount of "soft money."

Public funding

The Revenue Act of 1971 set up a fund to subsidize the public financing of presidential campaigns. Taxpayers could contribute $1 per annum of their due taxes by the simple expedient of ticking a box provided on their income tax return. Twenty-two years later the inflation in campaign costs persuaded Congress in 1993 to raise the potential contribution to $3.[13] The 1976 election was the first to operate under the public funding rules. By then the law set qualifying thresholds beyond which candidates for the presidency were eligible for public funding.

Prenomination candidates have to display a degree of widespread public support by collecting at least $5,000 in contributions of $250 or less in each of twenty states. This having been done, the candidate qualifies for federal funds matching all contributions up to a maximum of $250 per contributor. Technically, therefore, the presidential election fund could pay for up to half of a candidate's campaign, but since at least some individual contributions will reach the donation limit of $1,000, and matching funds are only available for the first $250, this 50 percent maximum public funding is likely never to be reached. The eleven candidates eligible for matching funds in 1992 received a total of $42,742,815, of which over $12.5 million went to the Bill Clinton campaign.[14]

These matching funds are only available on the condition that the candidate accepts the legally specified spending limits. The limits written into the law cover spending on the campaign in individual states (these were simplified in 1991), and an overall national limit. The state limits total more than the overall limit, leaving space for strategic spending decisions by the campaign. For the 1992 election the overall spending limit reached $27,620,000 for a candidate (plus a 20 percent allowance for compliance and fund raising costs). This phase of public funding gets the candidates for nomination as far as the party convention. The 1974 law included a provision giving a grant to cover the costs of each major party convention. In 1992 these grants exceeded $11 million each for the Republicans and Democrats.

Once nominated by one of the major political parties, the candidates qualify for federal funds designed to cover the whole cost of the general election campaign. This figure is also index-linked to inflation ($55,240,000 in 1992). Again, acceptance of public funding involves accepting conditions – in this case that the official campaign neither raises nor spends any money other than that received from the federal election fund, and again observes spending limits set for each state. Minor party presidential candidates may also qualify for public funding, but only retrospectively if they receive 5 percent of the vote in the general election. Once having qualified in this fashion, a new party can claim some public funding in the next election.

In each case these spending limits are imposed as a condition of receiving public funds – not as a blanket provision for all candidates.

A candidate wishing to compete entirely on private contributions would thereby avoid all limits. Prior to 1992 only one presidential hopeful, John Connally in 1980, had attempted this approach. Texan billionaire H. Ross Perot smashed all previous records and expectations in 1992 when he spent $64.7 million, over 95 percent from his own wealth, on his independent "United We Stand" presidential campaign.

Where is the action?

The 1980s began with a legal framework for campaign finance in place, structured by the cumulative reforms of the previous decade. Some organizational and public responses to this evolution were already evident. The expanded activity of PACs was particularly notable.

In 1974 the total number of federally registered political action committees was 608. By the end of 1980 this figure had more than quadrupled, to 2,551. The total number of PACs continued to grow rapidly, reaching 4,000 in 1984. PAC growth effectively reached a plateau around this level, peaking at 4,268 in 1988, but falling back moderately to 3,993 by July 1st, 1994.[15] By category, corporate PAC growth has been most explosive, increasing by a factor of twenty from 89 in 1974 to peak at 1,816 in 1988, with 1,715 on FEC records in 1993. The 201 Labor PACs operating in 1974 outnumbered their corporate counterparts, but growth in this category to 338 by 1993 was modest by comparison. The FEC puts "trade, health and membership" PACs together, embracing all types of membership associations. Starting with around 300 PACs in 1974, there were 767 PACs in this category by 1993. The final large category of PACs are the "Non-connecteds." Covering a broad spectrum, these are mainly ideological or single issue PACs. First listed separately in 1977, this category has since then grown almost ten-fold from 110 to 1,011 committees by 1993.

With donations from individuals to candidates limited, the PAC responds to several needs. Firstly, it allows individuals an alternative route to channel money into the political system through highly specified routes representing ideological, business or other interests felt important by the donor. Secondly, candidates, unable formally to solicit individual large donations, need either to reduce campaign expenditure, or instead to draw on large networks of contacts for multiple smaller contributions. PACs provide a large and well-signposted network, and can also legally donate somewhat larger amounts than individual donors.

Thirdly, organized interests in all categories may, through their PAC, create an access link to receptive politicians. The average PAC donation to a candidate in 1992 of $1,600 hardly looks overwhelming when compared with overall spending which in 1992 averaged around half a million dollars for those winning House seats, and just over three-and-a-half million dollars by winners in the Senate.[16] Nonetheless, in the restructured environment of campaign finance, an increasing number of interests felt that a donation was a worthwhile investment in access to significant politicians. Indeed, as the number of PAC donors increased, it may be that a donation was felt necessary for the sake of maintaining some visibility with political leaders.

Overall spending by PACs has become an issue. Very little PAC money is donated to presidential candidates (less than $800,000 in 1992). If anything the public funding contribution to presidential campaigns appears to have allowed politically interested money to find other channels. Also the nature of law making in the United States, through a highly defined congressional committee structure, allows donors to identify with some accuracy those members with whom they feel a clear common interest. In 1974 PACs contributed $12.5 million to federal candidates. By 1980 the figure was $60 million, and in 1992 it reached $188.7 million.[17] Donation is only part of the activity of PACs, and it gives some indication of the size of these organizations to realize that their total disbursements in the election cycle ending 1992 exceeded $394 million.

The proportion of congressional campaign funds provided by PACs increased through most of this period. In 1976 those winning Senate seats had received just under 15 percent of their campaign funds from PACs. This rose steadily to 26.8 percent in 1986, falling marginally to 26.7 percent by 1992. Winners in the House received 25.6 percent of their funds from PACs as early as 1976, which rose to 46.1 percent in 1990, slipping back a little to 41.7 percent in 1992.

Since those donating money wish to have an impact, contributions tend to favor those already occupying positions of influence. Incumbents attracted 71.7 percent of PAC donations in 1992, while challengers only picked up 11.7 percent. The rest went to candidates competing in open seats. One further consequence of this is that PAC contributions have a partisan favoritism. Democrats controlled the House for forty years until the 1994 elections, and, as the incumbent group, received 67 percent of PAC money in 1992. Democrats have recently held a small PAC funding advantage in Senate, although in 1986, when there was last a Republican majority, that party received most funds. Republicans can expect to benefit from their majority status in both House and Senate following the 1994 elections. Indeed, given the ideological preference of the Republican Party to many high-spending corporate, and conservative single-issue groups, PAC investment in incumbents may increase. The global effect of donated PAC money in congressional elections must therefore be perceived as bolstering incumbent Senators and Representatives, whatever status quo exists.

PACs have increased their value to campaigners by adopting a practice called "bundling." The practice is not restricted to PACs, and others who want political impact, including corporations banned from making direct campaign contributions, have become successful brokers of political cash. Bundling relies on good communications. Donors each have the legal right to donate direct to candidates up to the maximum limits. By identifying suitable candidates, PACs can simplify the routing of a donation, collecting multiple checks made out to a candidate campaign, and delivering them in a bundle. The donations are all individual and entirely legal, but arrive with the impact that togetherness adds.

Money can also be spent independently by a political committee to promote or criticize a favored candidate. As long as this is neither donated to a campaign fund, nor controlled by the official campaign in any way, there are no limits on this form of expenditure. In 1991–1992 PACs spent $10.4 million independently. The global figure is relatively small, but since this money can be highly targeted, it can have significant impact in particular races.

In some years PACs have played a part in presidential campaigns through independent spending, and sometimes this has been through committees created with the signal purpose of increasing the opportunity for a particular candidate. Ronald Reagan's "Citizens for the Republic" was the first such PAC. It distributed contributions to conservative Republican candidates and causes, underwrote the development of a fund raising operation, publicized and subsidized Reagan's public activities, and in various ways prepared the way for his official campaign. Nine presidential hopefuls for 1988 estab-

lished PACs on similar lines to the Reagan model, spending a total of
$25.2 million.[18]

Presidential candidate PACs were much less evident in 1992, but
these are just one example of the "leadership" PACs that have been
established by senior politicians with major fund raising potential. In
October 1988 fifty leading members of Congress had leadership
PACs which they could use to showcase themselves, while fostering
support for causes and candidates of their choice, thereby
reinforcing their own positions in office.[19]

Some PACs are demonstrably more successful than others in
collecting and distributing funds. The Realtor's PAC alone contributed $2.95 million to federal candidates in 1991–1992. The
American Medical Association PAC contributed $2.94 million.
Twenty-seven PACs, including the National Rifle Association ($1.74
million), the National Education Association ($2.32 million),
American Telephone and Telegraph ($1.30 million), and United
Steelworkers ($1.25 million) contributed over $1 million each. The
top fifty contributor PACs accounted for over one-third of all PAC
contributions. Some candidates are also particularly attractive to
PACs. In 1992 twenty-one Senate candidates received more than $1
million each from political committees, and twenty-eight House
candidates received more than $500,000 each. Not one of these was
challenging an incumbent, and only two were fighting in open seats.

The visible impact of this new political animal has alleviated some
analysts' concern that politicians are divorced from the public.
Curtis Gans, who moved on from the insurgent 1968 McCarthy
campaign eventually to become director of the Committee for the
Study of the American Electorate, claims that "PACs are a reflection
of American pluralism," and it is also said that campaign money
encourages competition, participation, and robust campaigning.
Others, acknowledging the apparent opportunities afforded by PAC
activity to avoid some finance limits, the favoritism shown to
incumbent politicians, and the emergence of particularly "fat" PACs
and PAC-favored candidates, are not so sanguine on the grounds of
pluralism. As Senator Robert Dole pointed out, "There aren't any
Poor PACs or Food Stamp PACs or Nutrition PACs or Medicare
PACs."[20]

Softly, softly

Political parties in the USA have been ailing for some time. While there is an ambivalent attitude to this among citizens, there was some concern that the reforms of the early 1970s further subverted parties by concentrating on presidential candidate campaigns. The presidential campaigns of 1976 had, incidentally, found the financial straitjacket under which the election had run severely cramped their sense of style. The 1979 amendment allowing unrestrained expenditure by state and local parties on traditional get-out-the-vote, party-building, voter registration, and similar activities was the legislative response. The funds channeled into campaigns through these routes are called "soft money."

Soft money can be used to print sample ballots, or other listings which mention three or more candidates for offices coming up for election. Traditional volunteer materials such as stickers, badges, small signs, and posters can be prepared. Voter registration and participation campaigns can be underwritten. Strategically used, this investment can pay off handsomely for candidates, and while it has been seen primarily as a way of supporting presidential campaigns, the generic effect must also benefit the parties' congressional teams.

In spite of its knock-on effect on federal elections, this is not defined as federal monies, and the federal regulations applying to donation do not apply. It took a little while for the full opportunity afforded to be realized, and the lack of disclosure requirements prevent an easy accounting for the 1980s. The Republican National Committee raised $9 million soft money in 1980, distributing it to states where the local law allowed, and the strategic impact would be greatest. In addition state and local parties raised money independently of the national effort to be spent on allowable activities.[21]

The Democrats were slower off the mark in using this legal loophole, but by 1988 an estimated $45 million of soft money was raised by the national parties, with the Democrats doing marginally better than the Republicans.[22] As of January 1st, 1991 national party committees were required to disclose their non-federal accounts. These showed the Republicans raising $52 million and the Democrats $37 million in soft money during that election cycle. These are substantial amounts to be freely available for use when set against the hard money spending limit for the general election of $55.24 million on the parties' presidential candidates.

Contribution limits do not apply to this money. Money can be solicited direct from corporations, trade unions, and others banned from hard money participation, and fed into states where the local law is favorable. Fund raising by both parties has included solicitation, usually by direct mail, of small contributions, but those prepared to be generous received special consideration, such as nominal membership of exclusive political clubs. Over $15,000 per annum qualifies the donor as a Republican Eagle, and over $100,000 is nomination for Team 100. Large-scale donors are invited to briefings with political leaders, and hope for high quality access to those they have helped.

Incumbency is advantageous. Laura Hartigan, the Democratic National Committee's national finance director, estimates that cabinet secretaries provide two or three briefings each month for major donors, and considers it important to "plug party high rollers into events at the White House."[23] Among recent big spenders have been Edgar Bronfman, chair of Joseph Seagram and Sons, with a $450,000 contribution to the Republicans; Steven Spielberg, who gave over $100,000 to the Democrats; the Las Vegas Golden Nugget Casino, which put $230,000 into Republican coffers, and the scores of couples who paid $25,000 each to attend a Democratic fund raising dinner in Hollywood.

Some hedge their bets, as for example Carl Lindner, donating $250,000 to Democratic funds in 1993, after his own company had given $865,000 to the Republicans during the Bush administration. Dwayne O. Andreas, and the giant grain company Archer–Daniels–Midland, of which he is chair, donated about $1.1 million in soft money to Republican Party organizations during the 1992 election cycle. In the aftermath of the Clinton presidential victory they gave more than $300,000 to the Democrats. This support is seen by some as part of a lobbying exercise that contributed to a regulation favoring the use of the corn-based fuel product ethanol to the considerable financial benefit of corn producers.[24]

The money to run

Total campaign spending in the 1992 election cycle was the highest to date. Congressional election spending reached $678 million. Estimates of the total presidential campaign expenditure were as high as $400 million. Federal level campaigning alone had become a billion dollar business. The expensively and vigorously pursued congressional campaigns of 1994, and the prospect of a major presidential battle in 1996, do not indicate that this expenditure is likely to decline soon.

The electoral process has become increasingly candidate-centered at all levels over the past quarter century. Campaigning techniques have changed with the increased use of electronic media, the introduction of computer and information technology based methodology, and the growth of an increasingly sophisticated expert consultancy system. All of these have inflated campaign costs, even when there is little evidence for their real value. Increasingly, participation at the highest levels of campaigning is dependent on being able to buy in to these facilities. Candidates have to rely on their personal campaign organizations in primaries, and this candidate-centered team continues to be at the core through the general election, its position strengthened by the need to mount formidable and continuous fund raising efforts.

Independent fund raising and campaigning contributes to a sense of independence from the political party. The parties have taken advantage of the laws where they can. There is some evidence that partisan loyalty in Congress is influenced by the partial underwriting of campaigns from party funds. It also seems clear that Republicans have so far been more successful than Democrats in the collection and strategic use of funds to maximize party impact in the world of entrepreneurial politics.[25] But generally the approach to policy has become more atomized.

Issues are the order of the day, as the numerous groups acting on the political scene use their access to the elected officials to press their case direct. The same groups sometimes publicize their specialist case to the electorate. The decline of self-consciously general purpose political organizations, such as the political parties, leaves the environment short of theaters within which broad policy aims can be developed out of competing issues. Incumbents look to their constituencies for guidance on the issues, but given the importance of fund raising, the "funding constituency" may begin to compete with the "electoral constituency" for attention, leading to a moral dilemma about the nature of representation in contemporary America.[26]

Two days after the 1992 elections the *New York Times* editorialized on "Ten Reasons to Feel Good," the first of which was "the remarkable turnout everywhere."[27] The 1992 voter turnout approached 55 percent. After years of decline bottoming out with half those eligible to vote staying away in 1988, this was seen as a glorious change of direction, but it is still a lower figure than that lamented by White in 1972 as a "shrivelled size," indicating a vague feeling that might be called alienation. Morning-after good vibrations notwithstanding, the sense of divorce from the political system remains with many members of the electorate. In the words of Wilson Carey McWilliams' 1992 analysis, "Voters, seeing money as dominant in elections and increasingly convinced that corruption is the political rule, feel a lack of voice and representation."[28]

This may have contributed to the extraordinary success of Ross Perot, who appeared to convince many citizens that a "world class campaign" purchased wholly with his personal wealth was less tainted than a campaign subject to the interests and pressures that accompany political fund raising. Perot was not the only wealthy candidate on the block. In 1992 House candidates invested $54.4 million of their personal wealth in their own campaigns. By spring 1994, seven months before election day, at least eleven House candidates had put $100,000 of their own wealth into their own campaigns, led by Republicans Eugene Fontenot (Texas; $850,000) and Richard Sybert (California; $430,000). Michael Huffington won California's 22nd House District in 1992 with an expenditure of $5.44 million, almost all of which came out of his own pocket. He reportedly spent over $20 million from the same source in his 1992 challenge for US senator from California. At least he could fairly claim not to be in debt to other interests – he accepted no PAC funds at all in 1990.[29]

In the mid-1990s campaign finance laws do not limit expenditure, do not limit donations, do not limit the extent to which the very rich may finance their own political ambitions, and do not restrict the overall costs of publicly funded presidential campaigns. The laws do require quite complex channeling of funds to achieve some of these ends, and insist on considerable documentation and disclosure. Anyone can find out who is spending the money and in what direction, if they have the time and inclination to investigate. Massive spending is not a guarantee of victory, but Jamin Raskin and John Bonifaz claim that there is now an effective "wealth primary," that is, immense sums have to be raised merely to participate in the candidacy system. This barrier imposes costs on the polity in terms of candidate choice, viability, and therefore representativeness.[30]

According to Everett Carll Ladd, "The public's criticism, as seen clearly in survey data, is that politics is too much captured by political insiders – for example, by the elected Democratic and Republican politicians in the national legislature – and in general that 'the system' is too insulated from meaningful day-to-day popular control. The call is to somehow check and limit the political class."[31] The attempts to check and limit have been varied. The tax revolt beginning in the late 1970s imposed decisions on state law makers, and influenced other legislators through the use of propositions and initiatives. Those same methods have been used more recently to attempt the imposition of term limits – unseating incumbents by changing the rules. These actions are intended, as was campaign finance reform, to focus the attention of the elected on the wishes of the voters.

Citizen criticism often argues that elected politicians are unresponsive, but this may be a misperception. In fact politicians are responsive, but to a range of demands made by donors, single-issue interests, and constituents, unfiltered by any accepted intervening broad policy structure. It may be a case of what Gary Jacobson has called "great individual responsiveness, equally great collective irresponsibility."[32] The difficulties are complex, and the temptation to look for a "quick fix" are considerable. Candidates and political organizations looking for short-term strategic advantage have capitalized on public disquiet, and the United States has suffered from an outbreak of candidates at all levels running against "the System," against "politics as usual," and against "big government." The chorus of unrestrained rhetoric along these lines can do nothing to restore the electorate's sense of efficacy.[33]

If the problem is a broad one of connectedness between voters and office holders, further campaign finance reform remains on the agenda as potentially part of the solution. At various times in recent years different reforms have passed in House and Senate, but a common wording has yet to be found. If more complete spending limits are to be included, then public funding is the *quid pro quo* demanded by the Supreme Court's interpretation of the Constitution, but there is little public support for public funding. Partisan differences exist which reflect the success of the main parties with different forms of fund raising; neither side wishes to see their money ox-gored. There is a sense that something must be done.

Representative Kay Shepherd (Democrat, Utah) has pointed out that "Failure to dampen the electorate's cynicism undercuts all of our achievements and leaves us open for a continuation of the attacks that have undermined our ability to govern," and called for "tough political reform."[34] The danger remains that the reform will be window-dressing, the results will be limited, and the electorate will continue to be disappointed.

Notes

1 Theodore H. White, *The Making of the President, 1972* (New York, Bantam Books, 1973), pp. 468–469.

2 Richard Hofstadter, *The Paranoid Style in American Politics and Other Essays* (New York, Vintage, 1967).

3 Theodore H. White, *The Making of the President, 1968* (New York, Pocket Books, 1970); Philip John Davies, "US Presidential Election Campaigns in the Vietnam Era," in *Vietnam and the Antiwar Movement*, edited by John Dumbrell (Aldershot, Avebury, 1989), pp. 124–136.

4 Joe McGinnis, *The Selling of the President* (Harmondsworth, Middlesex, Penguin, 1970).

5 Theodore H. White, *Breach of Faith: the Fall of Richard Nixon* (New York, Dell, 1975); J. Anthony Lukas, *Nightmare: The Underside of the Nixon Years* (New York, Penguin, 1988); Fred Emery, *Watergate: The Corruption of American Politics and the Fall of Richard Nixon* (New York, Times Books, 1994).

6 Arthur M. Schlesinger, Jr, *The Imperial Presidency* (New York, Popular Library, 1974); George Reedy, *The Twilight of the Presidency* (New York, Mentor, 1970); Rowland Evans and Robert Novack, *Lyndon B. Johnson: The Exercise of Power* (New York, New American Library, 1966).

7 Herbert E. Alexander, *Financing Politics: Money, Elections and Political Reform*, 4th edn (Washington, DC, Congressional Quarterly Press, 1992, pp. 26–27.

8 White, *1972*, p. 378.

9 Alexander, *Financing Politics*, p. 21.

10 Frank J. Sorauf, *Inside Campaign Finance: Myths and Realities* (New Haven, CT, Yale University Press, 1992), p. 11.

11 Talk by Herbert Alexander reported in "Alexander Sees New Campaign Reform Legislation . . . and More Litigation," *Public Affairs Report*, vol. 34, no. 5 (September 1993), p. 2.

12 Candice J. Nelson, "Money and its Role in the Election," in *The*

Election of 1992, edited by William Crotty (Guilford, CT, Dushkin, 1993), p. 103; Federal Election Commission press release, March 11th, 1993.

13 Federal Election Commission press release, August 20th, 1993.

14 Federal Election Commission, *Annual Report 1992* (Washington, DC, FEC, 1993).

15 Federal Election Commission press release, August 2nd, 1993; *National Journal*, July 30th, 1994 (no. 31), p. 1808.

16 Federal Election Commission press release, March 4th, 1993; "Campaigns: Lobbyists' Gifts . . ." (editorial), *Washington Post National Weekly Edition*, June 27th–July 3rd, 1994 (vol. 11, no. 35), p. 26.

17 Federal Election Commission press release, April 29th, 1993. These figures refer to the two-year election cycle ending in the year indicated.

18 Anthony Corrado, "Creative Campaigning: PACs as Presidential Campaign Organizations," *Vox Pop*, vol. 11, no. 2 (1992), pp. 1, 6–7.

19 Ross K. Baker, *The New Fat Cats: Members of Congress as Political Benefactors* (New York, Priority Press, 1989); Eliza Newlin Carney, "PAC Men," *National Journal*, October 1st, 1994, pp. 2268–2273.

20 Eliza Newlin Carney, "FYI: Don't Look Here for PAC-bashers," *National Journal*, July 16th, 1994, p. 1690; Elizabeth Drew, *Politics and Money: The New Road to Corruption* (New York, Collier Books, 1983), p. 96.

21 Brian A. Haggerty, "Soft Money in Presidential Elections," in *Political Parties and Elections in the United States*, edited by L. Sandy Maisel (New York, Garland, 1991), pp. 1028–1029.

22 Herbert E. Alexander and Monica Bauer, *Financing the 1988 Election* (Boulder, CO, Westview Press, 1991), p. 37.

23 James A. Barnes, "Greener Acres," *National Journal*, April 23rd, 1994, p. 950.

24 Charles R. Babcock, "Winning or Losing Is Like Money in the Bank," *Washington Post National Weekly Edition*, vol 11, no. 21 (March 21st–27th, 1994), pp. 13–14; Nelson, "Money and Its Role," p. 104; Barnes, "Greener Acres," pp. 952, 953; Peter H. Stone, "The Big Harvest," *National Journal*, July 30th, 1994, pp. 1790–1793.

25 Stephen A. Borelli and Kevin M. Leyden, "An Investment in Goodwill: Party Contributions and Party Unity in the 1980s," and Diana Dwyre, "Is Winning Everything? Party Strategies for the US House of Representatives," both papers presented to the Annual Meeting of the American Political Science Association, September 1992; Paul S. Herrnson, "Party Strategy and Campaign Activities in the 1992 Congressional Elections," paper presented to the conference "State of the Parties," Ray Bliss Institute,

University of Akron, September 1992.

26   James Eisenstein and Brian Werner, "Democratic Representation and the Transformation of State Legislative Funding Constituencies," presented to the Annual Meeting of the American Political Science Association, September 1992.

27   "Ten Reasons to Feel Good" (editorial), *New York Times*, November 5th, 1992, p. A34.

28   Wilson Carey McWilliams, "The Meaning of the Election," in *The Election of 1992*, edited by Gerald Pomper *et al*. (Chatham, NJ, Chatham House, 1993), p. 196. See also James Ceaser and Andrew Busch, *Upside Down and Inside Out: The 1992 Elections and American Politics* (Lanham, Maryland, Rowan and Littlefield, 1993), pp. 171–172.

29   Glenn R. Simpson, "Representative Moneybags," *Washington Post National Edition*, vol. 11, no. 27 (May 2nd–8th, 1994), p. 25.

30   E. J. Dionne, Jr, "Everything Money Can Buy," *Washington Post National Edition*, vol. 11, no. 17 (February 21st–27th, 1994), p. 29.

31   Everett Carll Ladd, "Of Political Parties Great and Strong," in *The American Enterprise*, July–August 1994, quoted in *National Journal*, August 6th, 1994 (no. 32), p. 1884.

32   Quoted in Brooks Jackson, *Honest Graft: How Special Interests Buy Influence in Washington* (Washington, DC, Farragut, 1990), p. 322.

33   E. J. Dionne, Jr, "The Big Lie About Government," *Washington Post National Edition*, vol. 11, no. 35 (June 27th–July 3rd, 1994), p. 29.

34   Quoted in editorial, *Washington Post National Edition*, vol. 11, no. 35 (June 27th–July 3rd, 1994), p. 26.

The transformation of the policy landscape

Tuesday January 20, 1981 dawned overcast and cold in Washington, DC – a typical winter's day. But, in fact, everything about that inauguration day was abnormal. In the White House, an exhausted Jimmy Carter prepared to hand the presidency to Ronald Reagan after a marathon forty-eight sleepless hours trying unsuccessfully to free the fifty-two US hostages held in Iran for what seemed an interminable 444 days. At 12:33 pm, shortly after Reagan swore to uphold the Constitution "to the best of my ability," the captives were ushered aboard a plane bound for a US military installation in Wiesbaden, West Germany. The picture of the newly-freed Americans made for an unforgettable day.[1]

But there was another dramatic scene unfolding on the Capitol steps. From the inauguration stand, Ronald Reagan proclaimed the Reagan Revolution:

> Government is not the solution to our problems; government is the problem . . . It is my intention to curb the size and influence of the federal establishment and to demand recognition of the distinction between the powers granted to the federal government and those reserved to the states or to the people; all of us need to be reminded that the federal government did not create the states, the states created the federal government.[2]

To accentuate the turnabout, Reagan's handlers decided to move the inauguration ceremonies from the cramped East Front of the Capitol with its uninspired view of the US Supreme Court to the West Front with the Smithsonian museums, Washington Monument, Lincoln Memorial, and Jefferson Monument serving as picturesque backdrops.

Reagan's distrust of the federal government he was about to command was widely shared by the American people. Eighty-three percent agreed with him that the size and influence of the government should be curbed.³ His proclamation that "government is the problem" was a crabbed rebuttal to the 1960s – a far cry from the grandiose pledge made by another new President, John F. Kennedy, thirty years before. In the most famous inaugural address of the twentieth century, Kennedy challenged his fellow citizens to "ask not what your country can do for you, but what you can do for your country." But in the decades following Kennedy's speech, a majority came to radically different conclusions about whether the federal government could be trusted and what role it should play in the American polity. In 1986, 67 percent agreed with the statement: "In the '60s and '70s, it was the federal government growing beyond our control that strongly contributed to the collapse of our economy, of confidence in our institutions, and a shaking of the very roots of our freedom."⁴

Surveys conducted by the University of Michigan Center for Social Research tracked the growing disillusionment. In 1958, only 18 percent thought that "the government is run by a few big interests looking out for themselves"; 1976, 60 percent; 1980, 77 percent; and in 1992, 75 percent believed it so.⁵ Moreover, the percentage who said that "the government cannot be trusted to do what is right most of the time" stood at 25 percent in 1958; 66 percent in 1982; and 73 percent in 1993.⁶ Other polls show that public distrust of big government had not wavered in the years following Reagan's inaugural address. A 1992 survey found 50 percent had "little" or "no confidence" that government can solve their problems; of these 60 percent said it was not due to the intractable nature of our difficulties, but because "the government is incompetent."⁷ One can envision Reagan sitting back at his California ranch saying, "See, I told you so."

One reason for the lack of confidence was the absence of continued government successes. From the 1930s to the 1960s, most Americans believed big government worked – not because they had an abstract faith in their leaders – but because together the government and the people could boast of some major triumphs: ending the Great Depression, winning World War II, permitting the returning GIs to attend college with federal assistance, building an interstate highway system second to none, extending civil rights to blacks, and permitting the former "have-nots" to join the burgeoning ranks of the middle class.

The US is a "results-oriented" society. But during the 1970s and 1980s, the federal government had relatively few successes. The US won small wars in Grenada and Panama and a big one in the Persian Gulf. It also had a major victory with the collapse of Communism in Eastern Europe that culminated in 1991 with the disintegration of the Soviet Union itself. But the US government lost the decade-plus conflict in Vietnam, saw a president resign to avoid impeachment, experienced an oil embargo, watched its middle class suffer from a declining standard of living, and saw another scandal nearly engulf another president. No wonder that by 1992 56 percent echoed the line from the movie "Network": "I'm mad as hell, and I'm not going to take it anymore."[8] Indeed, compared to other occupations, government officials and politicians took it on the chin (see Table 11.1).

Table 11.1

Public regard for government officials compared to other occupations 1992 (percentages)

Occupation	High %	High/fairly good Combined %
Teachers	46	91
Clergy	42	84
Police officers	36	84
Doctors	31	82
Business people	13	77
Advertising people	9	61
Reporters	12	61
Corporate executives	5	51
Labor leaders	9	50
Lawyers	11	49
Federal agency officials	5	43
US senators	5	39
Members of Congress	4	35
Politicians	3	24

Source: Survey by The Roper Organization, March 17–24, 1992.

This "crisis of confidence" permeated all aspects of American life. When asked, for example, what John F. Kennedy meant when he said in his 1961 inaugural address, "Ask not what your country can do for you, ask what you can do for your country," one person answered: "He's trying to remind the American people that they should try to be more responsible for themselves, and not be dependent on somebody taking over their responsibilities, such as providing you with benefits whenever you need it . . . Once you get on that track, why should you go back, because government is taking care of all your responsibilities."[9] A *Democrat* added, "I believe we are doing what we can for our country. We are not accepting any government programs and so-called handouts by being middle class."[10]

Lack of confidence in government is a 1970s phenomenon – not a 1960s one. Back then, Americans engaged in a "politics of consensus" which culminated during Lyndon Johnson's 1964 campaign against Barry Goldwater.[11] That year Johnson's political support extended from conservative Georgia senator Richard Russell to black activist James Farmer; from union boss Walter Reuther to auto magnate Henry Ford II; from Republicans in Vermont to Democrats in southwest Texas. In more of a consensual act than a majoritarian one, 61.1 percent confirmed Johnson as their president. But voters were engaged in something more than a plebiscite on Johnson, the man; they also provided a mandate to Johnson, the philosopher. A strong, active presidency – with states and localities yielding considerable authority to the federal government – had become universally acceptable to everyone except Goldwater and a few "extremists." One exception was California movie star Ronald Reagan. Sounding like a prophet of doom, Reagan stumped the countryside for Goldwater warning audiences: "Either we accept the responsibilities for our own destiny, or we abandon the American Revolution and confess that an intellectual belief in a far-distant capitol can plan our lives for us better than we."[12] He added, "Already the hour is late."[13]

Voters did not share Reagan's sense of urgency. An overwhelming majority perceived that the federal government was promoting the economic well-being of everyone, thereby enhancing the average citizen's freedoms. Franklin Roosevelt empowered the "common man" economically and politically. Harry Truman's Marshall Plan and Point Four Program brought an American version of the New

Deal to Western Europe. Dwight Eisenhower signed the first major civil rights bill since the Civil War. John Kennedy's New Frontier extended the idea of the "common man" to Third World countries through such initiatives as the Peace Corps.

By 1964, this string of success stories forged a new politics of consensus. Presidential assistant Eric Goldman suggested that Lyndon Johnson's 1964 State of the Union Address include the phrase: "Today, in a very real sense, we are all liberals, we are all conservatives – and we are moving toward a new American consensus."[14] Johnson did not use Goldman's words, but he did paraphrase Thomas Jefferson in his 1965 State of the Union Address: "We have achieved a unity of interest among our people that is unmatched in the history of freedom."[15] Two weeks later, taking the oath of office for the first time as an elected president, Johnson spoke of a "new American consensus" that would allow the country to "achieve progress without strife" and "change without hatred."[16]

Johnson sought to bring more "outcasts" into the political and economic mainstreams than any of his Democratic predecessors, save Roosevelt. After the 1964 election returns were in, Johnson was advised in a Goldman memo: "Consensus [politics] can . . . be an active, dynamic, rolling credo. It can be a springboard . . ."[17] Johnson forged ahead with his Great Society. At his insistence Congress passed the Civil Rights Act of 1964, the Voting Rights Act of 1965, a highway beautification program (a special project of Lady Bird Johnson), a food stamp program, and the Model Cities program. Congress also created the Office of Economic Opportunity and the cabinet departments of Housing and Urban Development and Transportation to administer the new programs.

Richard Nixon largely continued Johnson's initiatives. He signed into law the Occupational Safety and Health Act of 1970, the Clean Air and Water Acts of 1971, and added the Environmental Protection Agency to the growing morass of federal agencies. Nixon also imposed wage and price controls in an attempt to halt inflation. With an economy sliding into a recession, a Democratic Congress earmarked $250 million in 1974 for the Comprehensive Employment and Training Act program that was signed into law by Gerald Ford. Jimmy Carter enlarged federal authority by creating an Energy Department, and making good on a campaign pledge to the National Education Association by establishing a Department of Education.

By January 1981, the "consensus politics" of Lyndon Johnson was

no more. Reagan rewrote, or at least tried to, the compact between
the federal government and the states. Back in 1933 Luther Gulick, a
noted student of public administration, proclaimed: "The American
state is finished. I do not predict that the states will go, but affirm that
they have gone."[18] Two decades later Leonard D. White seconded
Gulick's diagnosis: "If present trends continue for another quarter-
century, the states may be left hollow shells, operating primarily as
field districts of federal departments."[19] Back then, Americans
seemed willing to let the states wither. A 1936 Gallup poll found a
majority favored a "concentration of power in the federal
government."

Gulick and his associates reflected a linear view of regime development. Explanations along these lines were devised and the attendant
public opinions were appropriate for the 1930s. In fact, they
remained credible rationales for policy development in the 1950s
and 1960s. Two generations of public administration scholars could
approvingly forecast the centralization and uniformity of public
policy. Such centralization was further strengthened by the development of the new national infrastructure that was supported by public
works, housing credit, and industrial-defense production that
fashioned the post World War II experience. Social and welfare
policies advanced along a similar centralized path.[20] This physical
and cultural policy landscape formed the picture of a national regime
that emerged in the 1960s and 1970s. These centralizing processes
were hastened by the professionalization of the public service into
the "best and the brightest." In some respects, the success of this
project provoked the groundswell that enabled the populist call for
the devolution and decentralization.[21]

In retrospect it appears that these centralizing impulses were spent
by 1975. The issue was clearly framed during the 1976 presidential
contest when the fiscal crisis of urban America went from blighted
neighborhoods to threaten the solvency of New York City. President
Ford refused to bail out the nation's largest city. His refusal met with
widespread public support. The revolt of the middle class[22] renewed
popular interest in the Declaration of Independence. They echoed
the Declaration's critique of government policies that were
unresponsive and unaccountable to the needs and concerns of the
people.[23] Public attitudes further soured when the national government was unable to act decisively and efficaciously. Inflation rates
spiralled, gasoline lines provoked frustration and violence, con-

fidence in savings and loans waned as persons invested in money markets, and deindustrialization increased plant closings. All this threatened the life of older industrial communities. The center was not holding. State and local governments, once at the periphery of power, became the focus for policy alternatives by default. Epochal forces of change related to a range of macro factors[24] fueled the rebellion against the halls of power concentrated in Washington.[25] Even if one sets aside economic and world monetary changes; the turmoil involving the renewal of civil rights for blacks; the Vietnam War and peace movements; religious, ethnic, and lifestyle changes; the plain fact is that by 1981 public opinion reported a massive loss of confidence in the federal government. Most supported a revival of state power. Six years later, as the nation was well into the Reagan Revolution, the public remained firmly committed to the decentralization of political power (see Table 11.2). A popular bumper sticker captured the popular mood: "Think globally, act locally."

Table 11.2

Public preference for federal or state power 1936, 1981, and 1987 (percentages)

	1936 %	1981 %	1987 %
Federal government	56	36	34
State government	44	64	63
No opinion	–	–	3

Sources: 1936: George Gallup, Survey; 1981: George Gallup, Survey, September 18–21; 1987: Decision/making/information, survey for the Republican National Committee, April 21–23. Text of question: "Which theory of government do you favor: concentration of power in the federal government or concentration of power in the state government?"

The popular preference to "let the states do it" has held during the 1990s. A 1994 *Time* magazine/CNN poll found 52 percent saying their state legislature "gets more done" than Congress; 56 percent agree states are "more efficient" in using taxpayers' money; and 64 percent believe their state legislators "care more about people like you" than do their congressional representatives.[26] These results reflect the widespread disillusionment with Congress. In 1937,

44 percent characterized Congress "as good a representative body as is possible for a large nation to have." By 1990, just 17 percent agreed. Moreover, back in 1937, just 16 percent thought that members of Congress "spend more time thinking of their own political futures than they do in passing wise legislation." By 1990, that figure rose to 41 percent.[27] That lack of confidence is directly correlated with the cry for limiting congressional terms. In 1947, just 40 percent backed term limits for House members; by 1990, 64 percent did. Similarly, in 1947, 54 percent favored limiting the tenure for senators; in 1990 support rose to 67 percent.[28]

Something more than a desire to return power to the states was at work. Pollster Daniel Yankelovich reported that the public's "search for community" – namely, the desire to compensate for the impersonal and threatening aspects of modern life by seeking mutual identification with others – grew from 32 percent in 1973 to 47 percent at the start of the 1980s.[29]

The administrative state and its accompanying reform impulses of technical and procedural accountability, standardization, and impersonal governmental regulation profoundly changed the relationship of citizen to government.[30] These new constellations initiated and legitimated the critique of national institutions and highlighted the importance of a new, unelected group. The "unelected" were often arrogant and disconnected from the state and local experience. Moreover, the needs and costs of state and local government fostered disagreements about the efficacy of federal missions. Public administration's paradigm was limited and its programs were disjointed and simple-minded. The perception that the federal government was unable to share the burdens of social, cultural, and economic restructuring grew.[31] The intersection of a new culture of public administration coupled with the added importance of state and local leaders created new opportunities and a latent political force for different approaches to public policy.

Translating opinion into reality

Translating opinion into reality is the process of forming and transforming the policy landscape. The policy landscape is most apparent at the intersections of public opinion, political leadership, and governmental institutions. The leading causes which have contributed to the formation of opinion – the transformation of the policy landscape and attendant shifts in confidence concerning national governance – are at the very core of the dynamic that drives representative government in the American tradition. Policy failures and successes clearly affect presidential elections. Yet, institutional factors are also important. The transformation of policy during the last twenty years and its attendant shifts in opinion are woven into the fabric of government.

American government is framed by the US Constitution which created federalism, checks and balances, and the separation of powers. Such a division of power is intended to conform to circumstances intrinsic to the pluralism of the US population, the size of the country, and the volatility of political preferences. The latter has been enhanced by the decline of political parties. Party decay is especially evident in the persistent division of party control of the national government; the successes of persons and organizations who bypass traditional party mechanisms; and the inability of various policy entrepreneurs to energize their political claims. These developments form a veil of contingency – the magic of politics and the illusions of persuasion – that cloud our understanding of recent and current events.

Notwithstanding these limitations, the fissures in the deeper structures of public opinion also define the policy landscape – including racial, ethnic, religious, regional, economic and cultural diversity. Their potential to shape or reshape public policy should not be underestimated. Thus, comprehensive accounts of policy transformation in this large and complex arena require attention to all elements in this public drama – their traditional forms of self-government, the fracturing of consensus and consent to specific national policies, and the force of the American Dream.

The persistence of the American ethos is observable in the existential tension of governmental prescriptions that echo the universalist claim of liberty and freedom and independence. The reciprocal relationship between this dream and the reality of the American spirit emerges in political appeals. The deterioration of various levels of confidence as well as policy successes and failures can be tracked in public opinion. This is not to say that governmental policy and the configuration of power at the national level have been shaped by opinion. On the contrary, institutional changes at the national level have shaped perceptions of government and have contributed to the public skepticism.

In 1972, Congress indexed[32] social welfare transfers and mandatory special budget categorization of these programs. This innovation protected entitlements and established their automatic and administrative character. Congress avoided biennial conflicts and appropriation battles by linking funding of these transfers to demographic as well as to economic and statistical indicators. The Consumer Price Index (CPI) inflation rate, age, income, rental rates, poverty rates, and population size triggered these entitlement payments. The following budget data reflect the "indexing" of mandatory transfers that began in 1972.

Another innovation was changing the budget process. In 1974 Congress empowered itself to assess policy by passing the Budget Control and Impoundment Act. The law created the Congressional Budget Office, established a new legislative calendar, and provided Congress with the capacity to assess policy options. That, along with the new Budget Committees, provided the framework for fiscal assessments which would become pivotal in future years. While this law is often associated with partisan conflict between Democratic Congresses and Republican presidents, its larger influence can now be understood more clearly. The budget process defined the relationships among the legislature, agencies, interest groups, and policy professionals. This cluster of forces transformed the policy process by institutionalizing the budget debate around policy spending categories such as defense, international, domestic discretionary (means-tested and non-means-tested), and interest. Other factors also altered the policy making process: the increase in unfunded mandates passed onto the states and local governments; monopolization of federal resources by ensconced interest groups, industries, and associations and their dependence on federal discretionary resources; exacerbation of the debt and deficit that occurred during this period; and the nationalization of civil liberties. But the most significant policy shift was congressional acquiescence to the Budget Reconciliation Act of 1981. The Reagan budget proposed a $40 billion cut and Congress, in a hurried panic to join the Reagan Revolution, approved it and the tax cut of 1982 that followed.

The latter was an affirmation of the Reagan pathway to economic growth, although the massive increase in military expenditures and the general power of the business cycle also explained the economic recovery that followed. Four years later the Tax Reform Act of 1986 flattened rates and removed thousands of sound incentives that peppered the economic landscape. Beginning in 1976 America pursued a policy of regulation: railroads (1978), airlines (1980), rates on motor transport (1980), Savings Banks and Savings and Loans (1982). Deregulation would have grave public consequences in the Savings and Loans industry when the margins between rates beckoned the Savings and Loans companies to take development risks that would have been unthinkable for an industry devoted to homeownership and stabilizing the social infrastructure. Thus, a classic institutional bulwark of middle class expansion which mediated the gulfs between the poor, working poor, and the wealthy was crippled. And a massive government-sponsored bailout was required.

Perhaps the policy change with the most enduring effect was the monetary policies adopted by the Federal Reserve Board. It attempted to control the spiralling inflation by tightening the money supply. Though a recession followed, the economic miracle based on increasing the federal debt sustained the American economy until 1992. The fiscal base-lines of this policy transformation can be quantitatively seen in Tables 11.3, 11.4, 11.5 and Figure 11.1 which present the fiscal data in their plainest form. The Office of Management and Budget (OMB) estimates for Fiscal Year 1994 are that federal revenues will be derived from the following sources: individual income tax, 37 percent; social security receipts, 31 percent; borrowing, 17 percent; corporate income tax, 8 percent; excise and other taxes, 7 percent. The distribution of federal expenditures intensifies the limits of the policy terrain: 46 percent of government outlays are paid to individuals, 18 percent to support national defense, 15 percent to assist state and local governments, 6 percent for federal operations and 1 percent for deposit insurance. From 1974 on, this pattern of spending has substantially increased the annual federal deficit. The 1993 US budget forecast a $5,000 billion debt. The pattern is clear: downsizing the national government will remain the central policy feature for the next generation. Thus, whatever substantive policy concerns arise will be molded into the structure inherited from the early 1970s.

Reaffirming federalism is related to energizing the representational dimension of Congress. In the 1970s, congressional reforms focused on streamlining its administrative capacity. While such professionalization was necessary, it was not sufficient to the deeper

Table 11.3 Discretionary outlays, Fiscal Years 1972–1992 (percentages of GDP)

	Means-tested programs			Non-means-tested programs							Total entitlements and other mandatory spending %
	Medicaid %	Other %	Total %	Social Security %	Medicare %	Other retirement and disability %	Unemployment compensation %	Farm price supports %	Other %	Total %	
1972	0.40	1.00	1.40	3.40	0.70	0.80	0.60	0.40	1.10	7.00	8.40
1973	0.40	0.90	1.30	3.80	0.70	0.90	0.40	0.30	1.50	7.60	8.90
1974	0.40	1.00	1.40	3.90	0.80	1.00	0.40	0.10	1.50	7.70	9.10
1975	0.50	1.20	1.70	4.20	0.90	1.20	0.80	0.00	2.00	9.10	10.80
1976	0.50	1.30	1.80	4.30	1.00	1.10	1.10	0.10	1.90	9.50	11.30
1977	0.50	1.20	1.70	4.40	1.10	1.10	0.70	0.20	1.50	9.00	10.70
1978	0.50	1.10	1.60	4.30	1.10	1.10	0.50	0.30	1.70	9.00	10.60
1979	0.50	1.10	1.60	4.20	1.20	1.10	0.40	0.10	1.50	8.50	10.10
1980	0.50	1.20	1.70	4.40	1.30	1.20	0.60	0.10	1.60	9.20	10.90
1981	0.60	1.30	1.90	4.70	1.40	1.30	0.60	0.10	1.60	9.70	11.60
1982	0.60	1.20	1.80	4.90	1.60	1.30	0.70	0.40	1.30	10.20	12.00
1983	0.60	1.20	1.80	5.10	1.70	1.30	0.90	0.60	1.10	10.70	12.50
1984	0.60	1.10	1.70	1.40	1.60	1.20	0.50	0.20	1.10	6.00	7.70
1985	0.60	1.10	1.70	4.70	1.80	1.10	0.40	0.40	1.20	9.60	11.30
1986	0.60	1.10	1.70	4.70	1.80	1.10	0.40	0.60	0.70	9.30	11.00
1987	0.60	1.00	1.60	4.60	1.80	1.10	0.30	0.50	0.50	8.80	10.40
1988	0.60	1.00	1.60	4.50	1.80	1.10	0.30	0.30	0.70	8.70	10.30
1989	0.70	1.00	1.70	4.50	1.80	1.10	0.30	0.20	0.60	8.50	10.20
1990	0.80	1.10	1.90	4.50	2.00	1.10	0.30	0.10	0.50	8.50	10.40
1991	0.90	1.20	2.10	4.70	2.00	1.10	0.40	0.20	0.60	9.00	11.10
1992	1.20	1.30	2.50	4.90	2.20	1.10	0.60	0.20	0.60	9.60	12.10

Source: derived from Congressional Budget Office.

Table 11.4 Outlays for major spending categories, Fiscal Years 1972–1992 (billions of dollars)

	Discretionary spending $ billions	Entitlements $ billions	Deposit insurance $ billions	Net interest $ billions	Offsetting receipts $ billions	Total outlays $ billions
1972	133.10	96.80	−0.60	15.50	−14.10	230.70
1973	135.00	112.20	−0.80	17.30	−18.00	245.70
1974	142.50	127.10	−0.50	21.40	−21.20	269.30
1975	162.50	164.40	0.50	23.20	−18.30	332.30
1976	175.60	189.70	−0.60	26.70	−19.60	371.80
1977	197.10	206.60	−2.80	29.90	−21.50	409.30
1978	218.70	228.40	−1.00	35.50	−22.80	458.80
1979	240.00	248.20	−1.70	42.60	−25.60	503.50
1980	276.50	291.50	−0.40	52.50	−29.20	590.90
1981	308.20	340.60	−1.40	68.80	−37.90	678.30
1982	326.20	372.70	−2.20	85.00	−36.00	745.70
1983	353.40	411.60	−1.20	89.80	−45.30	808.30
1984	379.60	406.30	−0.90	111.10	−44.20	851.90
1985	416.20	450.00	−2.20	129.50	−47.10	946.40
1986	439.00	459.70	1.50	136.00	−45.90	990.30
1987	444.90	470.20	3.10	138.70	−53.00	1003.90
1988	465.10	494.20	10.00	151.80	−57.00	1064.10
1989	489.70	526.20	22.00	169.30	−63.90	1143.30
1990	501.70	567.40	58.10	184.20	−58.80	1252.60
1991	534.80	634.20	66.30	194.50	−106.00	1323.80
1992	537.40	711.20	2.60	199.40	−68.80	1381.80

Source: derived from Congressional Budget Office.

Table 11.5
Discretionary outlays Fiscal Years 1972–1992 ($ billions)

	Defense $ billions	International $ billions	Domestic $ billions	Total $ billions
1972	79.30	4.60	49.20	133.10
1973	77.10	4.80	53.00	134.90
1974	80.70	6.20	55.60	142.50
1975	87.60	8.20	66.70	162.50
1976	89.90	7.50	78.20	175.60
1977	97.50	8.00	91.50	197.00
1978	104.60	8.50	105.50	218.60
1979	116.80	9.10	114.10	240.00
1980	134.60	12.80	129.10	276.50
1981	158.00	13.60	136.50	308.10
1982	185.90	12.90	127.40	326.20
1983	209.90	13.60	130.00	353.50
1984	228.00	16.30	135.30	379.60
1985	253.10	17.40	145.70	416.20
1986	273.80	17.70	147.50	439.00
1987	282.50	15.20	147.20	444.90
1988	290.90	15.70	158.40	465.00
1989	304.00	16.60	169.00	489.60
1990	300.10	19.10	182.50	501.70
1991	319.70	19.70	195.40	534.80
1992	304.30	19.20	213.90	537.40

needs of regime legitimacy. Without the political consensus that could be developed from the rootedness of Congress in the texture of pluralism that constitutes federalism, confidence in its ability to govern will not improve. The tension between representation and efficiency is an endemic reality of governing a large republic and the federal system. Moreover, the problems of policy implementation at the state and local levels which constitute an even more complex welter of human relationships – demographic, geographic, economic, social, and cultural – do not require the detailed uniformity imagined in the 1930s by the founders of modern public administration. The practice of the last two decades has revealed how important it is to be attentive to local dimensions and

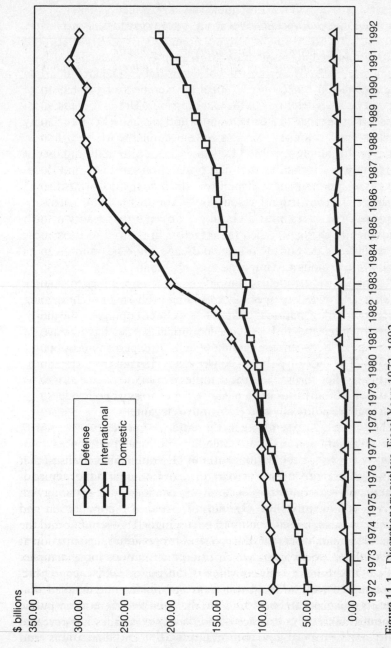

Figure 11.1 Discretionary outlays, Fiscal Years 1972–1992

Source: derived from Congressional Budget Office.

clusterings which have both political and policy saliency.[33] For example, the significant relocation of populations from urban centers as recorded in the reapportionments of 1970, 1980, and 1990 diminished the number of House members[34] elected by urban-dwellers as well as the proportion of senatorial dependence on urban constituents. In 1992 only 77 of 435 Members of the House of Representatives belonged to the Congressional Urban Caucus. Congress may give more authority to states and localities, but its capacity to assist cities is limited. Mayors have become the weakest interest group in Washington. Table 11.6 shows the decline in the number of representatives for states that had population increases and documents the apportionment disparities which have "disenfranchised" these states from federal resources.[35] The increasingly necessary focus on what states must do locally is driven by the reality of such fundamental changes. When these factors are linked to the deficit, the reconfiguration of the policy landscape could be ominous in its various dimensions and impacts.

Attention to the deficit simplifies the complexities of policy making, and poses an especially troubling problem of orchestrating consent regarding national policy. The welter of opinions, the multiplicity of interests, and weakened political parties have created a classic *stasis* between contending claims to expertise and popular consent. The lack of political consensus is derived from the multiplicity of policy thrusts and the complexity of governance as well as the paucity of institutions to mediate the process of policy development that are politically and electorally relevant.

The following presents a general pattern of policy prescriptions, interest group options, and attendant political preferences that uneasily coexist in the national arena: (1) state managerialism; (2) market choice private-sector control; (3) consumer advocacy and critique of self-regulatory sectors; (4) various long-standing or fleeting combinations of (1) and (2); and (5) populism, anti-institutionalism, and communitarianism. In the 1960s and 1970s the large-scale human-service industry and professional care-providers (especially those incorporated as non-profit entities for charitable and philanthropic purposes) entered the policy landscape. These entities often were allies of state managerialism and clients of the largesse of corporate contributions.[36] This web of governments, economic interests, entitlements and care-providers is a porous, yet secure form of social governance. During the 1970s disconnection

Table 11.6 State population growth and the 1991 apportionment

State	Present number of representatives	% population growth since 1980	Net population growth since 1980	Effect of 1991 apportionment on no. of representatives
Illinois	22	0.3	40,000	−2
Pennsylvania	23	0.5	61,000	−2
Michigan	18	0.7	66,000	−2
Louisiana	7	0.7	32,000	−1
Ohio	21	0.8	90,000	−2
Nebraska	3	0.9	15,000	None
Kentucky	7	1	38,000	−1
Indiana	10	1.3	74,000	None
Montana	2	2.1	17,000	−1
Mississippi	5	2.5	66,000	None
New York	34	2.7	486,000	−3
Arkansas	4	3.2	76,000	None
Alabama	7	4.1	168,000	None
Oklahoma	6	4.2	132,000	None
Massachusetts	11	4.8	292,000	−1
Kansas	5	4.9	122,000	−1
New Jersey	14	4.9	384,000	−1

Source: derived from US Bureau.

and disaffiliation from this nested and vested core of social policy makers extended into the polity.[37] Dissatisfaction with the policies it imposed empowered a massive shift of fiscal resources.

In sum, the following events are the major landmarks that shaped the policy landscape: the Budget Reconciliation of 1981, the tax reform of 1982, the military build-up and attendant diminution of other discretionary spending, the tax reform of 1986, the collapse of the Savings and Loans industry and its bailout (1989–2029), the Gramm–Rudman–Hollings Balanced Budget and Emergency Deficit Control Act of 1985, and the rising clamor among states and localities to end the process of mandating but not funding scores of policies. These political choices crystallized the deficit as the new foundation of public policy landscape. Thus, this terrain established the agenda for the 1990s: the downsizing at the national level dubbed "Reinventing Government."

Various voices will continue to influence the persuasive contentions regarding leadership and policy. The policy agendas of state legislatures, Congress, and the president are converging and include youth crime and sentencing reform, health care, industrial development, welfare reform, campaign finance, reinventing government, and gay rights. Items that are of concern in the states include school choice, school finance equity, and workers' compensation.[38] The civil rights agenda at the state and national level suggests an arena of policy differences that encompass the "color-blind" approach versus the "politics of inclusion" in race and ethnic policy, abortion policy, the impact of immigration on various states and the limits of multicultural and non-English languages in public affairs. Curiously, tensions between state courts and state legislatures have emerged as they raise funds for school equity and housing mandated by state courts. In this common need to pay for the public services, political leaders in Washington and in the statehouses are recognizing the importance of increased taxes. It is time to pay the bill and to readjust federal relationships.

The convergence of governing agendas at the federal and state level is reflected in the backgrounds of those seeking and winning the presidency. At the 1787 Philadelphia convention that formulated the US Constitution, Massachusetts delegate Elbridge Gerry suggested that state governors appoint the president because they could best judge the qualities of potential chief magistrates. Gerry's idea was not approved, but a variant of it initially was practiced.[39] Throughout much of the nineteenth century and into the early twentieth, several governors including Franklin Pierce, Rutherford B. Hayes, Grover Cleveland, William McKinley, Theodore Roosevelt, Warren G. Harding, and Calvin Coolidge followed a well-trodden path from the state house to the White House.

But the political powers of state governors became badly corroded following Franklin Roosevelt's regime. One lamented: "We don't have sovereign states anymore. All we have are a bunch of provinces ... We are becoming conveyor belts for policies signed, sealed, and delivered in Washington."[40] Members of Congress – especially senators – held an "inside track" to the Oval Office. One sign of the times: When Harry Truman delivered his Inaugural Address in 1949, four of his five successors were in the audience – John F. Kennedy, Lyndon B. Johnson, Richard M. Nixon, and Gerald R. Ford. Only Dwight D. Eisenhower was absent.

During the 1970s, the nation's governors, having endured a long period of political obscurity, regained some of their lost prestige. Former Georgia governor Jimmy Carter won the 1976 Democratic presidential nomination competing against another governor, Edmund G. Brown of California. On the Republican side, ex-California governor Ronald Reagan nearly took the top slot away from Gerald Ford. Four years later two ex-governors squared off in the general election. Carter and Reagan were not aberrations; instead they re-blazed an old trail to the White House – one forged anew by Arkansas governor Bill Clinton in 1992. While foresight is not as perfect as hindsight, these authors would venture that few, if any, of Clinton's successors (with the possible exception of Vice President Al Gore) were within shouting distance of his inaugural address. Given the new policy agenda, future presidents are more likely to come from the statehouses or have business backgrounds as voters demand that candidates have résumés congruent with their demand for local or state experience as opposed to foreign policy expertise.

The Clinton era: four-party gridlock

Bill Clinton's 1992 victory signaled the return to one-party government. Not since Jimmy Carter's reign have the Democrats controlled both the White House and the Congress. To many, Clinton's election heralded an end to the gridlock that characterized the Reagan–Bush years. During the first few weeks of the new administration, Clinton proposed and Congress passed the Family Medical Leave Act – legislation vetoed by George Bush that allowed workers to take time off from their jobs in case of a family crisis. It was, supposedly, a sign of things to come.

But with the passage of time, a new kind of gridlock – one not involving the political parties *per se* – has emerged. A 1992 exit poll showed that while 55 percent of Clinton backers wanted the federal government to provide "more services," 36 percent said government should "cost less." These results were *exactly opposite* from the overall totals: 55 percent wanted less taxes and fewer services while 36 percent wanted a more expansive and expensive government.[41] This division of opinion extends to all segments of the electorate, and shapes how the public evaluates Clinton's performance as president. As Table 11.7 indicates, American voters can be classified as populist, liberal, conservative, and libertarian. Populists believe that government should do more to solve the country's problems while at the same time promote "traditional values." Liberals agree with the populists' desire for an expanded government, but do not think it should get into the values business. Conservatives oppose an expanded government, but agree with former vice president Dan Quayle that it should promulgate traditional values. Libertarians share the conservative mistrust of big government, but do not think it should favor one set of values over another. Subsequent tables show the gridlock created by this new "four-way politics." Populists, liberals, and libertarians have been generally supportive of Clinton, but conservatives remain staunchly opposed (see Table 11.8). Moreover, while the Republican Party has a distinctly conservative hue, Democrats and independents are composed of nearly equal parts of the four ideologies (see Table 11.9). The Democratic division is particularly interesting since it means that Clinton must continue to finesse the internal divisions within his own party.

During the 1992 campaign, voters wanted "something done" about the economy, health care, and welfare, but they were skeptical about government's ability to solve these problems. Clinton heard the former cry, but he was overly optimistic that enactment of his agenda could restore faith in government. At midterm, Clinton has a much better understanding of the public's view than he did upon assuming the presidency. After the bitter wrangling over the 1993 budget, with its higher taxes and budget reductions, one White

Table 11.7
Four-way politics (classification of voters) 1993–1994 (percentages)

	Populist %	Liberal %	Conservative %	Libertarian %
April 1993	25	17	27	20
December 1993	23	13	31	22
January 1994	20	16	30	22

Source: Surveys by the Gallup Organization for *USA Today* and CNN. Text of questions: "Some people think the government is trying to do too many things that should be left to individuals and businesses. Others think that government should do more to solve our country's problems. Which comes closer to your own view?" "Some people think the government should promote traditional values in our society. Others think the government should not favor any particular set of values. Which comes closer to your own?"

Table 11.8
Approval of President Clinton by ideological group 1993–1994 (percentages)

	Populist %	Liberal %	Conservative %	Libertarian %
April 1993	71	67	35	46
December 1993	67	75	36	50
January 1994	65	64	36	54

Source: Surveys by the Gallup Organization for *USA Today* and CNN. Text of question: "Do you approve or disapprove of the way Bill Clinton is handling his job as president?"

House political adviser grudgingly admitted that his colleagues "didn't understand how serious the lack of faith in the federal government was and the amount of work they had to do to reconstitute the center . . . before they could go and propose all these new little programs."[42] The conundrum Clinton faces is neatly captured in Tom Robbins' novel, *Even Cowgirls Get the Blues*, when one of the characters asked: "You really don't believe in political solutions

Table 11.9
Four-way politics by party 1994 (percentages)

Ideology	Republicans %	Democrats %	Independents %
Populist	16	25	19
Liberal	8	19	18
Conservative	51	18	28
Libertarian	18	21	25

Source: Survey by the Gallup Organization for *USA Today* and CNN, January 15–17, 1994.

do you?," to which the startling response is given: "I believe in political solutions to political problems. But man's primary problems aren't political; they're philosophical. Until humans can solve their philosophical problems, they're condemned to solve their political problems over and over and over again. It's a cruel, repetitious bore."[43]

Until the public believes once more in government's ability to make a difference, Clinton will be forced to tinker at the margins. After a year in office, Clinton has changed some things – but the reach of the government initiatives he advocates (with the glaring exception of health care) has been smaller than he envisioned as a candidate. For example, Clinton promised in 1992 that he would create community development banks designed to empower poor people. To date, the House of Representatives has appropriated only $338 million over the next five years to subsidize the creation of lending institutions in some of the nation's most distressed neighborhoods.[44] In many ways, Clinton has fulfilled the prophecy of his one-time rival for the Democratic presidential nomination, Paul Tsongas. Back in 1982 Tsongas, then a US Senator from Massachusetts, bluntly declared that the Democratic Party "should take the best of what (Reagan) did and embrace that without embarrassment," adding that if the Democrats were returned to the White House "not all the spending cuts (Reagan initiated) are going to be restored."[45]

Out on the hustings, many Americans continue to lustily cheer calls for spending cuts. In 1993, New Jersey voters ousted Democratic governor Jim Florio after he enacted a massive tax increase – a result that reverberated through the White House. Less known, but equally significant, voters in Texas and Washington State approved ballot initiatives requiring legislators to receive voter approval for major tax increases. The National Taxpayers Union estimates that similar proposals could be on the ballot in as many as eight states in 1994 – including Florida, Oregon, and Missouri.[46] Until a modicum of public confidence in government is restored – confidence that can come only when the government has a string of major successes – voters will remain cynical, and Clinton stymied. Clinton polltaker Stanley B. Greenberg describes a scenario for ending the gridlock:

> Passage of programs by themselves does not guarantee success. There has to be restructuring of the American economy . . . there has to be health care that is secure . . . there has to be a government that is leaner and more efficient. [Clinton] has got to show government can be successful. That's the way out of this mess – the way we can create a new coalition."[47]

Until that confidence is restored, the mess referred to as "gridlock" is likely to continue.

Notes

1   See Jimmy Carter, *Keeping Faith* (New York: Bantam Books, 1982), especially pp. 3–14.

2   Quoted in Ronald Reagan, *Ronald Reagan: An American Life* (New York: Simon and Schuster, 1990), pp. 226–227.

3   Louis Harris and Associates, survey, January 22–25, 1981.

4   Decision/Making/Information, survey for the Republican National Committee, January 11–12, 1986.

5   University of Michigan, Center for Social Research, selected surveys, 1958, 1976, and 1980. The March 26–29, 1992 poll was conducted by CBS News/*New York Times* and the question was changed slightly to read: "Would you say the government is pretty much run by a few big interests looking out for themselves?"

6   University of Michigan, Center for Social Research, selected surveys, 1958 and 1982. The 1993 result is from CBS News/*New York Times*, survey, January 12–14, 1993.

7   ABC News, survey, April 8–9, 1992. Asked of those who have just a little or no confidence at all the government will solve problems (50 percent): "Is it because those problems [the government in Washington decides to solve] often are very difficult to solve, or is it because the government is

incompetent?"

8   CBS News, survey, January 14–19, 1992. Text of question: "I'm sure that you've heard the phrase 'I'm mad as hell, and I'm not going to take it anymore.' When you think about the way things are going in this country these days, do you ever feel that way?"

9   Stanley B. Greenberg, "Plain Speaking: Democrats State Their Minds," *Public Opinion*, summer 1986, p. 48.

10   Ibid.

11   See Eric F. Goldman, *The Tragedy of Lyndon Johnson* (New York: Alfred A. Knopf, 1969), p. 51.

12   Summary of Ronald Reagan's speech to General Electric employees found in Ronald Reagan with Richard G. Huebler, *Where's the Rest of Me?* (New York: Duell, Sloan, and Pearce, 1965), p. 303.

13   Ibid.

14   Goldman, *The Tragedy of Lyndon Johnson*, p. 51.

15   In his Inaugural Address of March 3, 1801, Thomas Jefferson said, "We are all Republicans, we are all Federalists. The Johnson quotation is taken from Lyndon B. Johnson, State of the Union Address, Washington, DC, January 4, 1965.

16   Lyndon B. Johnson, Inaugural Address, Washington, DC, January 20, 1965.

17   Goldman, *The Tragedy of Lyndon Johnson*, p. 276.

18   Everett Carll Ladd, *The American Polity* (New York: W. W. Norton, 1987), p. 322.

19   Quoted in Larry Sabato, *Goodbye to Good-time Charlie: The American Governorship Transformed* (Washington, DC: Congressional Quarterly, Inc., 1983), p. 161.

20   See Donald L. Horowitz, *The Courts and Social Policy* (Washington, DC: The Brookings Institution, 1977. The nationalization of the Bill of Rights and the vigorous use of litigation and the activism of the Supreme Courts as well as the legislative agenda of the Johnson years and congressional protection of significant social and welfare initiatives won in the federal courts established the backdrop for the policy transformation that would reflect the preference for state concentration over federal concentration of power.

21   See Jonathan Rieder, *Canarsie: The Jews and Italians against Liberalism* (Cambridge, MA: Harvard University Press, 1985) and Ronald P. Formisano, *Boston Against Busing: Race, Class and Ethnicity in the 1960s and 1970s* (Chapel Hill: The University of North Carolina, 1991).

22   See Donald I. Warren, *The Radical Center: Middle Americans and the Politics of Alienation* (University of Notre Dame Press, 1976). This first

empirical analysis and in fact the discovery of a population cluster that held a perspective that did not fit the liberal or conservative molds points to the experiential source of the opinions that energized the new political and policy forces of populism, communitarianism, and libertarianism. When combined with some sort of traditional political or regional base these three new voices would combine to fashion electoral majorities.

23 See Kevin P. Phillips, *The Emerging Republican Majority* (New Rochelle: Arlington House, 1969), Sylvano Tomasi, Geno Baroni, et al., *Pieces of A Dream* (Staten Island: Migrations Studies, 1973), and Richard Krickus, *Pursuing The American Dream: White Ethnics and The New Populism* (Garden City: Anchor Press/Doubleday, 1976).

24 See Joshua S. Goldstein, *Long Cycles: Prosperity and War in the Modern Age* (New Haven: Yale University Press, 1988) for a comprehensive discussion of factors and models of long-term developments of political economies, and Edward R. Tufte, *Political Control of the Economy* (Princeton University Press, 1978) for the short-term calculus in America.

25 See Phillip J. Cooper, *Hard Judicial Choices: Federal District Court Judges and State and Local Officials* (New York and Oxford: Oxford University Press, 1988). These case studies of the implementation of federal directives and remedies illustrates the issues of political consensus and the mismatch of governmental branches at the intersection of federal policy driven by litigation and the strains in national–local relationships that were delegated to the courts.

26 Yankelovich Partners for *Time*/CNN, survey, January 17–18, 1994. Only 30 percent thought Congress "gets more done;" 17 percent said Congress was "more efficient in its use of taxpayer's money;" and 16 percent said their member of Congress "cares more about people like you."

27 Surveys by the Roper Organization, latest that of December 1–8, 1990.

28 Gallup, Surveys, January 17–22, 1947 and November 8–11, 1990.

29 Daniel Yankelovich, *New Rules: Searching for Self-Fulfillment in a World Turned Upside Down* (New York: Random House, 1981), p. 251.

30 See Ralph P. Hummel, *The Bureaucratic Experience*, 2nd edn (New York: St Martin's Press, 1982). This account of the language and relationships induced by administrative and procedural dicta provides theoretical and historical background of the transformation of citizens into clients.

31 See Jonathan Rieder, *Canarsie*, Ronald P. Formisano, *Boston against Busing*, and Anthony Downs, *Opening Up the Suburbs: An Urban Strategy for America* (New Haven: Yale University Press, 1973), Jennifer L. Hochschild, *The New American Dilemma: Liberal Democracy and School Desegregation* (New Haven: Yale University Press, 1981), and Paul E.

Peterson, *City Limits* (University of Chicago Press, 1981). These analyses of housing, school, and urban policies span the period under review and illustrate the web of national action and inaction that ruptured consensus in this arena of policy.

32   See R. Kent Weaver, *Automatic Government: The Politics of Indexation* (Washington, DC: The Brookings Institution, 1988).

33   See Michael J. Weiss, *The Clustering of America* (New York, Harper & Row, 1988). This data base for forty types of clusters illustrates the variegated, geo-coded patterns of market and political preferences that reflect income, education, housing, and other social indicators of enormous importance patterned into the political economy and the moral anatomy of American society.

34   See Charles A. Kromkowski and John A. Kromkowski, "Why 435?: A Question of Political Arithmetic," *Polity*, fall 1991, pp. 129–145.

35   See Stephen L. Elkin, *City and the Regime in the American Republic* (University of Chicago Press, 1987), and Brian D. Jacobs, *Fractured Cities: Capitalism, Community and Empowerment in Britain and America* (London/New York: Routledge, 1992). These treatments of the recovery of participation and citizenship reveal the potential and the profound difficulties that have been structured into the policy landscape.

36   Carroll L. Estes, *The Aging Enterprise: A Critical Examination of Social Policies and Services for the Aged* (San Fransisco: Jossey-Bass, 1979). This pioneering analysis of nationally directed social policy identifies the limits of "top-down" programming for the elderly.

37   See Jim Sleeper, *The Closest of Strangers: Liberalism and the Politics of Race in New York* (New York: W. W. Norton, 1990).

38   Charles Mahtesian, "Ten Issues To Watch," *Governing*, January 1994, pp. 42–43.

39   Sabato, *Goodbye to Good-time Charlie*, p. 196.

40   Ibid., p. 161.

41   Voter Research and Surveys, exit poll, November 3, 1992.

42   Ronald Brownstein, "Clinton's Job One: Reversing the Anti-Government Tide," *Public Perspective*, May/June 1994, p. 3.

43   Tom Robbins, *Even Cowgirls Get the Blues* (Boston: Houghton Mifflin, 1976), quoted in Yankelovich, *New Rules*, preface.

44   Brownstein, "Clinton's Job One," p. 3.

45   Paul E. Tsongas, speech to the National Press Club, Washington, DC, October 5, 1982.

46   Brownstein, "Clinton's Job One," p. 5.

47   Ibid., p. 6.

Leadership: the presidency and Congress

Since the middle of the 1970s Americans have seen a significant redefinition of the working relationship between the US Congress and the American president in the struggle to direct American public policy making and administration. This most basic relationship in the national government has changed the capacity of these American institutions and reallocated authority between them. This institutional redefinition originated in several sources inside and outside the national political institutions and has produced a "decentering" of American politics. Critical events, the struggle over Vietnam policy in the late 1960s to early 1970s and the Watergate scandal, created opportunities for institutional change. Some more basic factors such as a cultural demand for greater democracy in government, the rise of more complex Washington politics in the face of an enormous growth in interest groups, new realities in international politics, slow economic growth, divided party government, and the declining importance of the political party ties have also contributed to the definition. As well, the institutions themselves have reformed their structures, rules, and procedures and have sometimes chosen to assert themselves more aggressively in areas of policy formerly left to the other branch. Finally, part of the change, especially in the presidency, but in Congress as well, can be attributed to changes in the personnel holding office.

The presidentially driven style of government, the legacy of the New Deal of the 1930s, World War II, and the Cold War, has given way to a system whose process is more difficult to lead and whose product is less predictable. It is a system which expects active presidential leadership but also expects Congress to play a greater role and demands that many more interests are fully represented. The president now has become only a principal actor and no longer the sole, dominating figure on the American political stage. As an institution, Congress has become more assertive of its powers and, as individuals, members of Congress have become less willingly led by the White House.

This adaptation of the leadership institutions in the national government has taken place within confines of the relatively stable constitutional structure and political culture of the US. A shifting of the balance of power between the institutions has occurred several times in American political history. The current struggle is notable because it has produced a situation where neither institution is in a position necessarily to prevail. In fact, the common complaint of this period is that American politics is characterized by "gridlock" where the Congress and president have the ability and the desire on many occasions to frustrate the policy making process.

The American system is, by design, decentralized. The twin emphasis in Madison's model on separation of powers coupled with a system of checks and balances, creates incentives for cross-institutional conflict in the interest of restraining government power. Unlike cabinet systems which concentrate power in the hands of the governing team in the parliament, the American system does not guarantee that the President and the Congress will approach the policy making process from a common political basis. In the recent past, the two political parties have split the control of the Congress and the president in all but six of the last twenty-five years. The institutions differ in their interests and their orientation to policy making. Congress represents localized interests of states and communities and presidents respond to international issues and concerns of large widespread interests. House members, and some senators, survive politically by cultivating the local constituency with casework, adroit use of local media, and grantsmanship. Presidents, by contrast, turn to the mass media in an effort to mobilize popular support on behalf of administration goals. Electorally, the branches confront the citizenry divided in different ways and on different election cycles. With the exception of Reagan, presidents through much of this period found public support exceedingly difficult to maintain and faced electoral vulnerability. Incumbent members of Congress, by contrast, enjoyed much individual approval by constituents and much electoral security.

The politics of the 1970s and the 1980s often seemed to put the

Congress and president in competition with each other more regularly than in the past. Although the constitutional logic of Madison's model of government saw the contest between the president and the Congress as vital, in much of American political history the branches of government have in fact cooperated in policy making.[1] These long periods of institutional "comity" – cooperative relations between the branches – have resulted from the integrating effects of the party system in pulling government officials together, a degree of social agreement about the proper role and limits of government, and some clarity about the issue agenda of the national government. In these periods there existed shared motives and shared means to pull the branches together and to resolve conflicts within the majority party. At some points in American history, leadership in this process has rested with the president and at other times has resided in Congress. The contemporary period, by contrast, is one of divided democracy where weakened partisanship in the electorate has weakened the linkages between the branches. As a result, the institutions face more complex political demands, weaker incentives for interbranch cooperation, and a greater willingness of political leaders to assert the prerogatives of their branch.

An understanding of the developing relation between the president and Congress considers a number of factors. Structural change and political circumstances in Congress, institutional responses to a changing political environment, and changes in the career pattern, political needs and skills of the incumbent politicians within the institutions have affected the politics of the American leadership. I consider the institutions in turn. The Congress has become more assertive, yet lacks the tools needed to direct the political process. The political position of the president has become weaker and the tools of presidential influence have changed.

Conflict between the branches is to be expected. Political scientist James Thurber identified six factors that are most important as root causes of divided democracy and the inter-branch conflict it has produced.[2] The ambiguity of the boundaries of the powers given to each branch means that there are potentially many opportunities for either branch to contest the claims of the other. Secondly, the Congress and the presidency are chosen from and respond to differently defined constituencies who possess differing interests. Thirdly, differing terms of office means that the office holders respond to their electorates with different senses of time. The reality that most congressional incumbents have been electorally secure, while presidents have been vulnerable, limits presidential claims for support even on members of his own party. Fourthly, the decline of the party system over the last twenty-five years has reshaped politics as the shared fate of individual members became separated from that of the president. Members of Congress increasingly run on their own with custom designed appeals made to constituents. Fifthly, divided government affects policy making as both attempt to control policy, obtain credit, and win further voter support. Finally, Thurber notes that power in the institutions and among them has been in flux, reflecting both issues of institutional capacity and larger questions of the desired role of government in society. We will see that these factors are helpful in tracing trends in the relationship of president and Congress.

Congress

In the late 1960s critics of Congress, including some of its most thoughtful members, described the institution as the "broken branch" of American national politics and called for institutional reform.[3] The congressional reform movement peaked in the early 1970s, partly in reaction to the Vietnam War and partly in reaction to the politics of the Nixon administration and the Watergate scandals. The reformers emphasized two key themes: the need for greater democracy within Congress so that the institution would more appropriately represent the demands for public policy expressed by the citizenry and the need for greater institutional capacity so that the Congress could confront the president on a more equal footing in policy making and in the direction of government administration.

Internal reforms to make the Congress more internally democratic and responsive sought to alter major features of the congressional power structure at the time. Reform initiatives reduced the disproportionate influence and prerogatives of the relatively small group of major committee chairs who effectively controlled the legislative process. These chairs were mostly conservative, senior, Southern Democrats, whose positions allowed them life and death control of legislation. They held chairs by virtue of their seniority rather than any commitment to the policy program of the national Democratic Party. Because of the historic lack of party competition in the South, and the distinctive conservatism of the Southern wing of the party, many of the incumbent chairs were out of touch with the liberal, urban mainstream of the majority Democrats. That so many power holders in the Congress tended to come from conservative, rural states and districts meant that the views of such constituencies were represented far out of their proportion in the United States. Not only did the chairs block the policy initiatives sought by Democratic Party progressives, they tended to be more willing to accommodate the president's assertion of power. This arrangement made it easier for presidents to bargain with Congress since only a relatively small number of critically influential members needed to be considered.

Reformers, as well, were concerned with the capacity of Congress to be a coequal partner with the president in national policy making. For these reformers, the constitutional authority and practical influence of the Congress had diminished in a wide range of areas over the twentieth century. Executive budgeting, widespread delegation of legislative authority to the executive, presidential warmaking, tighter executive control of the executive departments, and the pivotal role the president occupied in setting the policy agenda and mobilizing the public had all worked to the disadvantage of Congress. Low public esteem for Congress added to the perception that reform was desirable. Perhaps the most important factor leading to congressional reform was frustration over presidential warmaking in Vietnam and the domestic policy challenges of the Nixon administration. Both suggested to many members of the Democratic Party majority the dangers of presidential actions which were not subject to congressional checks. Recapturing power from the president required not only a willingness to assert institutional prerogatives, but also a greater capacity to gather and organize ideas and information for policy making.

The reforms adopted in the early 1970s changed the organization and power structure in four main ways.[4] Firstly, they sought to democratize the power structure of Congress, particularly in the House of Representatives. Efforts at democratization brought about changes in rules so that it would be more difficult for any small group of members to control the legislative process against the will of the majority party. Such rules limited some of the historic prerogatives of the committee chairs by limiting the seniority system and making the appointment of the chairs subject to challenge in the party caucus. Likewise, the absolute control of the committee over the legislative calendar of the committee and over the structure and jurisdiction of the subcommittees was ended. Greater flexibility was granted the leadership in referring bills to committees and floor procedures were also changed in 1973 to limit the power of the House Rules Committee and to allow for easier amending on the floor and for greater participation by members in debating legislation. Congressional rule changes opened the legislative process to the public and organized interests in a number of ways, reduced secrecy, and limited the monopoly on information that some members had enjoyed. For example, the introduction of electronic voting in the House greatly increased the number of recorded votes members make, thus producing more visibility for individual decisions among interest groups, voters, and other political leaders. In all, the reform process reduced hierarchy and diminished the independence of major committees and their leaders from the larger Congress.

A decentralization of power within the Congress was a second major characteristic of the institutional reforms. Reformers sought to redistribute influence by shifting power from the standing committees to the more than 300 subcommittees in the Congress.[5] The Subcommittee Bill of Rights did much to free subcommittees from their parent committee and its chair. Subcommittees were separately empowered and rule changes allowed far more members of the majority party to hold a leadership role and use institutional resources and opportunities to pursue public policy aims. Subcommittees received budgets of their own and quickly added staff to support their initiatives. Rule changes allowing multiple referrals meant that many subcommittees in various parts of Congress might be independently acting in a policy area and claim some share in legislating. Formal rule changes were supplemented by changes in the informal norms and practices of the Congress. For example, the decline of the apprenticeship norms and the committee reciprocity norms legitimated the participation of quite junior members in areas where they lacked either recognized expertise or status on the relevant committees.

A third element of congressional reform brought large increases in the professional staff of the Congress in order to increase its capacity to make judgments independently of the executive.[6] Reformers had noticed that the Congress suffered from disadvantages in its working relationship with the president, especially relative to public advocacy of legislative programs and independent analysis of government budgeting and foreign policy issues. In order to give itself greater ability to frame up alternatives for itself and to judge the information and arguments of the executive, Congress greatly increased the number of its committee and subcommittee staffs; and enlarged and created special research agencies such as the Office of Technology Assessment, the Congressional Budget Office, and the Legislative Research Service. Growth in the personal staffs of members, driven in part by members' electoral need to do casework for constituents, also contributed to the ability of members to regain some of the initiative in policy making. Not only can Congress gather and analyze far more information than in the past, the openness of the process means that few members may any longer routinely enhance their power by manipulating information.

Finally, the reforms sought to strengthen the role of party leaders in the Congress.[7] Although this initiative is somewhat at odds with the desire to decentralize power, it was consistent with the desire to increase institutional democracy. Reformers believed that stronger party leaders, chosen by the party caucus and relying on a stronger set of party policy committees, actually increased the possibility of a cohesive majority party that reflected the views of its membership. In the House, the Democrats moved the important question of determining committee appointments toward the party's steering and policy committee and thus increased the leadership's role. The Speaker's influence over the floor – and the increasing importance of the floor as an arena for shaping legislation – has increased because of his ability to choose the members of the Rules Committee and through them to influence the conditions by which legislation is considered.

Although the initial effect of the reforms did not greatly increase the power of the leadership, over time problems arising from the dispersal of legislative activity produced a need for coordination that the leadership was uniquely suited to provide. In the 1980s in particular, the majority party leadership provided a center around which policy alternatives to Reagan administration proposals might be developed. By bargaining among the various participants, the leadership has become instrumental in forging the final legislative package that goes to the floor. Since the leadership ultimately controls access to the floor by determining the agenda and the terms of the debate, the Speaker and the floor leaders have become far more central to the legislative process. As well, the party leaders became more active in presenting their proposals and explaining congressional activity to the mass public through the mass media. In this way they somewhat offset the president's natural advantage as a national media figure and congressional leaders became more significant figures in American national politics.

Some of the changes in the Congress since the mid-1970s result from changes in members of Congress themselves.[8] New personnel are significant because they bring to the institution a different orientation to the congressional career, different motivations, and different political skills. Since the president, the national party leadership, and the congressional leadership all have little influence over who is nominated or elected to the Congress, changes in the membership are one way that external pressures are felt and a factor that the institution must accommodate. Probably the most significant consequence has been the rise of individualism in Congress where members pursue their individual electoral strategies and independent legislative agendas, largely by effective use of interest groups, with relatively little regard to larger party aims.

Several developing trends in congressional elections became apparent around the time of the post Watergate election of 1974. First, greater degree of turnover developed in the early 1970s largely as the result of retirements and, with the end of Watergate, with the election of a number of Democrats to historically Republican seats. The greater success of Democrats even in historically unfriendly territory was no short-term aberration. Rather, it marked several important changes both in the electorate and in the Congress. An increasing proportion of voters demonstrated that they would split their ballots and would vote for attractive candidates of any party. In order to be successful in reaching electoral support, members reduced their reliance on party appeals and emphasized constituency responsiveness, policy positions, and personality attributes in campaigning for support. With adequate campaign funds and effective use of mass media, candidates for Congress could pursue an entrepreneurial campaign approach independent of party and president. Thus, elections need not tie members either to a particular program, to the fellow partisans in the Congress, or to the president if he is of their party.

The opportunity structure became more open, at least where incumbents were not involved, and prospective candidates could begin a successful nomination campaign to a seat without having served a lengthy apprenticeship in other offices or without significant ties to local party organizations. Skillful use of media and campaign technology, reliance upon other interest groups as a political base for the primary, and use of other non-political factors to attract campaign money and voters opened the congressional career to a cohort of younger, well educated, and entrepreneurial men and women. In the Senate in particular, a remarkable number of senators have entered the body from occupations as different as professional athlete, astronaut, and actor.[9] Because campaigns were customized to a constituency, heavily focused on the person of the candidate, and dependent upon selective issues to mobilize an activist strata among local interest groups, these members felt little obligation toward fellow members, the larger interests of Congress, party, or president.

The new style member of Congress was motivated by a personal ambition, characterized by a focus on policy, an emphasis on rather theoretical expertise gained by formal education (rather than prior experience), an impatience with institutional norms and structures, expertise in both the substance and process of policy, and a heavy emphasis on personal self-promotion. In many respects this style has been highly successful. Rates of incumbent reelection reached historic highs during the 1980s with as many as 97 percent of the incumbents seeking a new term succeeding.[10] Likewise, the contemporary Congress member is exceedingly well educated and possesses an enviable depth in intellect and skill. Yet, the individual style has not helped the Congress perform its essential function of accommodating interests and aggregating demands for public policy. Habits of teamwork and a larger perspective on policy have often been lacking and members have sometimes exploited the institution for their political benefit. The most widespread tendency is for members to build their political support by running against the institution and the "rascals" who are their colleagues. It is a successful ploy which enhances public cynicism and explains the apparent contradiction that Americans tend to despise the Congress and love their own member of Congress.

The efforts of the Congress to reassert itself against the president led to several major initiatives in the mid-1970s that have helped to define the course of institutional politics in the following years. Three areas in particular seem most important and were direct responses to the confrontational strategies of the Nixon administration and a rethinking of foreign policy and presidential war-making after Vietnam. Taking advantage of a weakened presidency after the Watergate scandals and Nixon's resignation, the Congress acted in these main areas. Firstly, the Congress set out to reclaim its power of the purse that had slipped away gradually since the 1921 Budget and Accounting Act. Secondly, through the War Powers Act, passed over the president's veto, Congress attempted to become more involved in major issues of foreign policy. Thirdly, the Congress sought greater control over the administration of laws in order to recover prerogatives that had slipped away by delegation and lack of use.[11]

The power of the purse is one major source of congressional authority because government spending affects how congressional efforts at policy making are implemented. Up to the early 1970s presidents tended to dominate budget-making and were largely unsupervised in its execution. Conflict over budget priorities and Nixon's liberal use of impoundment to frustrate congressional wishes resulted in the Budget Control and Impoundment Act of 1974. This Act sought to offset the president's advantage in directing government spending and focused on two main issues. Firstly, it aimed at enhancing Congress's ability to legislate on the federal budget by creating new Budget Committees to examine the budget as a whole, a budget process that sought to focus responsibility for budget questions, and institutional and informational resources to give Congress an independent understanding of the budget. Secondly, the Congress recognized officially the custom of presidential impoundment and sought to restrict the president's use of it, by requiring congressional approval of impoundments. In practice, the reformed budget process has had mixed results. Clearly Congress is more active in budget matters and better informed, but the process hasn't provided the hoped-for tools to allow Congress to provide greater coherence and accountability. The status of impoundment has been clarified and flagrant abuses controlled, although the impoundment provisions have not worked out wholly as intended.

In the 1980s, the budget problem was transformed by the emergence of massive budget deficits. The diffuse power structure in Congress made it difficult to respond to this challenge by raising additional revenue from taxation or reducing spending by cutting back on programs or entitlement spending. As public ire about government deficits grew, Congress responded with the Balanced Budget and Emergency Deficit Control Act which is usually referred to as Gramm–Rudman–Hollings. This Act set a target to reduce the deficit and created a mechanism that would automatically reduce spending if the ordinary process did not produce budgets below the target. Although this effort has contributed somewhat to the centralizing of authority for budgeting in Congress and given the leadership new opportunities to negotiate, experience with Gramm–Rudman–Hollings does not suggest that Congress has sufficient political will to address the basic problem of "uncontrollable" spending – those budget items such as Social Security (Pensions) defined by legislation as non-discretionary.

In foreign policy and the war powers, Congress responded to the experience of Vietnam War era decision making by passing, over the veto of President Nixon, the War Powers Resolution which sought to engage the president in consultation with Congress concerning the decision to commit American troops to conflicts. Although the power to declare war was clearly constitutionally reserved for Congress, deployment of troops has often taken place under the president's powers as commander in chief and his status as chief agent of diplomacy. Moreover, in the National Security Act after World War II, Congress had greatly enhanced the presidential role in foreign affairs as a consequence of America's changed place in the world. The War Powers Act sought to recover congressional participation by formalizing a process of notification and review when troops went into combat situations abroad. It required consultation in advance when possible or notification in emergency situations. Congress established a 60–90 day time period in which congressional approval must be obtained or the troops returned home. The Act, which presidents have routinely described as unconstitutional, ill considered or inapplicable to the case at hand, has proven an awkward device for regulating military action.

In practice, Congress has not been able to force the president to consult and it has proven difficult for Congress to develop a sufficient consensus to force presidents to withdraw troops. Even in controversial cases of presidentially directed intervention in Grenada, Lebanon, and Panama, it has been difficult for Congress to respond as long as the commitment is short-lived. The primary value of the War Powers Act may be felt by anticipated reactions. It forces presidents to consider whether they have sufficient political support to weather protest. Decision making on the Gulf War does illustrate the political value of presidential efforts to lead a public debate through the Congress.

Greater congressional assertiveness in other areas of foreign policy also occurred through Congress's ability to investigate and publicize actions, the use of the treaty approval process, and through often detailed specifications of the duties and reporting requirements imposed on the diplomatic and national security establishment. Foreign policy questions in many areas have implications well beyond traditional national security concerns. While some issues, such as the Panama Canal Treaty during the Carter administration, are essentially symbolic, other international issues such as energy, trade relations, environment, and international financial exchanges all had domestic economic consequences and became increasingly interesting to Congress.

Enhancing congressional influence over the institutions of government administration was a third area in which the newly assertive Congress of the 1970s began to act. Historically, Congress has possessed significant influence in domestic agencies in the US through its role in budgeting, its influence in the appointments process, its ability to legislate on the structure and powers of agencies and in cultivating ties with interest groups and agency leaders. Presidents have long been frustrated by the extent of congressional influence in the executive branch and the Nixon administration sought to assert greater presidential control through management improvement, proposals for widespread executive reorganization, and tighter staff control of policy decisions and top administrators from the White House. In the conflict which ensued, Congress lost its confidence that administrative officials would respond to congressional intent and met this challenge by changing the budget and spending process and closer scrutiny of appointees. Congress effectively thwarted most efforts at large-scale administrative reform and limited the impact of executive efforts to gain greater managerial control by introducing devices such as Management by Objective and Zero-Based Budgeting and, in addition, the use of a "legislative veto," a procedure which allowed Congress to reverse specific decisions of administrators by congressional resolution. Although the Supreme Court struck down many applications of the legislative veto in 1983, it remains in some forms. Greater use of congressional hearings and increased efforts at oversight activities also provide Congress with more information and an opportunity to influence agency administrators. From the 1980s forward, this area has been relatively quiet because the Reagan administration adopted a largely negative approach to the bureaucracy in which it put in place administrative leadership with little commitment to government activism. Stringent budgets, outside of defense, further limited the possibilities for congressional action in this area.

The congressional reforms of the 1970s did not all match the expectations of their advocates. In particular, the dispersal of power into the subcommittees made determination of the direction of the policy making process extremely difficult. While the system was open to influence to an unprecedented degree, the sheer number of subcommittees made legislating far more difficult and increased the number of actors with claims to be accommodated. The decline of the party system outside of Congress, the more complex public agenda, and the rise of interest group politics created greater strains between constituency and party which tended to be resolved in favor of the constituency preferences. Because members had to demonstrate that they represented constituents, interest groups and campaign contributors effectively, floor activity increased and the role of the committee process with its specialization declined.

The 1980s produced a counter response within the Congress, especially in the House.[12] The effectiveness of Congress became a more central concern, especially in the face of the more ideological Reagan administration. Two changes are critical in this period. Firstly, Congress became more partisan. Even though party was less important outside of Congress, it served within Congress to define sides and to structure the dynamics of the negotiation between the branches. Internally, the 1980s substantially strengthened the hand of the leadership. Frustration with the decentralized, individualized policy process created an opportunity for House and Senate majority leaders to broker among the various committees, subcommittees, caucuses, and external interests in creating legislation. The product has been fewer bills presented to Congress, far more creative use of the rules to structure floor action, and larger bills covering an enormous range of issues so as to create both a solid legislative coalition and to reduce the president's temptation to veto. The effects of these changes in Congress continue to be felt. The institution still struggles with its decentralized nature, yet its leadership has become sufficiently important to national policy making that even a Democratic president such as Clinton cannot take it for granted. If only in a negative way, the Congress of the 1990s has more impact on policy and administration than any since the 1930s.

Presidency

In the late 1960s the presidency was commonly seen as the core institution of American politics and virtually the sole source of initiative, leadership, and innovation in the American system. Executive ascendancy, the logical outcome of New Deal era economic and social policies and the foreign policy and defense imperatives of World War II and the Cold War, reached its zenith at the end the 1960s. Presidential war-making in Vietnam, undertaken with little consultation and only the indirect assent of Congress, created fears of an imperial presidency broken loose from its constitutional moorings.[13] Not only did the president appear to dominate the public landscape by the effective use of the national mass media, he had accumulated substantial influence over the tools of administration – the budget, agency reorganization, the deployment of military forces, and the appointments process.

Within a decade, however, the picture was startlingly different. A visible weakening of the presidency had occurred and commentators observed that the presidency had become "imperiled" rather than "imperial."[14] Although effective presidential leadership is still possible – witness President Bush's mobilization of public opinion and Congress on the Gulf War – it is far more difficult than before. Explanations for the deflating of the American presidency can be found in several sources. America's drawn out involvement in Vietnam proved expensive for the presidency once public support turned away from the war. The so-called credibility gap between the official messages and the apparent realities of the war eroded the special relationship of trust between the president and the public. The Watergate crisis, leading to the resignation of President Richard Nixon in 1974, similarly portrayed an disillusioning image of deceit and criminal misconduct within the 1972 Nixon campaign and in the White House. In addition, presidents faced difficult economic conditions, the Arab oil embargo, domestic problems that often seemed to defy solution, and highly visible events such the Iranian hostage crisis. These difficult problems often defied presidential solution and undercut the image of presidential invincibility.

The reversal of the president's fortunes reflects a weakening of the underlying forces in American politics that had empowered the presidency in the first place.[15] These included: A central emphasis on presidential leadership in foreign policy bolstered by the norm that "politics stops at the water's edge"; the president's role as administrative leader of government, a national party that limited and organized politics around a limited set of issues; a nominating process that produced presidents with political stature in the Washington establishment; and a strong bond between the president and the mass public that was facilitated by a supportive mass media. Changes in these areas, along with the more assertive Congress discussed earlier, left contemporary presidents less able to act and at risk of what political scientist Larry Berman has called "constitutional insolvency."

The management of international relations, one of the factors which contributed to growth in the power of the president up to the end of Vietnam, has become more problematic for presidents and a less secure basis for presidential power. Disillusionment with presidential leadership in Vietnam and the subsequent domestic turmoil over war policy undercut the Cold War's consensus on foreign policy. Periods of *détente* and the eventual end of the superpower conflict made less compelling to the public and Congress the argument that the president should be the sole actor in foreign policy. Presidents after Nixon could no longer function free from competition in the conduct of foreign policy. The nature of international issues changed as complex questions of international economics and a concern with human rights were added to the traditional national security concerns. Questions of energy supply, trade relations, and currency matters had various implications for domestic constituencies and invited congressional attention. Rose and other scholars point out that other nations have grown more equal with the US and were less likely to accept automatically the president as "leader of the free world."[16] No longer can presidents be certain that their allies will cooperate with policy created by the administration. One domestic result is that presidents are sometimes seen as weak or ineffective by other Washington actors and by the larger public when others in the world do not accommodate American stands. Rogue states such as Iran, Iraq, Libya, and North Korea have all posed visible challenges to the US and to presidential authority. Finally, foreign policy after the Cold War has become enormously complex and politically risky for the president. National interests are sometimes difficult to explain to the public and Congress, multinational efforts are no longer automatically under presidential direction, and visible failure even in minor trouble spots poses political risks for presidents at home.

Information and the control of the administrative apparatus of the national government can provide presidents with many opportunities to pursue their political objectives in both foreign and domestic policy domains. In reality, leadership of the executive has proven vexing for presidents in the last twenty-five years. Not only did Congress become more assertive, the demands for influence from the myriad interest groups associated with the president's support coalition have grown. All recent presidents have struggled with the reality that many of their appointees have political imperatives beyond the interest of the president. Efforts to integrate administration appointees and to tie them to the president led to the major growth in the size and power of the White House staff and to greater managerial centralization.[17] The result in the Nixon White House was presidential isolation and a series of decisions which alienated civil service employees and Congress alike. In reaction to Watergate and the high-handed tactics of the Nixon administration, both Ford and Carter adopted more open staff styles and sought to use the cabinet to integrate and direct government. More active use of the cabinet was supposed to reduce presidential isolation, inform the president and staff of the operational realities of governing, and achieve more coherence in policy. These efforts to create "cabinet government" in its American variation have proven largely futile and the idea was abandoned by the end of the Carter administration. The problem for the president, however, remains. Cabinet officers often come to identify strongly with their agency and its interest group and do not share the president's perspective, serve as a source for presidential initiative, or pursue presidential aims.

The White House staff as a result has become the key to the president's administrative and legislative strategy.[18] However, effective use of the staff has proven difficult, even though the staff is populated primarily by those with personal loyalty to the president. Two problems have become especially important. Firstly, ambitious staff members have desires of their own which they want the president to adopt. Secondly, the expertise of the staff leans heavily toward political tactics rather than substantive expertise in government because so much of the staff is initially recruited from the president's campaign organization. Because of its large size, the varying ambitions of its members, its distance from the operational concerns of government, and the relatively unpredictable political environment surrounding the presidency, organizing and managing the staff effectively toward the president's purposes has been a recurring problem. Presidents have had to decide on either a centralized management approach under a strong chief of staff or a more open staff style in which many aides have access to the president, claim his time, and attempt to influence his decisions. Neither has been satisfactory and every president has faced at least one staffing crisis. The open staff style, especially in the Carter and Clinton administrations, compounded problems with priority setting and in the appropriate management of the president's time. More centralized strategies of staff management were used in the second Reagan administration and in the early Bush administration. In both cases the chief of staff was to "protect" the president from external and internal conflict and defend his time. Neither was especially successful and both cases illustrated that a centralized approach tends to exaggerate weaknesses of the chief of staff's managerial style. In Reagan's first term he employed a troika rather than a single chief of staff in a structure that proved well suited to his rather uninvolved approach to government. Finally, staffing problems affect administrations most acutely at the beginning and have complicated efforts to pursue a legislative agenda precisely at the point where Congress and the public are most likely to accept presidential leadership. Failure to find a suitable approach to staffing, thus, has been costly.

The decline of the New Deal party system has forced presidents to deal with a more complex range of issues.[19] The issue basis of which presidents seek support and attempt to exercise influence now includes everything from social issues such as abortion, to crime, to economic growth, racial harmony, gender equality, budget deficits, international trade, environmental regulation, and more. Activists within the parties, a crucial group in the nominating process, and to an extent the larger electorate, have become issue specialists who respond to candidates in terms of narrowly defined and intensely held issue concerns. Because the party system no longer organizes issues or structures an agenda as it once did, presidents attempt to influence an enormous range of issues in order to respond to current public concerns and to their activist supporters. In reality, presidential ability to affect even a fraction of the issues mentioned are sharply limited because of the need for congressional cooperation, tight financial constraints, and lack of consensus solutions to many issues. Presidents thus have assumed responsibilities without the necessary policy tools. Moreover, modern campaigns induce candidates to make commitments on a broad range of issues in order to garner support. Once in office presidents, especially Carter and Clinton, find that there are too many groups demanding action and presidential pledges are often at odds with the median preferences of the larger public. The results are a lack of focus, disenchanted activists, unviable policy proposals, frustrated activist presidents. Presidents with a more limited agenda, if they can manage to forge a large enough alliance of supporters, have fared better. For example, the first Reagan administration with its rather narrow, ideological program coupled with a pragmatic political style was probably the most successful of the post Watergate administrations when evaluated in terms of their stated goals.

Not only has the electoral process left presidents with a complex issue agenda in office, the kind of individuals chosen differ. Changes in the presidential nominating system in the early 1970s produced presidential nominees lacking political ties within government and serious preparation for governmental leadership. The growth in the number of primary elections and the reduced influence of party officials and party office holders in nominating politics has created more open contests for the presidential nomination. Campaigns by political "outsiders," often capitalizing on public distrust of government, have produced presidential contenders such as George McGovern, Jimmy Carter, Michael Dukakis, or Bill Clinton, who have skillfully managed the campaign process in the early caucus and primary states and utilized successful media strategies to capture the nomination. Although the "outsider" candidates are skillful politicians, they lack experience with the national government and the policy making process in Washington. Unlike Lyndon Johnson or Richard Nixon, most recent presidents have not been deeply knowledgeable about the personalities and processes of national policy making and have had to develop a reputation for effectiveness with others who participate in governing.

The decline of the party system and the changes in campaign technology mean that presidents do not share with members of Congress, even those of their own party, a common issue agenda.[20] In the American system, of course, the separation of congressional and presidential elections means that presidents may not have a party majority in either house of the Congress. Indeed, since 1972 only the Carter and Clinton administrations have worked with a majority of co-partisans in both houses. Not only are more voters willing to split tickets, they are responding to essentially different appeals – the president's campaign tends to focus on issues with a national and international focus, where the House and Senate elections are directed to domestic questions and to locally significant concerns. Because campaigns now run essentially independent of each other, presidents cannot count on the support of fellow partisans once in office. Other than Reagan in 1980, recent presidents have have little in the way of electoral coattails. Indeed, in the cases of Carter, Bush, and Clinton, most members of Congress ran more strongly in their constituencies than the president did. In such cases, the member of Congress will not feel strongly obliged to cooperate with the president when the president's need runs counter to the member's need to satisfy the constituency. Presidential sanctions of uncooperative members, never very strong, have minimal effect if the member is secure in his or her district.

More than any other factor, public support for the president is credited with empowering the office in the twentieth century.[21] The claim to act on behalf of the people is always powerful in a democratic society and the president's standing with the public serves as a cue for other office holders who are attempting to decide what positions to take. Using the national mass media, presidents have established a direct relationship with voters and have used public support to gain political leverage in pursuit of their objectives. Presidents try to present themselves as non-partisan, national leaders rather than as political figures to make the broadest appeal possible. Public support helps presidents in the struggle with Congress over the direction of public policy and reconciles presidential activism with a democratic political culture. However, public support can weaken as well as strenghten the president. The habit of trusting and supporting the president was shaken by by Vietnam and Watergate. Both raised doubts about presidential truthfulness and political integrity. Presidents since Watergate have found a different relationship with the public. Firstly, because presidents from Ford to Clinton have portrayed themselves as "ordinary" Americans, there has been a decline in deference and respect for presidents. Presidents are viewed more cynically, have become easy targets for humor, and are easily dismissed by their fellow citizens. Secondly, presidential prestige has become significantly more volatile in response to presidential performance in office. In part this occurs because the "outsider" presidents often lacked a support base with a strong attachment to them, and in part it occurs because of the tendency of the mass media to inflate the importance of each presidential success or failure. Dramatic fluctuations occur routinely in relatively short periods of time. For example, President Bush's popularity ratings are among the highest ever recorded at the end of the Gulf War and fell within a year to among the lowest. Thirdly, media presentations of presidents have become more critical, and perhaps more realistic, with the effect that alternate interpretations of presidential plans are more likely to be presented to the public.

The politics of popular support have become a principle concern of the contemporary presidency. Because the "outsider" presidents often lack the connections and resources to deal effectively with others in Washington directly, presidents have come to rely on direct appeals to the public to gain leverage over Congress and to mute the opposing interest groups. This strategy of governing by invoking the public, termed the plebicitary presidency by Lowi, allows the president to use the familiar skills and rhetoric of campaigning. Appeals to the public, however, have limitations: the public soon tires of presidential appeals, arguments for policy change are often too complex to make effectively via the media, some actions are just unpopular, and the president's natural advantage can be countered by effective interest group activity. Over time, administrations often face a vicious cycle in public support. As some withdraw support, the stature of the presidency appears to decline, leading to less success in policy, and resulting in still more unfavorable ratings. In the absence of a dramatic event to reverse the cycle and revitalize the presidency, the potential for presidential leadership shrinks back to the constitutional minimum. A larger risk of this search for public support is the possibility that it becomes an end in itself or makes it impossible for the government to take decisive action. The inactivity of the first two years of the Bush administration and the inability of the Clinton administration to confront foreign policy problems in the former Yugoslavia and Rwanda may well reflect a belief that taking actions would cost too much public support. To the extent that the search for public support diverts presidential effort and encourages short-term fixes at the cost of more solid policies, long-term national interests may be harmed.

In the absence of coherent parties, and given the explosion of interest groups of all types, presidential administrations have adopted strategies for governing which attempt to activate groups in pursuit of legislative and public support. Just as interest groups of various forms mobilized various blocks of voters and supplied campaign resources, such groups become the building blocks of a governing strategy. This changed environment moves national politics from what Samuel Kernell has called "institutional pluralism" to "individualized pluralism."[22] Where institutional pluralism predictably structured the working relationships of presidents, Congress, the interest groups, and the parties, individualized pluralism leaves each office holder to assemble his or her own support coalition and produces a great deal of fluidity in governing because coalitions must be assembled issue by issue. The pursuit of group support by presidents has proven difficult because of the sheer number and complexity of interest groups and the limited amount of assistance they can and will offer the president across areas of policy. As a result, assembling support is time consuming and politically difficult. This tendency of interest groups to slow down the process and force accommodation is, of course, felt more acutely by activist presidents such as Carter and Clinton than by a president such as Reagan with his limited agenda and relatively passive approach to government.

Over the past twenty years, presidents have found it more difficult to mobilize majorities in the Congress in order to direct policy. With the declining importance of political party and the frequent lack of a party majority, appeals to party loyalty or to a shared commitment to the president's program will not persuade Congress. Although presidential leadership has sometimes proven difficult in this setting, it has not proven wholly impossible. Presidents have responded by assembling a custom designed legislative coalition for each major issue. In one way, the weakening of party ties has benefitted the president since he can attempt to assemble a legislative majority from anywhere in Congress either inside or outside his party. As long as some portion of the membership of the opposing party can be attracted by compromise, constituency interests, or other bargains, the skillful president can obtain at least a portion of his legislative program. A notable example of this strategy were the so-called "Reagan Democrats" who dependably supported Reagan's initiatives on questions of budget, defense, and tax policy early in the administration. An occasional victory obtained with the assistance of members of the opposing party may even help a president contain the demands of the more extreme members of his legislative party. Finally, the strengthening of the congressional party has assisted presidents by providing once again a negotiating partner who can actually deliver acceptable legislation.

Bargaining case by case is not ideal from a president's perspective, for several reasons, although a president seeking an active role in shaping policy may have little choice. Firstly, the process of assembling coalitions is time consuming and vulnerable to a variety of forces unrelated to the issue at hand. Secondly, presidents have a limited stock of resources for bargaining, especially given current budgetary constraints. Thirdly, in close votes bargaining encourages members to withhold support in order to gain more for themselves. As a result some efforts never achieve the critical mass or momentum to proceed and the greatest rewards appear to go to the president's least loyal supporters. Finally, the price for agreement may become too high and pose a dilemma for a president. The failure to pass a major bill that the administration has endorsed raise concerns about its effectiveness with the public and the press; but accommodation with Congress may lead to policies which alienate the president's supporters.

There are two alternatives to bargaining. Presidents, such as Reagan in the first year or Bush in mobilizing support for operation Desert Storm in the Gulf War, who believe they have strong public support may forgo the bargaining strategy in favor of a public offensive to demonstrate to members that their constituencies support the president. This approach works well with high visibility issues on which public attitudes about appropriate policy are fluid. The alternative, presidential efforts to evade the Congress, can be far more problematic. To a greater or lesser extent, Presidents Nixon, Reagan, and Bush, all Republicans facing strong Democratic majorities in the Congress, adopted political strategies which sought to govern by avoiding Congress.[23] Such strategies require that the presidency have at hand alternative means to accomplish political aims. Some strategies use long-accepted methods of presidential administration, such as an executive agreement in foreign policy, to avoid bringing controversial questions to Congress. In other cases, such as Nixon's expansion of the Vietnam War into Laos and Cambodia or the Iran–Contra affair in the Reagan administration, off-budget financial dealing or extra-legal maneuvers may be attempted to flout the efforts of the Congress to control executive actions. Always dependent upon maintaining a substantial level of public support, these strategies have increased conflict between the branches and risked the administration's political position if things go wrong, as they did during the Iran–Contra affair.

The weaker presidency produced by these changes in the political landscape is not incapable of governing nor in danger of being superseded by the Congress. Presidents and the Congress have adapted to the new realities. Indeed, David Mayhew has shown in *Divided We Govern* that the extended period of divided party government from 1968 to 1992 has not been one of legislative deadlock or inaction.[24] The somewhat deflated view of the contemporary presidency may well be a sign of political health in the United States. The post World War II image of the presidency as the primary source of leadership, initiative, and innovation in the American system was certainly overdrawn. In so far as the public develops a greater appreciation of the complexity of government and the constraints on presidency, a more balanced view of national leadership may emerge.

Summary

For both the Congress and the presidency, the last twenty years have been ones of change. The adaptation of the leadership institutions to an unfamiliar political landscape have remade the institutions and affected their capacity for policy making. Not all of these changes have, in fact, worked out as intended. The gradual recentralizing of power in the hands of congressional leaders reflects the limits of institutional democracy. Vigorous representation of the interests of one's constituents does not lend itself to the accommodation of differences and timely movement toward decision making. The deflating of the presidency, a mostly unintended result of a great many other changes in the political system, has reduced the potential for transformational leadership.

Public expectations, as measured in polling and through elections, send contradictory signals to elected officials. Americans expect different things from the branches: national leadership in a complex world on the one hand, vigorous defense of local interest on the other; tax cuts and deficit reduction from one and the defense of treasured entitlements on the other. Some commentators have described the situation as a kind of "cognitive Madisonianism" where a public somewhat cool to government sets branches against each other in a conflict in which neither branch can succeed. The nature of current American politics offers few true opportunities to educate and lead public opinion since there are relatively few incentives for office holders to invest in political activity with longer-term benefits. The end of divided party government with the election of President Clinton in 1992 did not essentially resolve the problem. Clinton's electoral victory was a hollow one. While Americans agreed that "change" was needed, there was little agreement upon what that change should look like. The Clinton victory was not sufficient to bridge the gap between the Congress and the president in order to address the agenda, in health care, for example, that Clinton had posed. As we have seen, the gap between the institutions rests on other factors beyond the identification of party leaders.

Government has not been impossible under these conditions and every administration can point to major policy accomplishments. However, these accomplishments are fewer in number and less dramatic in practice than advertised. Here there is something of a vicious cycle in which office holders, in their efforts to bid for support, raise expectations for a kind of policy which can not be produced. The result is disappointment with the administration and with government in general that compounds future efforts. The bargaining process that is essential to legislative strategy can produce laws, as Mayhew has shown. Whether or not the solutions produced constitute a coherent or effective response to public problems, however, remains open to question. The sharpened partisanship within and across the institutions has not sharpened the policy process since it is based on a search for tactical advantage rather than clear differences in inter-party strategies of government. The bitter confirmation battles over Robert Bork and Clarence Thomas illustrate this problem. The recurring temptation to escape the efforts of control by the other branch to break out of the gridlock of governing in a separated system guarantees that inter-branch conflict will remain. Where the Congress and president have been unable to resolve the direction of policy clearly, a range of other strategies have been employed.[25] The increased political role of the courts (as distinct from their traditional legal role), the use of mandates on the states and the private sector, and a range of cross-governmental devices to negotiate differences allow government to proceed when the primary relationship for policy making fails to respond. Governing in this climate is possible, it just isn't very pretty.

Notes

1 L. Fisher, *The Politics of Shared Powers: Congress and the Executive*, 2nd edn (Washington, DC, CQ Press, 1987).

2 J. A. Thurber, *Divided Democracy: Cooperation and Conflict Between the President and Congress* (Washington, DC, CQ Press, 1990). pp. 2–7.

3 L. N. Reiselbach, *Congressional Reform* (Washington, DC, CQ Press, 1986). J. A. Sundquist, *The Decline and Resurgence of Congress* (Washington, DC, Brookings Institution, 1981).

4 Steven S. Smith, *Call to Order: Floor Politics in the House and Senate* (Washington, Brookings Institution, 1989), pp. 15–28. Rieselbach, *Congressional Reform*, pp. 41–67.

5 R. Davidson, "Subcommittee Government: New Channels for Policy Making," in T. Mann and N. Ornstein (eds.), *The New Congress* (Washington, DC, American Enterprise Institute, 1981) pp. 99–133. R. Hall, "Committee Decision Making in the Postreform Congress," in L. Dodd and B. Oppenheimer (eds.), *Congress Reconsidered* (Washington, DC, CQ Press, 1989).

6 M. Malbin, *Unelected Representatives: Congessional Staff and the Future of Representative Government* (New York, Basic Books, 1980).

7 D. Palazzolo, "From Decentralization to Centralization: Member's Changing Expectations for House Leaders," in R. Davidson (ed.), *The Post-Reform Congress* (New York, St Martin's Press, 1992). D. Rohde, *Parties and Leaders in the Postreform House* (University of Chicago Press, 1991).

8 B. Loomis, *The New American Politician: Ambition, Entrepreneurship and the Changing Face of Political Life* (New York, Basic Books, 1988). J. Hibbing, *Congressional Careers: Contours of Life in the U.S. House of Representatives* (Chapel Hill, University of North Carolina Press, 1991).

9 D. Canon, *Actors, Athletes and Astronauts: Political Amateurs in the United States Congress* (University of Chicago Press, 1990).

10 G. Parker, *Characteristics of Congress: Patterns in Congressional Behavior* (Englewood Cliffs, Prentice-Hall, 1989), pp. 65–94.

11 R. Spitzer, *President and Congress: Executive Hegemony at the*

Crossroads of American Government (New York, McGraw Hill, 1993). Fisher, *Politics of Shared Powers*. Sundquist, *Decline and Resurgence*.

12 R. Davidson, "The New Centralization on Capitol Hill," *Review of Politics*, 50:3 (1988). Rohde, *Parties and Leaders*.

13 A. Schlesinger, *The Imperial Presidency* (Boston, Houghton, Miffli, 1973). T. Cronin, *The State of the Presidency* (Boston, Little, Brown, 1975).

14 R. Rose, *The Post-Modern Presidency*, 2nd edn (Chatham, NJ, Chatham House, 1991), p. 52. C. Jones, *The Presidency in a Separated System* (Washington, DC, Brookings Institution, 1994).

15 L. Berman, *The New American Presidency* (Boston, Little Brown, 1986), pp. 3–8.

16 Rose, *Post Modern Presidency*, pp. 237–251.

17 Berman, *New American Presidency*, pp. 99–125. R. Nathan, *The Administrative Presidency* (New York, John Wiley, 1983).

18 S. Hess, *Organizing the Presidency*, 2nd edn (Washington, DC, Brookings Institution, 1988).

19 J. Fishel, *Presidents and Promises* (Washington, DC, CQ Press, 1985).

20 G. Edwards and S. Wayne, *Presidential Leadership*, 3rd edn (New York, St Martin's Press, 1994), pp. 312–325.

21 T. Lowi, *The Personal Presidency: Power Invested, Promise Unfilled* (Ithaca, NY, Cornell University Press, 1985). P. Brace and B. Hinckley, *Follow the Leader* (New York, Basic Books, 1992).

22 S. Kernell, *Going Public: New Strategies of Presidential Leadership*, 2nd edn (Washington, DC, CQ Press, 1993), pp. 25–39.

23 C. Tiefer, *The Semi-Sovereign Presidency* (Boulder, CO, Westview Press, 1994).

24 D. Mayhew, *Divided We Govern* (New Haven, Yale University Press, 1991).

25 B. Ginsberg and M. Shefter, *Politics by Other Means* (New York, Basic Books, 1990).

Index